Deborah Hicks Midanek
The Governance Revolution

M000309416

Deborah Hicks Midanek

The Governance Revolution

What Every Board Member Needs to Know, NOW!

ISBN 978-1-5474-1644-8
e-ISBN (PDF) 978-1-5474-0027-0
e-ISBN (EPUB) 978-1-5474-0038-6

Library of Congress Control Number: 2018949267

Bibliographic information published by the Deutsche Nationalbibliothek
The Deutsche Nationalbibliothek lists this publication in the Deutsche Nationalbibliografie;
detailed bibliographic data are available on the Internet at http://dnb.dnb.de.

© 2018 Deborah Hicks Midanek
Published by Walter de Gruyter Inc., Boston/Berlin
Printing and binding: CPI books GmbH, Leck
Typesetting: MacPS, LLC, Carmel
www.degruyter.com

Dedication

This book is dedicated to just a few of the many extraordinary people I am privileged to know and have worked with:

- Coley Bailey, my beloved husband, whose belief that I can do anything makes me get up every morning and try.
- Adolph A. Berle, professor of law at Columbia University, member of FDR Brains Trust and significant architect of the New Deal; author with Gardiner Means of the enduring and still influential 1932 book *The Modern Corporation and Private Property*, and patient teacher of the little girl across the street who needed to know how to spit watermelon pits farther than anyone else.
- Alexandra Reed Lajoux, PhD, chief knowledge officer emerita of the National Association of Corporate Directors and a constant friend since she first published my work in *Directors Monthly*. Her unwavering support and keen insight made this book possible.
- Ira Millstein of Weil Gotshal, senior statesman attorney and governance leading light who helped me get the board of his client restructured to favor the independent directors whom I recruited and led in resolving the bankruptcy of the infamous firm. He acted with courage and integrity, always.
- Claude D. Montgomery, now a partner at Dentons LLP and visionary attorney who answered my plea for legal counsel to the court appointed Equity Security Holders Committee in the Drexel Burnham Lambert Group, Inc. Chapter 11 when no one else would. His remarkable vision, skill, and audacity helped me as committee chair chart a path through complex, ambiguous issues and achieve an extraordinary result for all parties, including the unsung equity holders, the firm's former employees. And that same penetrating vision and intrepid boldness have assisted me time and again in my later service as independent board member for various companies.

To all of you and many more, my eternal gratitude.

DOI 10.1515/9781547400270-201

Praise for the Governance Revolution

The Governance Revolution is a must-read for any current or aspiring corporate director. Deborah Hicks Midanek has created an eminently readable, incredibly pragmatic, and extremely valuable playbook for corporate directors. This is the one book every director should read to gain a better understanding of the current corporate governance revolution!

> — Harvey Pitt, CEO, Kalorama Partners, LLC; Former Chairman,
> United States Securities & Exchange Commission

Moving our corporations toward sustainable business practice requires that boards of directors stand and deliver. This powerful book is ideal for every director and member of senior leadership who wants to make a difference.

> — Halla Tómasdóttir, CEO,
> The B Team

This is truly brilliant. Frankly I opened it with a sense of obligation to skim, but that did not last. I read the whole thing word for word. The scope is breathtaking. It is well researched, exhaustive and deeply thoughtful. Frankly I was expecting a modest "how to" and instead got a definitive history. Congratulations!

> — Robert J. Rosenberg, retired partner and co-chair of Insolvency Practice
> Group at Latham & Watkins LLP; frequent independent director

I'm still reading the book and I have to say WOW.

Most of us take some facts and surround them each by 1000+ words. You take a fact and add two more to make a sentence. I've rarely seen such an information packed book.

I've been a non-executive director and trustee of various companies/ charities but this is opening my eyes to all the things that directors forget or get steered away from.

> — Stefan Drew, Author, Futurist, Director,
> Marketing Magician Enterprises, Ltd

A thorough and thought-provoking consideration of the role of the board in modern business, and why we ought to be talking more about it. With mix of research, legal insight and personal example, Midanek demonstrates not only how boards ought to function, but how more thoughtful approaches

DOI 10.1515/9781547400270-202

to governance can and should restore business to a more sustainable and trusted force in society. I wish I'd had this book in business school!

— Michele Miller, Author & Television Writer,
The Underwriting

Ms. Midanek combines historical research, personal experience, and current debates in a compelling read. Her book provides context for many of today's discussions about the role of corporations and who's in charge.

— Gwen Finegan, Board Member and Strategic Advisor to
Health Care Systems

This book has opened my eyes to many important concepts, and confirmed my beliefs about others. While much of the material may not be new, I think it is both new and important to see these ideas written down. Never have these principles been so important for people to understand. While the ideas can be complex, they are explained in human terms. I like this book!

— Chantha Nguon, Executive Director,
Stung Treng Women's Development Center, Cambodia

Drawing on her encyclopedic knowledge of business history and decades of practical experience inside corporate boardrooms, Deborah brilliantly illuminates and breathes life into dry and dusty concepts like fiduciary duties, maximizing shareholder value, and exercising reasoned business judgment. Deborah encourages corporate directors to flex their collective corporate governance muscles to enthusiastically participate in building robust businesses that serve and reward every constituency today and lay foundations of opportunity for future generations."

— Peter A. Chapman, Publisher,
Beard Group, Inc.

This book is a must-read not only for current and prospective directors but for anyone who wants to understand the concept of corporations and the way in which they are and should be managed. Bravo to this author who dives into the real heart of how we arrived at corporate America as it exists today and the right path to righting our ship! She has gone in depth to the complexities of the relationships between shareholders, management and directors and has explained it so that a general readership can understand. This book is enlightening, provocative and fun!

— John L. Cook Esq., Cofounder & Partner (Ret.),
Cook, Barkett, Ponder & Wolz, L.C.

The author is an anthropologist who brings back great stories of that weird tribe of corporate directors; she describes boardroom cultures, often dysfunctional, and shows us how to move and improve them. She is a social psychologist, alert to examples of conformity pressures, groupthink, and emergent leadership in board meetings. She is an economist, bringing the interests of creditors, stockholders, and customers into board deliberations. Her voice is personable and inviting; the experience and examples in this book can encourage seminar discussions across the social sciences.

— Clark R. McCauley, Jr., Research Professor of Psychology, Bryn Mawr College; Founding Editor *Emeritus*, Dynamics of Asymmetric Conflict; Co-Director, Solomon Asch Center for Study of Ethnopolitical Conflict

Ms. Midanek's book has not only helped me as the CEO understand how better to use my board, but it will be required reading for all members of the board and senior management.

Board members who can challenge, collaboratively, are the best board members a CEO can have; they promote useful discussion, new ideas, and are generally more supportive of the process. A board member who believes he or she is the smartest person in the room, however, will spew the most irrelevant anecdote, be the worst listener, and the least productive. This book provides useful perspective to help all of them to work better as a group in service to the company."

— Darren Latimer, Chief Executive Officer, Stonegate Capital Holdings

By tracing how corporations and their boards have evolved, Ms. Midanek provides a unique historical perspective on the role of corporations in society going back to the trading companies in the Netherlands and Britain in the 17th century. This well-written history is a valuable read for business and law students and teachers as well as for today's officers and directors and their advisors.

— Lewis H. Lazarus, Partner, Morris James

"All directors want to help the companies they serve to flourish," writes Deborah Hicks Midanek in her valuable book. Drawing on her store of boardroom experience, this specialist in how boards of directors think and act tackles the big questions such as "Who owns the company?"

— James Kristie, Editor-in-Chief and Associate Publisher, Directors & Boards, Retired

The Governance Revolution is a must read for board members and risk and legal professionals advising boards. Deborah Midanek makes the case for a new look at the purpose of corporations and the need for long term perspectives...something sorely missing today. This book will help you in your board service.

> — Catherine Allen, Chairman and CEO, The Santa Fe Group; a multi-board director and 2018 NACD Directorship Honoree

The release of this publication could not be more timely or on point. Directors face more challenges and exposure than they ever have. This book is extremely informative and a tremendous resource tool for directors especially those that are independent. Kudos to Ms. Midanek for having the insight and tenacity to write this book.

> — Trey Monsour, Esq., Shareholder, Polsinelli, PC

About De|G PRESS

Five Stars as a Rule

De|G PRESS, the startup born out of one of the world's most venerable publishers, De Gruyter, promises to bring you an unbiased, valuable, and meticulously edited work on important topics in the fields of business, information technology, computing, engineering, and mathematics. By selecting the finest authors to present, without bias, information necessary for their chosen topic *for professionals*, in the depth you would hope for, we wish to satisfy your needs and earn our five-star ranking.

In keeping with these principles, the books you read from De|G PRESS will be practical, efficient and, if we have done our job right, yield many returns on their price.

We invite businesses to order our books in bulk in print or electronic form as a best solution to meeting the learning needs of your organization, or parts of your organization, in a most cost-effective manner.

There is no better way to learn about a subject in depth than from a book that is efficient, clear, well organized, and information rich. A great book can provide life-changing knowledge. We hope that with De|G PRESS books you will find that to be the case.

DOI 10.1515/9781547400270-203

About the Author

Deborah Hicks Midanek is an independent director, a pioneer in the corporate restructuring industry, a veteran of Wall Street trading floors, and a serial entrepreneur. Widely respected for her turnaround skills, she has diagnosed and remedied problems for over 60 corporations and facilitated the growth of nearly 30 other ventures, including her own. She has been described by the late Fletcher Byrom, chief executive officer of a Fortune 25 company, as a "pure thinker"—quickly gaining a deep understanding of complex problems and demonstrating an extraordinary ability to assimilate conflicting desires and craft lasting solutions.

Deborah has been directly involved in much of the extraordinary innovation that has taken place on Wall Street over the last few decades, and in handling the consequences of its excess. With solid knowledge of capital markets from all points of view and a long record of success in building and rebuilding companies from the bottom up, Deborah focuses on defining transitions as positive processes.

Deborah has served as chairman, lead director, and director as well as committee chair (audit, compensation, governance, special independent) for 23 public and private companies. In her first role as a director, she organized the shareholders of beleaguered Drexel Burnham Lambert Group to achieve recognition by the bankruptcy court and restructured the incumbent board to favor independent directors, whom she recruited and led.

Deborah founded advisory firm Solon Group in 2005 and continues to lead it today. She is a 2011 NACD Board Leadership Fellow, and also a Certified Turnaround Professional, based on career achievement. She has served as chief executive officer of several companies, built and sold her own institutional investment management firm and grew a retail no load mutual fund complex to $1 billion in assets in record time. She joined Drexel to start its interest rate swap (derivatives) function and then led the firm's structured finance department.

DOI 10.1515/9781547400270-204

Deborah earned her MBA from the Wharton School and an AB from Bryn Mawr College. A frequent writer and speaker on governance, resilience, and leadership, she is deeply involved in promoting entrepreneurship. A New Yorker now living in Mississippi, she is in the middle of a downtown turnaround, renovating and repurposing the twenty-two 19th century commercial row buildings she has acquired.

About the Series Editor

Alexandra Reed Lajoux is Series Editor for De|G PRESS, a division of Walter De Gruyter, Inc. The series has an emphasis on governance, corporate leadership, and sustainability. Dr. Lajoux is chief knowledge officer emeritus (CKO) at the National Association of Corporate Directors (NACD) and founding principal of Capital Expert Services, LLC (CapEx), a global consultancy providing expert witnesses for legal cases. She has served as editor of *Directors & Boards, Mergers & Acquisitions, Export Today,* and *Director's Monthly*, and has coauthored a series of books on M&A for McGraw-Hill, including *The Art of M&A* and eight spin-off titles on strategy, valuation, financing, structuring, due diligence, integration, bank M&A, and distressed M&A. For Bloomberg/Wiley, she coauthored *Corporate Valuation for Portfolio Investment* with Robert A. G. Monks. Dr. Lajoux serves on the advisory board of Campaigns and Elections, and is a Fellow of the Caux Round Table for Moral Capitalism. She holds a B.A. from Bennington College, a Ph.D. from Princeton University, and an M.B.A. from Loyola University in Maryland. She is an associate member of the American Bar Association.

DOI 10.1515/9781547400270-205

Contents

DOI 10.1515/9781547400270-206

Prologue: What Is the Governance Revolution?

It is of the essence of revolutions of the more silent sort that they are unrecognized until they are far advanced. This was the case with the so-called Industrial revolution, and is the case with the corporate revolution through which we are at present passing. The translation of perhaps two-thirds of the industrial wealth of the country from individual ownership to ownership by the large, publicly financed corporations vitally changes the lives of property owners, the lives of workers, and the methods of property tenure. The divorce of ownership from control consequent on that process almost necessarily involves a new form of economic organization of society. Manifestly the problem calls for a series of appraisals.

—Berle & Means: *The Modern Corporation and Private Property*, 1932

In 1932, Adolf A. Berle and Gardiner C. Means named a revolution, the corporate revolution, that, following the industrial revolution before it, transferred considerable control of wealth to the organization. Today we face continuing battles for control of the organization and the wealth it provides, and it is the clearly the responsibility of its guardians, the board of directors, to protect that wealth and the future direction of the corporation. We are, therefore, in the midst of a third revolution: the governance revolution.

Directors of the public corporation enter this revolution poorly armed. Their job, not well understood by many, including directors themselves, is not to maximize shareholder value. They are there to protect and enhance the health and value of the corporation as the guardians of its perpetual life. Focus on maximizing shareholder value in the short run, recently a dominant focus, can be seen as a dereliction of the director's fiduciary duty. Each director singly, and the board of directors collectively, owes its loyalty to the corporation, not to its shareholders' short-term wishes.

Shareholders of public companies do not own them, but instead own interests in residual income with specific and narrow rights attached, including the right collectively to elect the directors. Just because they assert rights does not mean they have those rights, unless the board falls for their bluster and gives them rights.

Shareholder activists may employ very smart people, and may have ideas worth listening to and acting upon. That does not give them the right to abuse and harangue sitting directors, or do anything more than vote them out, fair and square. Companies also employ and can hire very smart people to analyze alternative scenarios just as the activists do, and implement those they find to be in the best interests of the corporation, with assistance from their boards.

DOI 10.1515/9781547400270-207

Much short-term pressure in the markets today derives from the need of pension fund managers to realize returns above public market norms. As hard working pension fund managers seeking to garner enough money to pay escalating, unfunded pension obligations, they have been increasingly investing in alternative asset classes such as hedge funds and private equity vehicles whose returns are alleged not to correspond with broad market behavior. Addressing the pension crisis would change the investment landscape and significantly ease the chronic pressure for short-term profits.

For their part, if directors take ownership of their true roles, they can drive the companies in their charge toward long-term sustainable value creation over short-term sophistry. They can just say no to activists, and can boldly lead their companies to better futures if they will do the job before them. By building an understanding of the origins and legal basis for their role, these directors will arm themselves to prevail in the governance revolution.

The role to be played by the board of directors has never been more critical to our nation's prosperity. Much work needs to be done. Now is the time.

Introduction

Boards are mysterious, and imperious; cloistered and powerful; revered and reviled. Their members are a breed apart, to be treated warily as we just do not know exactly what to make of them—sometimes even when we serve alongside them.

Long accustomed to operating in obscurity, directors have found their peace and quiet disturbed lately by all kinds of clamor at the board room door. Many of our major enterprise failures are blamed on failure of governance. Activist shareholders believe they know better. Proxy advisors grade board performance. Women and minorities lament their lack of inclusion, and the lovely phrase "board refreshment" has taken hold as a polite way of saying that new blood is needed. Regulators debate whether and how to add more new rules to ensure that boards perform.

Improving Governance Now Urgently Important

At the same time, several corporations are now larger than small countries and have operations that span the globe. Technological change, already disruptive, continues to accelerate. Financial markets and their derivative instruments and computer directed trading are volatile, unpredictable, and opaque. Accounting rules do not always correspond to measures of health. Customers and vendors alike are fickle as all are under pressure to show growth, which often means cutting cost or quality. Employee loyalty has been eroded by perceived lack of employer loyalty, and by the constant search for green grass. And of course, we have terrorists and cyber thieves attacking our information systems and sometimes our people.

It is hardly surprising that board members may want to hide behind that door to the boardroom, as their job has become extremely demanding. There are many legitimate needs for their attention, and many distractions. How to tell the difference?

To my mind, to separate the wheat from the chaff in governance, we start with the definition of the role, which needs to start with an exploration of what governance is, and how it came to be practiced in the forms we know today. Without that foundation, board members will flounder. In fact, many do flounder, as they lack a basic understanding of their purpose and thus are left believing that their job is simply to follow the checklist du jour.

DOI 10.1515/9781547400270-208

Governance Defined

A quick Google search of "corporate governance" can create the impression that it is a recent invention, coming to life late in the 20th century. Though public focus on governance increased in the 1980s as a wave of hostile takeovers occurred, and in the 1990s and the New Millennium with various huge failures in the United States and abroad, governance itself is as old as the hills. Wherever humans have had to divide resources and allocate risks among themselves, governance has been at work. Over the centuries, various governance systems have been codified as ownership and control inevitably become separated.

Definitions of governance abound, each one more detailed and sophisticated than the last, but to me the most robust one is this: Governance is the system by which decisions about enterprise resource allocation and risk tolerance are made. Such systems, implicit or explicit, are everywhere, in families, countries, homeowner's associations, tribes, wolf packs, and so on. Some are good and productive, and others are disorganized and destructive. But wherever there are resources to be acquired or divided and more than one consumer of same, there is governance. It comes down to who decides who gets what, for the achievement of which purpose.

Governance Structures

What we have now, and what has evolved significantly since the corporate form of organization became so dominant during the 20th century, are established systems, in many cases developed by regulatory authorities and/or stock exchanges where company shares are listed for trading, that codify behaviors developed over centuries and seek to improve upon them. When ships set out to sea, agreed rules were needed regarding how operations were handled, expenses and rewards allocated, and risks and disasters addressed. Marco Polo, the Medicis, Christopher Columbus were all subject to governance structures.

These structures take different forms in different countries and industries, but certain universal themes recur, among them the use of groups of intermediaries between multiple owners and operating control, requirements for periodic reporting of financial results to owners, and an identified authority to appoint the leader. Nevertheless, throughout its evolution, the concept of governance, while lively in the minds of many regulators, has often been misunderstood, since few of those who write the rules and evaluate corporate decisions and results have sat in the director's seat and wrestled with the myriad issues the board must handle.

Meanwhile, governance requirements have remained obscure to investors, the public at large, and, at times, directors themselves.

Vulnerability of Boards

Boards of directors are considered all but irrelevant by many financial players, who tend to see them as mushrooms at worst, a nuisance but necessary evil at best. Management is also often eager to placate directors and keep them out of the way, so they can get on with the serious work of running the enterprise. The proxy advisor cohort, per the 2017 Conference Board report on their view of the role of the board, largely views the position through a disjointed lens and seems to recognize no board responsibility to apply independent judgment. The public at large has little understanding of the function of boards and board members, except when Enron or Lehman Brothers or the Weinstein Companies collapse, at which point everyone is eager to pin the tail on the board of directors as the donkey.

Board members, busy doing other things and coming together only periodically for brief periods of time in structured settings to consider information that has been carefully culled for them, are all too vulnerable to attack. Many do not fully understand the job they are there to do, but feel nonetheless that they are supposed to know, or they would not have been selected. Eager to fit in and be accepted, they do not ask. Worse, they fall prey to believing that someone will tell them if there is something they need to know.

Helping Board Members Move from Passive to Active

It is time for board members to fight back. How, you ask? The old-fashioned way: by being as well prepared as possible, studying the context of corporate governance, and learning the ins and outs of the role. By understanding that good governance is based on values and a systematic approach. That checklists and regulations are important, but the real requirement is the courageous exercise of good judgment. That all that needs to be exercised adroitly, as the group dynamics of the board itself can make their application challenging.

Finally, the struggle to be effective, address risk management, strategy and now culture, currently popular preoccupations, are about making it possible for the board to exercise forethought in a structure that has largely been considered by design to be reactive rather than active. In a rapidly changing world that puts a premium on agility and innovation, this issue needs to be looked at carefully.

Key Audiences for this Book

For serving directors, I hope this book will be helpful and perhaps serve as a device to foment discussion and, whether you agree with me or not, help to achieve greater alignment among fellow directors, between directors and management, and between enterprise and shareholders as well as other stakeholders. For aspiring directors, the book may give you some useful insight into what you are in for and help you to prepare for the journey.

For those not serving as board members, I hope this practical guide to the demands and challenges of board service will be useful in understanding better how to work with companies and their boards. Audiences beyond directors and would-be directors that may find these comments helpful include company management and employees as well as investors, attorneys, lenders, policy makers, teachers, and students.

Structure of the Book

Part I: The System and How it Came to Be

The use of the corporate form and its constant companion the board of directors has succeeded in transforming the world many times for over four centuries. Understanding their evolution and relationship to raising capital provides a necessary foundation for directors today.

Part II: The Players and Capital Market Forces

Stakes are high as boards are now significantly comprised of independent directors who must manage the challenges inherent in having less information than management while also playing defense in the face of pressure from short-term activists, longer-term investors, and increasingly active regulators.

Huge shifts in our capital markets compound the challenges as institutional investors dominate as never before, activist investors boldly assert rights they may or may not have and pursue various aggressive tactics seen and unseen, and "innovation" in capital market instruments has led not only to a huge private equity sector but also to a complex intertwined network of largely obscure derivative instruments. We have painfully seen the cascading effect of their mysterious complexity as we drove ourselves into the abyss of the 2008 financial crisis and struggled to claw our way back out.

Part III: The Role of the Board

Perception of the board's role has changed quite a bit in the last seventy-five years, and there are many legacies of former conventions clouding the thinking in and about today's boardrooms. New directors can easily be disoriented, and it is easy for all directors to lose perspective. Functioning of the board can only be as strong as its weakest link, which is often weak due to lack of a clear and common understanding of board role and responsibilities. The debate over the board's proper role has never been as loud or litigious, though the principles have been in place for over four hundred years. Here we review the issues.

Part IV: Doing the Job

Only directors themselves can improve governance, and then only if they know the rules of the game and play, as Einstein said, better than the rest. Learn the rules, play as a team with clear goals, and work together to win, which means winning and keeping the confidence of customers, investors, and stakeholders by delivering sustainable results in an ethical manner and leading them all toward well-developed corporate goals. It is time and past time for directors and boards to move from defense to offense in fulfilling their responsibilities.

Part V: Hazards and Their Navigation

Trauma is inevitable, and that is when the board comes into its own as the guardian of the perpetual life of the corporation, a responsibility management does not share. Board members function much like parents raising a child, protecting it while it develops its own judgment, teaching the child how to perform responsibly as a citizen in a changing world, and stepping in when the child is facing challenges.

The biggest such challenge can occur when the money is rolling in. It is human nature to relax then, and way too easy for all parties to become complacent and take their eyes off the ball. In the wonderfully apt statement of economist Hyman Minsky, "stability breeds instability," and our job is to combat that tendency with every fiber of our ability. To do that we as the board must build a corporate culture that is resilient, able to both acknowledge and learn from mistakes, and driven by enduring values that go beyond the value of the dollar.

Before We Begin

If I achieve nothing else, I hope to drive home the fact that governance is not boring, but deeply engaging and full of drama and impact. While this volume is not definitive in any respect and largely reflects my own experience and point of view, I do hope it is interesting and readable; possibly provocative. I hope to instigate discussion, not necessarily to be right, though of course I hope I am. Though there are many more expert than I in each aspect we explore, few are foolhardy enough to try to provide an integrated view of the entire subject, even once over lightly. Above all, I hope that the ideas and context discussed herein add to the confidence and discernment of all involved in the current governance revolution. Please forgive the inevitable errors.

In the Beginning . . .

Adolf Berle and Gardiner Means observed in their seminal 1932 work *The Modern Corporation and Private Property* "It is of the essence of revolutions of the more silent sort that they are unrecognized until they are far advanced. This was the case with the so-called industrial revolution, and is the case with the corporate revolution through which we are at present passing. . ."

We as citizens are living through a period of profound transformation, the shape of which, like the industrial revolution and the corporate revolution described by Berle and Means, we will likely not fully understand for decades to come, should we survive. It is disturbing, disruptive, and hopeful, all at once. Having brought ourselves to the brink of system collapse ten years ago, we can see and feel the downside of present circumstances in the way that our parents and grandparents saw and felt the impact of the Great Depression and World War II. We also know well the enervating effects of chronic failure to resolve conflict among the zealots we fight now, in whatever guise they take, religious or political ideology, nation state, or just plain terrorists.

As a long-time corporate director and an experienced turnaround executive who has seen countless instances of governance failure leading to corporate collapse, I find myself hopeful. I am hoping that the clamor of new regulations following the scandals of Enron, WorldCom, and hosts of other corporate disasters and the radically increased global focus on corporate governance following the 2008 financial crisis will achieve what no amount of exhortation in the form of principles and policies has done. Whether we follow the system described in the article published by the Harvard Law School Forum on Corporate Governance and Financial Regulation entitled "Corporate Governance: The New Paradigm" espoused by well-known attorney Martin Lipton, a founding partner of law firm Wachtell, Lipton, Rosen, & Katz, or prefer the individually focused concepts set forth by Lipton's crosstown rival attorney Ira Milstein in his 2016 book *The Activist Director*, we are in a state of emergency that requires bold action.

That bold action must be taken by directors themselves from within the boardroom. These directors and those that succeed them have a very difficult, often ambiguous job. Those brave souls that undertake the role deserve respect, but just as they are surrounded by change, they themselves must change. They must roundly reject being treated as a necessary nuisance to be placated, along with the passivity and ritualized behavior that allowed otherwise smart and sensible directors to fail to notice the radical changes in the balance sheets of Lehman or Enron, or to willfully overlook the fraudulent sales practices apparently endemic to Wells Fargo.

"Change is constant" is now a constant refrain. In view of that change it is imperative that board practices change. Successful and vigilant directors are out there, but there are far too many who have seen the job as a sinecure or a retirement pastime, or who have deferred to custom or been dulled by boredom in the face of endless slide presentations. Serving as a corporate director is a serious calling requiring dedication and courage. Directors individually and collectively as boards must show up with their A game ready to take on the challenges of our turbulent world.

As humans we face both unprecedented prosperity and a growing number of challenges that are undermining the environmental, economic, technological, and institutional systems on which our future rests. Having achieved the distinction taking the world to the brink of collapse, we know firsthand that in our world of complex and interconnected systems, a single disruption can lead to cascading and dramatic breakdowns. If we want to sit at the leadership table, we must learn to protect and sustainably grow our corporations, our citizens, and ourselves.

Survival of the Fittest Corporations

Out of approximately six million companies in the United States, less than 1 percent are publicly traded and an even smaller number, roughly five thousand, are traded on exchanges such as the New York Stock Exchange and NASDAQ. These five thousand play an outsized economic role—by some estimates they employ nearly one-third of the American workforce.

The composition of major stock market indices shows significant change over time. This supposedly exceptional turbulence in corporate rankings, according to business historian Leslie Hannah, is also observed in earlier periods. According to her, corporate dinosaurs are ubiquitous in an ever-changing world. Because no company, no matter how successful, lasts forever, and because only a fraction of companies survive more than a few decades, turnover of varying degrees is entirely natural. Hannah has also found that of the one hundred largest companies in the world in 1912, twenty remained among the one hundred largest in 1995.

. . . And Directors

Boards of directors, too, will soon experience long awaited and massive turnover, as suggested by a new study, *Age Diversity Within Boards of Directors of the S&P 500 Companies*, conducted by Board Governance Research LLC and funded by the Investor Responsibility Research Center Institute (IRRC). The report shows little age diversity within the boardrooms of S&P 500 companies, which boast a median average age for all boards of 62.4 years, and that the average is persistent across companies by size and industry segment. While the data are presented to bemoan this lack of age diversity, to my eyes this means that within the next ten years we will see many new directors at many companies.

. . . And Institutional Investors

Investors are also facing new challenges. Over the past few decades, the ownership of public corporations has been turned on its head. While private individuals owned approximately two-thirds of U.S. equities in 1970, today it is institutional investors like Blackrock, Vanguard, and State Street that control two-thirds of such shares.

This increase in institutional assets, often referred to as fiduciary capitalism, came with the rise of pension funds and mutual funds, and more recently, the popularity of exchange traded funds (ETFs) has shifted assets from active to passive investment strategies. The concentration of ownership and the growth of passive assets are now so great that engagement with portfolio companies is far more practical for the largest institutional investors than simply selling their positions, as there are limited remaining places that can host their money. Even as institutional investors have become more powerful, their enormous size compels them to be more involved in corporate affairs.

Regulators Also Evolve

Regulators are stirring. As Jerome H. Powell, chairman of the Federal Reserve Board appointed in 2018, commented in a speech in August 2017, "Across a range of responsibilities, we simply expect much more of boards of directors than ever before. There is no reason to expect that to change."

Mr. Powell served as the top Federal Reserve official overseeing the negotiations with Wells Fargo & Company regarding the early February 2018, settlement announcement: no further growth above its current level of about $2 trillion in assets until it proved that its governance was substantially improved. In a marked shift from its historically hands-off approach to corporate boards, the Fed's top regulator chastised former Wells chairman John Stumpf in a published letter, excerpted below:

> The Federal Reserve Board is issuing this letter to you with respect to your tenure as Chair of the board of directors of Wells Fargo & Company (WFC) from 2010 to 2016. As Chair, it was your responsibility to lead the WFC board in its oversight of the firm's business and operations. With respect to that responsibility, it was incumbent upon you as leader of the WFC board to ensure that the business strategies approved by the board were consistent with the risk management capabilities of the firm. It was also incumbent on you to ensure that the WFC board had sufficient information to carry out its responsibilities. . . The settlement is an attempt by the Fed to impress upon banks that their boards of directors should be vigorous, independent watchdogs—and if they fail, there will be consequences.

Join the Governance Revolution

As we move through this period of profound and constant change, serving as a corporate director has never been more important—or more demanding. I invite you to join me in the Governance Revolution. I would love to hear from you at DHMidanek@SolonGroup.com.

Read More

The Modern Corporation and Private Property, Preface. Adolf A. Berle and Gardiner C. Means; Harcourt Brace, & World, Inc., 1932

The Modern Corporation and Private Property; The Implications of Corporate Control, Revised Preface, Gardiner C. Means, 1967

The Global Risks Report 2018, World Economic Forum

What Does Fortune 500 Turnover Mean? Dane Stangler and Sam Arbesman, Ewing Marion Kauffman Foundation, June 2012

Letter to Former Wells Fargo Chairman John Stumpf, Federal Reserve Board Press Release, February 2, 2018

Part I: **The System and How It Came To Be**

Boards of directors are sitting ducks. Shareholders complain and even attack, management manipulates, and individual board members have no power, able to act only as part of the board as a whole. Worse, the board meets only occasionally, typically quarterly, in fairly ritualized circumstances, and board members rarely have the opportunity to speak candidly to each other or to management.

And yet, the board bears ultimate responsibility for the health of the corporation. The director's role is not an easy one, and we can empathize with the many directors who stand on ceremony rather than substance, hoping at best that they look good in the proxy statement and the photo in the annual report. As they seek strategies to boost company health and shareholder wealth, today's board members must also navigate unprecedented investor scrutiny and deliver greater transparency and accountability while protecting against cyber and other kinds of terrorism and understanding the potential impact of new technologies such as cryptocurrency.

How can board members fight back when the deck is so seriously stacked against them? What is required is a revolution in governance, powered by a revolution in the thinking and behavior of corporate directors. The role is an ambiguous one and requires much effort and attention not only in meetings but in the many hours between them.

In this part, we explore the current dominant system of corporate governance and how it came to be. Our primary focus is on the United States, and the public company. You may think we are spending too much time on history and skip ahead, but to my mind, we all need the insight that the history of the corporate form offers to provide a firm foundation for the way corporations are governed today, so bear with me. Today's directors operate in a complex environment composed of many markets, players, and instruments. Every director's toolkit should include a sense of how these have evolved.

Chapter 1
How Our Governance System Began

Boards of directors and their perceived poor performance have been castigated for over 400 years. As economist Adam Smith wrote in *The Wealth of Nations* in 1776, corporate directors managed "other people's money" and this conflict of interest meant directors were prone to "negligence and profusion."

Yet the corporate form of organization and its use to raise and deploy capital has had an extraordinarily positive impact on global development. And every jurisdiction in the world requires that a board of directors be appointed in order to form a corporation and maintain it. To understand this apparent conundrum, we look first at how the corporation and its companion, the board, evolved. Its history is fascinating, at least in part due to its durability over the centuries. Very little has changed.

The First Limited Liability Corporation

In 1597 four tattered and battered Dutch ships struggled home from the East Indies with a few bags of peppercorns. With decimated crews and cargo, a far cry from the riches imagined, the merchants who paid for the voyage were disappointed. Their expedition nonetheless galvanized Dutch determination to best the dominant Portuguese in the battle for control of the spice trade with the East Indies, known today as Southeast Asia. To do this, they needed what none alone had: capital to build ships and to staff and provision them for long and dangerous journeys.

Bold action was needed. The government of the Dutch Republic mandated the combination of all the trading companies, then competing in separate shipping guilds, into a single entity in exchange for a monopoly on trade with the East Indies for 20 years as well as certain sovereign rights in territories discovered. In 1602, the resulting Dutch East India Company ("Verenigde Oostindische Compagnie" or "VOC") received its charter.

This may sound simple, but first consider the distance, the dangers and the plain unknown. These merchants had long operated independently, choosing and financing their own journeys and paying out to investors, or collecting to fund losses, at the end of each journey. Think how novel it was to decide collectively how to allocate capital, and to be trusted with keeping the capital rather than returning it at journey's end. Add to that the danger of the Portuguese rivals,

DOI 10.1515/9781547400270-001

the native peoples in the New World, and the demands of long sea voyages. It was a remarkable series of actions the Dutch undertook.

VOC was organized as a stock company with two types of shareholders: the *participanten*, economic participants but not managers; and the *bewindhebbers*, who acted as managing directors. In this case the liability of not just the *participanten* but also of the *bewindhebbers*, whose exposure, in the past, was typically unlimited, was limited to the paid-in capital. The VOC therefore was a limited liability company, likely the world's first.

Amsterdam Stock Exchange Established to List VOC Securities

VOC also appears to have pioneered the use of investing in the company rather than in a specific venture governed by the company and required that the capital remain invested (or be "locked up" in modern parlance) for the life of the company. To make this palatable to investors, the Dutch needed a mechanism to allow investors to access their capital. The world's first stock exchange was thus created, and VOC listed its shares on the Amsterdam Stock Exchange, the first company in history to list its shares on a formal stock exchange. Although it listed only VOC instruments at first, it soon grew.

VOC Completes Initial Public Offering, Possibly World's First

In VOC's next pioneering move, the company's stock as well as bonds were offered to the general public, with a minimum participation level of 3,000 guilders, a price that allowed many merchants and entrepreneurs to participate. This offering was unprecedented and became the first recorded initial public offering or IPO. Remarkably, the annual dividend paid out averaged around 18 percent of capital over the course of the company's ensuing 200-year existence.

The capital VOC was able to raise using these new techniques put it far ahead of any rival. Estimates suggest that the company raised more than ten times the capital acquired by the English East India Company, chartered by Queen Elizabeth in 1600, which appears to have continued the practice of financing voyages one-by-one at least until mid century.

In 1688, Joseph de la Vega, an Amsterdam trader as well as a successful businessman, published the delightfully entitled *Confusion of Confusions*, about the workings of the city's stock market. The earliest book about stock trading, it took the form of a dialogue between a merchant, a shareholder and a philosopher. He described a market that was sophisticated but prone to excesses, and de la

Vega offered advice to his readers on such topics as the unpredictability of market shifts and the importance of patience in investment.

To see VOC's achievements in perspective, consider this: not only was it granted quasi-governmental powers in the areas it explored, allowing it to maintain its own army and rule certain colonies itself, but between 1602 and 1796 VOC sent almost a million Europeans to work in the Asia trade on 4,785 ships, and netted more than 2.5 million tons of Asian trade goods. By contrast, the rest of Europe combined sent only 882,412 people from 1500 to 1795, and the fleet of the English East India Company (EIC), VOC's nearest competitor, was a distant second to its total traffic with 2,690 ships and a mere one-fifth the tonnage of goods carried by VOC.

The Governance of VOC Establishes the Model

VOC was a private enterprise, organized in six chambers (*kamers*) based on the various ports and predecessor guilds. Seventeen delegates were selected from the *bewindhebber* shareholders and convened as the *Heeren XVII* (the Lords Seventeen), including eight delegates from Amsterdam (one short of a majority on its own), four from Zeeland, and one from each of the smaller chambers, while the seventeenth seat rotated. The *Heeren XVII* defined the VOC's general policy and divided operating tasks among the chambers, which carried out the necessary work, built their own ships and warehouses, and traded the merchandise.

The same governing structure that had previously existed to enact and enforce rules governing the conduct of independent merchants in the guilds found itself pressed into service to manage a large business venture in the joint stock company. This appears to have happened without evident consideration as to the different nature of these tasks, or whether an institution developed for one task best fit the needs of the other function, though it is likely that including the members of the prior structure with careful balancing of representation was the most effective way to assure adoption and compliance by all.

The Lords Seventeen Governance Structure Drawn from Guild System

We will dig more deeply into this, but for now, note that this first fairly autonomous board of directors did not originate in the joint stock company with its passive investors. It was instead a form of governance inherited when the business corporation evolved out of societies of independent merchants in which the members each conducted their own businesses. These earlier merchant societies or guilds, in turn, had apparently adopted boards to replace decision-making by assemblies of the entire guild membership. Instead of having an oversight function, the role of the board in these earliest trading companies was legislative (passing ordinances to regulate the membership) and adjudicative (hearing disputes involving the members). Nonetheless, they provide a useful mechanism to use as ownership and control were increasingly separated.

VOC Confronts a Large Activist Shareholder

VOC's Lords Seventeen may also have been the first to confront dissident shareholders. Isaac Le Maire was the largest shareholder in VOC and a *bewindhebber* sitting on the board of governors. Le Maire apparently attempted to divert the firm's profits to himself by undertaking fourteen expeditions under his own accounts instead of those of the company, which had been the traditional method under predecessor forms of organization. Since his large shareholdings were not accompanied by greater voting power, Le Maire was ousted by the *Heeren XVII* in 1605 on charges of embezzlement, and forced to sign an agreement not to compete with VOC.

Mr. LeMaire seems not to have taken his removal lightly. In 1609, he complained of VOC's shoddy corporate governance, and petitioned for the liquidation of VOC. Failing in that effort, he later sought to create the French East India Company, in continuing efforts to break the Dutch government sanctioned monopoly on trade routes and the lucrative spice trade. Notably, he approached Henry Hudson, to lead an expedition for LeMaire and the French. VOC, learning of this plan, made Hudson a better offer, which financed the voyage searching for the northeast passage to the Pacific that led to the discovery of the Hudson River and the settlement of New Amsterdam.

. . . And a Bear Syndicate

Again thwarted, and still the largest shareholder with close to 25 percent of VOC stock, LeMaire next formed a secret company with eight others, for the purpose of trading in VOC shares. This new company sold short shares of VOC, hoping to force the price down. In 1609 the share price fell significantly, perhaps owing to rumors spread by LeMaire. VOC in turn complained to the States-General of the Netherlands, who decided in 1610 to prohibit the sale of shares not in the seller's possession. During 1610 and 1611 the stock price of VOC increased, causing Le

Maire and company to suffer big losses when they had to deliver shares at a lower price than market.

Here we have the first known instance of the use of the corporate form and its ability to transform the world. Though limited in life by the terms of its charter, which was periodically renewed through payments of fees to the Dutch government, VOC brought to life a social contract that allowed for a publicly traded joint-stock corporation, an entity with rights similar to those of states and individuals, with limited liability and significant autonomy.

The stage was set for transferable ownership interests in which voting power can depend upon the number of interests purchased. And in a further step, by being publicly offered and traded, that voting power could become widely dispersed among passive investors and began the long running discussion of what tools are needed to govern the corporation when ownership is so clearly separated from control. Importantly, even then, it was clear that the fiduciary duty of the directors was owed not to LeMaire as the largest shareholder, but to the enterprise and its prospects. Remember this as we move forward.

The Corporate Form Advances and Spreads—And with It, the Board

To track the history of the corporation is to see the evolution of the corporate board. The English East India Company (EIC) may have been the first (or at least the first well documented) corporate charter to grant the power to the governing board to elect the corporation's governor, rather than keep that power for the crown or leave it in the hands of the company's members. Somewhat later, the board elected a chairman and deputy chairman to preside over their meetings, thereby establishing an office of chair separate from that of governor. In another example, an act of Parliament in 1773 introduced staggered terms to the company's board of what were by then referred to as directors, with one-quarter of the directors elected every year.

King William III sought to modernize the kingdom's finances to pay for its wars, and thus the first government bonds were issued in 1693 and the Bank of England was set up the following year. Soon thereafter, English joint-stock companies began going public.

London's first stockbrokers, however, were barred from the old commercial center known as the Royal Exchange, reportedly because of their rude manners. Instead, the new trade was conducted from coffee houses along Exchange Alley. By 1698, a broker named John Castaing, operating out of Jonathan's Coffee

House, was posting regular lists of stock and commodity prices. Those lists mark the beginning of the London Stock Exchange.

Corporations Arrived in the New World

As sovereign focus shifted from how to expand territory through discovery into how to develop said territories into profitable activities, the model of the joint stock corporation was again used to raise the capital and govern the new colonies. Not only did the various trading company boards help preserve political ideas of governance through representative bodies that first took root in medieval times, but they also assured the spread of these ideas into new territories and political venues.

In 1606, James I granted a charter for purposes of trade and colonization in North America. Governance of the London Company was provided through a local resident council of thirteen members appointed by the king, while at the same time, a "Council of Virginia" of thirteen members in England for "superior managing and direction." In 1609, a new charter was issued for the London Company, now called the "Treasurer and Company of Adventurers and Planters of the City of London for the First Colony of Virginia" in which the company's council was elected by the members of the company, rather than appointed by the king. Membership in the company, in turn, was available to persons who contributed money toward the colony.

In 1620, another similar charter was granted, to "The Council established at Plymouth, in the County of Devon, for the planting, ordering, and governing of New England, in America." The Plymouth Colony charter limited membership to forty members, who were named in the charter and held memberships for life, and who filled vacancies by vote of the existing members.

In 1628, John Winthrop and others secured from the Plymouth Company a grant of land between the Merrimac and the Charles River and were granted a charter to form a corporation named the "Governor and Company of the Massachusetts Bay in New England" (aka the Massachusetts Bay Company). The charter called for a governor, deputy governor, and eighteen so-called "assistants", one of the earliest English designations for what we now call directors.

The charter for the Massachusetts Bay Company did not specify that the company's general courts and council had to meet in England. As a result, the elected governing board of the Massachusetts Bay Company became, in effect, the Massachusetts colonial legislature.

Further examples of these charters continued. In 1670, the English crown granted a charter creating the Hudson's Bay Company—officially titled "The Governor and Company of Adventurers of England trading into Hudson's Bay"—for the purpose of trade in what is now Canada. In 1711, the South Sea Company—officially named "Governor and Company of Merchants of Great Britain Trading the South Seas and other parts of America, and for Encouraging the Fishery"—received its charter as a joint-stock company with a monopoly granted over British trade in South America.

And Bubbles Burst

When the Treaty of Utrecht, however, acknowledged Spain's claim to South America, the South Sea Company was left without trading purpose. According to Scottish journalist Charles Mackay in his 1841 book *Extraordinary Popular Delusions and the Madness of Crowds,* by January 1720, its directors were promulgating rumors about their success trading in the endless bounty of South America. By June the share price had increased tenfold before investors, starved for facts, started selling shares in July. In August the stock collapsed, devastating the English markets. Prosecutions of the company governor, sub-governors, its board and government officials followed.

In a similar story in France, Louis XIV's long reign had nearly bankrupted the French monarchy. Rather than reduce spending, the Regency of Louis XV of France endorsed the monetary theories of Scottish financier John Law. In 1716, Law was given a charter for the Banque Royale under which the national debt was assigned to the bank in return for extraordinary privileges. The key to the Banque Royale agreement was that the national debt would be paid from revenues derived from opening the Mississippi Valley. The Bank was tied to other Law ventures —the Company of the West and the Companies of the Indies, together known as the Mississippi Company. The Mississippi Company had a monopoly on trade and mineral wealth from North America and the West Indies.

In 1720, the bank and company merged and Law was appointed by the monarchy as Comptroller General of Finances. Law exaggerated the wealth of Louisiana, which led to wild speculation on the shares of the company in 1719. When shares appeared to generate profits, investors were paid out in paper bank notes. Law's pioneering note-issuing bank thrived until the French government was forced to admit that the number of paper notes being issued by the *Banque Royale* exceeded the value of the amount of metal coinage it held. At the end of 1720, Law's opponents attempted to convert their notes into specie *en masse*, a bank run which forced the bank to stop payment on its paper notes. The value of the new paper currency was cut in half.

In London, Parliament passed the Bubble Act, which stated that only royally chartered companies could issue public shares. In Paris, Law was stripped of office and fled the country. The downside of public ownership of the corporation was becoming clear. The limited liability of the shareholder was a critical hook for successful capital raising, but at the same time, it can be said to have motivated excessive risk-taking. Yes, we do wonder what the boards thought they were to do, but we will see again and again how hard it is for boards to act when the rewards are or appear to be huge.

Read More

A History of Corporate Governance, 1602–2002. Frentrop, Paul, Amsterdam: Deminor, 2003

Putting LeMaire into Perspective: Business Organization and the Evolution of Corporate Governance in the Dutch Republic, 1590–1610, Gelderblom, Oscar; De Jong, Abe; Jonker, Joost; 2010

Origins of Shareholder Advocacy, J. Koppell, ed., New York: Palgrave Macmillan

The Oxford Handbook of Capitalism, Mueller, Dennis C., ed. Oxford University Press, 2012

The First Crash: Lessons from the South Sea Bubble, Dale, Richard, Princeton University Press, 2004

The South Sea Bubble: An Economic History of its Origins and Consequences, Helen Paul, Routledge Explorations in Economic History, 2013

Chapter 2
The Emergence of the Corporation in United States

We have now tiptoed quickly through the guild halls to the age of exploration, wandered through colonization, and into the industrial age. We have been talking about structures that married government goals with structures that incentivized private pursuit of them, and along the way may have built a good deal of independent power. As the colonies moved through the revolution and out the other side, learning to operate as a confederation of states, we see different agendas emerge.

The following sections of this book will take the reader through the first 150 years of corporate evolution in America, to help shed light on how contemporary board practices and the varied perceptions of what they should be came to be. For much of that period, the board, while legally required to exist, was a largely invisible part of business history; its behavior not codified, and rarely mentioned as in any way distinct from the company for which it is responsible.

At the time of the 1776 Declaration of Independence, the only corporations allowed had received specific authorization via royal charter or other government action. Though VOC and EIC and The Massachusetts Bay models had been successful beyond imagination, memories of the spectacular losses incurred in the South Sea Bubble and the Mississippi Company left the lasting impression that corporations were risky, and perhaps dangerous given the outright power once held by VOC and EIC.

Following the 1788 ratification of the Constitution, the formation of corporations, still distrusted, became part of the difficult debate surrounding the definition of state versus federal power. State governments could and did form corporations through special legislation, and the privileges of incorporation were granted selectively to enable projects that directly served the public interest: the construction of turnpikes, bridges and canals, the operation of banks and insurance companies, and the creation of fire brigades. Banks and insurance companies had just begun to assume corporate form and numbered sixty-seven at the opening of the century.

New York Pioneers Simple Incorporation Procedure

From inception of the United States, the states handled corporate law, since all desired to attract capital and promote economic growth, often in competition with each other. It was not until 1811, however, that the first state created an

DOI 10.1515/9781547400270-002

incorporation law that provided a simple registration procedure to form a corporation without specific permission from the legislature.

New York took the honors, and despite alleged fears of the potential for undue risk-taking, also allowed investors limited liability. Importantly, New York required that every corporation be under the control of a board of directors. Interestingly, rather than worrying about undercapitalized corporations, New York's pioneering general incorporation law limited the maximum amount of capital corporations could raise to $100,000. This may reflect an ongoing thread throughout political and corporate history: mutual fear of tyranny. Just as businesses fear that government will exceed its powers, so governments fear an overreach by the corporate powers as they grow.

Boston Manufacturing Company is First Private Corporation in United States

Manufacturing activity continued dominated by the use of partnerships until the Boston Manufacturing Company, the first of the large New England textile firms, was incorporated by Francis Cabot Lowell in Waltham, Massachusetts, in 1813. Mr. Lowell envisioned a fully integrated textile factory, building upon the success of the Slater Mills in Rhode Island in 1793 in inventing a machine process for spinning cotton thread.

While the bloody war for independence was finished, the war for economic independence was in full swing. The economic model of the time was based on raw materials from the United States being shipped to England and Europe and finished there. The United States remained dependent, therefore, on England and Europe for finished goods, which were expensive.

Not surprisingly the English were not eager to share their technological advances, which included the development of the power loom. In 1810 Lowell went on a two-year trip around England and Scotland, trading on family ties when he could to secure visits to production facilities and posing as a peasant worker when he could not gain access any other way. Though he was suspected of industrial espionage at that point and stopped and searched in Nova Scotia on his return, no stolen plans were ever discovered. Mr. Lowell had memorized the pertinent details of the looms he wanted to replicate and managed to create an even better loom for his factory.

His factory needed capital however, which he raised using the corporate form, as it had the capacity to attract larger sums than could a partnership. He assembled a board and eleven initial stockholders, built his factory, created finished goods for the domestic market, and along the way revolutionized American business practice. He pioneered the use of water to power his big looms, carefully selected his workforce, paid them in cash and provided safe onsite housing for them. As time went on, the novelty of this non-farm employment for what became known as mill girls wore off. Mr. Lowell's factory and its shift ending bell also served as catalysts for the first strikes and efforts of labor to organize to secure better conditions.

As production grew, more power and space were needed, and the factory moved to East Chelmsford on the Merrimack River. Renamed Lowell in honor of Francis Cabot Lowell at his premature death at 42 years old in 1817, Lowell became the first planned factory town in the U.S. and boasted dozens of textile factories by the 1840s. Maybe more importantly, by that time the U.S. produced cloth at a lower cost than England could, and England finally lost her dependent colonies. Allegedly even Thomas Jefferson, famously dedicated to the notion of the United States as a bountiful agrarian economy, began through his acquaintance with Lowell and his innovations to see the need for large-scale mechanization to allow the U.S. to compete on the world stage.

In an early demonstration of the use of the corporate form in a private enterprise that separated economic ownership from management control, by 1830 the stockholders had grown from 11 to 76, no individual owned more than 8½ percent of the stock, and the board of directors' combined holdings amounted to only 22 percent. Twenty years later there were 123 stockholders, while the board held only 11 percent.

Corporations Gain Power Under State Control

Over the course of the 19th century, more and more states allowed incorporation of limited liability corporations with a simple registration procedure. In the late 19th and early 20th centuries, one industry after another found the corporate form attractive, in part because it was the only legal form that allowed the corporation to offer limited liability to investors. This is a very important attraction when large amounts of capital are required for huge undertakings such as railroads and canals.

State legislators tried to maintain control of the corporate chartering process: incorporated businesses were prohibited from taking any action that legislators did not specifically allow. Unless a legislature renewed an expiring charter, the corporation was dissolved and its assets divided among shareholders. Many required a company's accounting books to be turned over to a legislature upon request. The power of large shareholders was limited by scaled voting, so that large and small investors had equal voting rights. Interlocking directorships were outlawed. Shareholders had the right to remove directors at will, and so on.

The penalty for abuse or misuse of the charter was not a plea bargain and a fine, but dissolution of the corporation by the legislature. In 1819 the U.S. Supreme Court tried to strip states of this sovereign right by overruling a lower court's decision that allowed New Hampshire to revoke a charter granted to Dartmouth College by King George III. The Court claimed that since the charter contained no revocation clause, it could not be withdrawn. State legislators saw this as an attack by the Court on state sovereignty, and laws were re-written, and state constitutional amendments passed to circumvent the *Dartmouth v. Woodward* ruling.

Over several decades starting in 1844, nineteen states amended their constitutions to make corporate charters subject to alteration or revocation by their legislatures. In 1855 it seemed that the Supreme Court had adjusted its position when in Dodge v. Woolsey it reaffirmed states' powers over "artificial bodies."

Government spending during the Civil War brought some corporations significant wealth. Political power began flowing to absentee owners, rather than locally rooted enterprises. Legislators were persuaded to extend durations of charters, and slowly their control diminished as corporate power grew. Importantly, the 1886 Supreme Court case of Santa Clara County v. Southern Pacific Railroad set the precedent for seeing a corporation as a "natural person."

Economic Opportunity Expands; Farmers and Artisans Suffer Disruption

The growing impact of the industrial age, as demonstrated by the Boston Manufacturing Company discussed above, provided both expanding economic opportunity and began the conversion of a nation of farmers and artisans to wage earners no longer self-employed and self-reliant. Dependence on the larger employer grew, along with the concomitant fear of unemployment.

From the era of reconstruction to the end of the 19th century, the United States underwent an economic transformation marked by the maturing of the industrial economy, the rapid expansion of big business, the development of large-scale agriculture, and the rise of national labor unions and industrial conflict.

An unprecedented surge in immigration and urbanization after the Civil War contributed significantly to economic growth. American society was in transition as waves of immigrants arriving from Europe, Asia, Mexico, and Central America were creating a new American mosaic. And the dominance of the Anglo-Saxon Protestants who founded the nation, once so important to the development of political and economic organization, began to wane.

Corporate Control is Concentrated

Technological innovation in the late 19th century also fueled this surging economic growth. However, the accompanying rise of the American corporation and the advent of big business resulted in the concentration of the nation's productive capacities in fewer and fewer hands. Mechanization brought farming into the realm of big business as well, making the United States the world's premier food producer—a position it has never surrendered.

Agricultural modernization disrupted family farms, for example, provoking the country's farmers to organize and protest as never before. Social and economic tensions created by industrial development fueled the rise of national labor unions and ugly clashes between capital and labor.

Business and industry were undergoing enormous changes during the 1890s. The first class of multimillionaires had made their fortunes in the Civil War, and during subsequent decades they began to consolidate their holdings, dominating a number of industries with national and international reach. One historian estimates that 1,800 firms disappeared during that period, resulting in the formation of ninety-three trusts.

Public antagonism toward "trusts" and "monopolies" boiled over. Critics of "The Trusts" often targeted silver and gold mines in the West and other large companies whose employees faced hazardous conditions and low wages. Others attacked "The Trusts" and "Wall Street" in the same breath, identifying J.P. Morgan and other financiers as the agents of industrial consolidation. In rural areas, the most dangerous monopolies appeared to be the railroads, which controlled shipping rates along their lines.

Farmers also denounced grain elevators and speculators: the rise of agricultural futures markets, accompanying mechanization of harvesting and processing, caused many farmers to feel increasingly helpless in the face of large institutions beyond their control. In short, denunciation of "The Trusts" symbolized broad fears about the size and power of big business in America.

How J.D. Rockefeller Went from Rags to Riches

To gain some perspective on the scale of what was going on, consider this: John D. Rockefeller, J. Pierpont Morgan, and Andrew Carnegie were worth, according to the series on them produced by the History Channel, more than $1 trillion in 2018 dollars when combined. Even by today's standards, that is an enormous amount of wealth, and it was gained in less than a single generation.

Let us look at just one of them, to gain insight into how this was done. John Davison Rockefeller, the son of a traveling salesman, was born on 1839, in Richford, New York. An industrious youngster, he earned money by raising turkeys, selling candy and doing odd jobs for neighbors. In 1853, the Rockefeller family moved to the Cleveland, Ohio area, where John attended high school then briefly studied bookkeeping at a commercial college.

In 1855, at age 16, he found work as an office clerk at a Cleveland firm that bought, sold and shipped grain, coal and other commodities. In 1859, Rockefeller and a partner established their own similar firm. That same year, America's first oil well was drilled in Titusville, Pennsylvania. In 1863, in the middle of the Civil War, he entered the fledgling oil business by investing in a Cleveland, Ohio refinery. In 1864, Rockefeller married Laura Celestia "Cettie" Spelman, an Ohio native whose father was a prosperous merchant, politician and abolitionist active in the Underground Railroad. The Rockefellers ultimately produced four daughters and one son.

In 1865, at age 26, Rockefeller borrowed money to buy out some of his partners and take control of the refinery, which had become the largest in Cleveland. In 1870, at age 31, Rockefeller formed the Standard Oil Company of Ohio, along with his younger brother William, Henry Flagler, and a group of other men. John Rockefeller was its president and largest shareholder.

Standard Oil gained a monopoly in the oil industry by buying rival refineries and developing companies for distributing and marketing its products around the globe. In 1882, these various companies were combined into the Standard Oil Trust, which would control roughly 90 percent of the nation's refineries and pipelines. Standard Oil was vertically integrated and did everything from build its own oil barrels to employ scientists to figure out new uses for petroleum by-products. The trust avoided listing on a major stock exchange, in order to keep its financial information private.

The Government Fights Back, Kind Of

But this secrecy was to no avail. The success of Standard Oil was too obvious. In 1890, the U.S. Congress passed the Sherman Antitrust Act, the first federal legislation prohibiting trusts and combinations that restrained trade. Two years later, the Ohio Supreme Court dissolved the Standard Oil Trust; however, the businesses within the trust soon became part of Standard Oil of New Jersey, which functioned as a holding company. In 1911, after years of litigation, the U.S. Supreme Court ruled Standard Oil of New Jersey was in violation of anti-trust laws and forced it to dismantle. It was broken up into thirty individual companies.

Rockefeller's enormous success made him a target of muckraking journalists, reform politicians and others who viewed him as a symbol of corporate greed and criticized the methods with which he'd built his empire. As *The New York Times* reported in 1937: "He was accused of crushing out competition, getting rich on rebates from railroads, bribing men to spy on competing companies, of making secret agreements, of coercing rivals to join the Standard Oil Company under threat of being forced out of business, building up enormous fortunes on the ruins of other men, and so on."

Rockefeller retired from day-to-day business operations of Standard Oil in the mid-1890s, even as the contest between Main Street have-nots and Wall Street haves reached new intensity with the presidential election of 1896, in which William Jennings Bryan galvanized the public with his promises to bust the trusts. Rockefeller joined forces with Andrew Carnegie, his contemporary who made a fortune in the steel industry, and J.P. Morgan to help finance the ultimately successful campaign of then Ohio Governor William McKinley.

Following Carnegie's model in which he became a philanthropist and gave away the bulk of his money, Rockefeller donated more than half a billion dollars to various educational, religious and scientific causes. Among his activities, he funded the establishment of the University of Chicago and the Rockefeller Institute for Medical Research, now Rockefeller University. Laura Rockefeller became the namesake of Spelman College, the historically black women's college in Atlanta, Georgia. In 1909, the Rockefeller Sanitary Commission was founded. Less than 20 years later, its primary goal was achieved: the successful eradication of hookworm disease across the southern United States. In 1920, after decades of adventure, and with little to lose, Standard Oil of New Jersey, a remnant of Rockefeller's empire finally listed on a major stock market, the New York Stock Exchange.

Early Days of the New York Stock Exchange

The exchange was in place, ready for the listing. Almost 200 years after the Amsterdam Stock Exchange listed VOC shares, the NYSE was founded on May 17, 1792, when twenty-four brokers met beneath a buttonwood tree in lower Manhattan to sign the Buttonwood Agreement, which set a floor commission rate charged to clients and bound the signers to give preference to the other signers in securities sales. Previously the exchange of securities had been intermediated by the auctioneers who also conducted auctions of commodities such as wheat and tobacco. The group made its first headquarters at the Tontine Coffee House.

The earliest securities traded were primarily government securities such as war bonds from the Revolutionary War along with the shares of the First Bank of the United States stock. Formed In 1791 by the first Secretary of the Treasury, Alexander Hamilton, the goals of the First Bank of the United States were to allow the federal government to assume the Revolutionary War debts of the several states and pay them off; to establish a national bank and create a common currency, and to raise money for the new government. As states allowed the formation of more corporations and more capital was needed for the building of the new country's infrastructure, trading volume grew.

The War of 1812 led to greater commercial activity in the post-war United States. In 1817, the brokers operating under the Buttonwood Agreement adopted restrictions on manipulative trading as well as a formal governance structure, specified listing criteria, and rented space exclusively for securities trading. The organization officially became the New York Stock & Exchange Board, later simplified to the New York Stock Exchange. The invention of the telegraph improved communication and consolidated markets, and New York's market rose to dominance over Philadelphia. Speculation in railroad stocks in the 1830s increased demand for capital and stimulated trading at the exchange. After the Civil War (1861–65), the exchange provided the capital for the accelerating industrialization of the United States.

In 1869, following the end of the Civil War, the rival Open Board of Stock Brokers, with 354 members, merged with the NYSE, which had 533. At that point, membership was capped, and the value of a seat on the Exchange took on importance in its own right. Caps would be increased from time to time. Robert Wright of Bloomberg writes that the merger increased both NYSE's members and trading volume, important as by then "several dozen regional exchanges were also competing with the NYSE for customers. Buyers, sellers and dealers all wanted to complete transactions as quickly and cheaply as technologically possible and that meant finding the markets with the most trading, or the greatest liquidity in today's parlance.

Minimizing competition was essential to keeping a large number of orders flowing, and the merger helped the NYSE to maintain its reputation for providing superior liquidity. The Civil War had stimulated securities trading and the late nineteenth century saw continued rapid growth, with no mechanisms in place beyond the Exchange's own governance procedures to control the nature of the instruments traded. Later, we will look at the exchange's listing requirements, bellwethers for companies with publicly traded stock.

Teddy Busts the Trusts

With the dawn of the 20th century, the gap between rich and poor continued to be a central political issue, even as President McKinley, pro-business, won reelection. He traveled to upstate New York in 1901 to speak, and was shot, the third president to be killed while in office. Moving from vice president to president in the blink of an eye, the zealous trust buster President Theodore Roosevelt went on the attack.

Apparently convinced that a bloody revolution was not far off, Roosevelt believed the Wall Street financiers and the powerful trust titans were being foolish. Although himself a man of means, he was concerned that continued exploitation of the public could result in an uprising that could destroy the whole system. He also believed that the basis of his power was the will of the people, and when he was elected in 1904 he had a strong foundation on which to stand. Government power was very different from commercial power.

The president's weapon was the Sherman Antitrust Act, passed in 1890. The Sherman Act was the first important federal effort to limit the power of corporations that controlled a high percentage of market share. For the first 12 years of its existence the Sherman Act was a paper tiger as the courts routinely sided with business when any enforcement was attempted. Ironically, in the volatile labor/management wars of the 1890s the act was used primarily to block strikes, since it prevented any "conspiracy to restrict trade," and businesses like the Pullman Railcar Company successfully argued that labor unions were such conspiracies and won enforcement support from state and federal militia.

The Supreme Court ruled in 1895 that many business combinations did not constitute "trusts" that restrained interstate trade, and thus could not be prosecuted under federal law. For example, the American Sugar Refining Company, founded in 1891, controlled 98 percent of the sugar industry. Despite this virtual monopoly, the Supreme Court refused to dissolve the corporation in an 1895 ruling.

Government Power Takes on Commercial Power: Teddy v J.P.

Roosevelt nonetheless sensed that he had a sympathetic Court by 1902, and rapidly took action, choosing as his target the most powerful industrialist in the country. J.P. Morgan controlled, among many other ventures, Northern Securities, a railroad conglomerate that dominated railroad shipping across the northern United States.

Legend has it that Morgan was enjoying a peaceful dinner at his New York home on February 19, 1902, when his telephone rang. He was furious to learn that Roosevelt's Attorney General was bringing suit against the Northern Securities Company. Stunned, he muttered to his equally shocked dinner guests about how rude it was to file such a suit without warning.

Four days later, Morgan was at the White House with the president. Morgan bellowed that he was being treated like a common criminal. The president informed Morgan that no compromise could be reached, and the matter would be settled by the courts. Morgan inquired if his other interests were at risk, too. Roosevelt told him only the ones that had done anything wrong would be prosecuted.

Roosevelt sought to apply a moral standard of right versus wrong and good versus bad to evaluating the trusts. If a trust controlled an entire industry but provided good service at reasonable rates, it was a "good" trust to be left alone. Trusts that exploited their monopoly power, jacking up rates and exploiting consumers came under attack. The Supreme Court, in a narrow 5 to 4 decision, agreed and dissolved the Northern Securities Company. Roosevelt said confidently that no man, no matter how powerful, was above the law. As he landed blows on other "bad" trusts, his popularity grew and grew.

Unintended Consequences Lead to More Antitrust Laws

The Sherman Act, however, also kicked off a wave of mergers that even further concentrated corporate power, as companies realized the advantages of creating a single large corporation were even better than acting as the now outlawed cartel. Defining the behavioral meaning of restraint of trade is not easy, especially when the methods of operating had a prior existence and seemed like the normal course. Thus, much of the interpretation of antitrust legislation has been left to the courts to determine case by case.

To address this enforcement challenge, the Clayton Antitrust Act of 1914 was added to the body of United States antitrust law. It sought to prevent anticompetitive practices before they occurred by prohibiting particular conduct, not deemed in the best interest of a competitive market. The Clayton Act specified particular prohibited conduct, the three-level enforcement scheme, the exemptions, and the remedial measures.

In expanding upon the concepts introduced by the Sherman Act, the Clayton Act thoroughly discusses the following four principles defined as restraining economic trade and business:

- Price discrimination between different purchasers if such a discrimination substantially lessens competition or tends to create a monopoly in any line of commerce (Act Section 2, codified at 15 U.S.C. § 13)
- Sales on the condition that (A) the buyer or lessee not deal with the competitors of the seller or lessor ("exclusive dealings") or (B) the buyer also purchase another different product (commonly called "tying") but only when these acts substantially lessen competition (Act Section 3, codified at 15 U.S.C. § 14)
- Mergers and acquisitions where the effect may substantially lessen competition (Act Section 7, codified at 15 U.S.C. § 18) or where the voting securities and assets threshold is met (Act Section 7a, codified at 15 U.S.C. § 18a)
- Any person from being a director of two or more competing corporations, if those corporations would violate the anti-trust criteria by merging (Act Section 8; codified 1200 at 15 U.S.C. § 19)

Read More

The Boston Manufacturing Company and Anglo-American Relations 1807–1820, Bergquist Jr, H. E., Business History, 1973

Enterprising Elite: The Boston Associates and the World They Made, Dalzell, Robert F., 1987

Daniel Webster, the Boston Associates, and the US Government's Role in the Industrializing Process, 1815–1830, Prince, Carl E., and Seth Taylor, Journal of the Early Republic, 1982

John Marshall and Heroic Age of the Supreme Court. Newmyer, R. K., Baton Rouge: Louisiana State University Press, 2001. ISBN 0-8071-2701-9

The Oyez Project, *"Dartmouth College v. Woodward"*, 17 U.S. 518 (1819)

The Presidency of Theodore Roosevelt (2nd ed.) Gould, Lewis L., 2011

Theodore Roosevelt and the Rise of America to World Power, Beale, Howard K., 1956

Mergers and the Clayton Act, Martin, David Dale, University of California, Berkeley, 1959

An International Antitrust Primer. Kintner; Joelson, Macmillan, 1974

Chapter 3
Post–World War I Developments

Through the 1920s, however, power continued to be concentrated in fewer hands as corporations issued shares with multiple classes of voting rights, while other shares were sold with no votes at all, salable in the post–World War I economic boom of the 1920s. More and more ordinary people, those wage earners we discussed above, were looking to the stock market to save the new money they were earning. The law did not, however, guarantee good information or fair terms.

The first three decades of the 20th century saw economic output surge with electrification, mass production and motorized farm machinery. Due to the rapid growth in productivity there was excess production capacity and the work week was reduced. The dramatic rise in productivity of major industries in the U.S. and the effects of productivity on output, wages and the work week are discussed by Spurgeon Bell in his book *Productivity, Wages, and National Income* (1940).

The Stock Market Crashes

And then, the stock market crashed on October 23, 1929. Share prices dropped 89 percent, and the country slowly moved into the Great Depression as confidence was shaken and banks failed at an increasing rate. Reflections on its cause prompted calls for reform. Controls on the issuing and trading of securities were virtually nonexistent, allowing for a variety of frauds and other schemes. Further, the unreported concentration of controlling stock interests led to various abuses of power.

At the beginning of the 1930s, more than 15 million Americans, one-quarter of all wage-earners, were unemployed. President Herbert Hoover did not do much to alleviate the crisis: Patience and self-reliance, he argued, were all Americans needed to get them through this "passing incident in our national lives." But in 1932, Americans elected a new president, Franklin Delano Roosevelt, who promised "a New Deal for the American people." This New Deal would use the power of the federal government to try and stop the economy's downward spiral.

The Great Depression and FDR's New Deal

With another determined Roosevelt (note that distinguished name offers another nod to the Dutch) in office, bold action was again taken. FDR had formed a group

DOI 10.1515/9781547400270-003

of academic advisers, known as his Brains Trust, comprised of three Columbia University professors: Raymond Moley, Rexford Guy Tugwell, and Adolph A. Berle, Jr, author with Gardiner C. Means in 1932 of *The Modern Corporation and Private Property,* a landmark book whose ideas still resonate. Basil ("Doc") O'Connor, Samuel I. Rosenman, and Hugh Johnson joined shortly thereafter. These men helped FDR develop an economic plan which became the backbone of the New Deal, aimed at providing relief for the unemployed and poor, recovery of the economy back to normal levels, and reform of the financial system to prevent a repeat depression.

Safety Net for Banks Created

The new president acted swiftly to, he said, "wage a war against the emergency" just as though "we were in fact invaded by a foreign foe." First, he shored up the nation's banks.

In all, 9,000 banks failed during the decade of the 1930s. It is estimated that 4,000 banks failed during 1933 alone. By then, depositors saw $140 billion disappear through bank failures.

The last wave of bank runs continued through the winter of 1932 and into 1933. Almost immediately after taking office in early March, Roosevelt declared a national "bank holiday," during which all banks would be closed until they were determined to be solvent through federal inspection. In combination with the bank holiday, Roosevelt called on Congress to come up with new banking legislation to further aid the ailing financial institutions of America. In June of that year, FDR signed into law the Banking Act of 1933, often referred to as the Glass-Steagall Act after its two Congressional sponsors, ending the banking panic.

The Banking Act established the Federal Deposit Insurance Corporation (FDIC) and extended federal oversight to all commercial banks for the first time. It also separated commercial and investment banking. At the time, overzealous commercial bank involvement in the stock market was considered the main culprit behind the crash. Banks were seen to have invested depositor money in the stock market and encouraged their depositors to invest in the same companies. When the market fell, the compound impact made the banks an easy target to blame.

The FDIC protected depositors by insuring commercial bank deposits of $2,500 (later $5,000) with a pool of money collected from the banks. The FDIC did not insure investment products such as stocks, bonds, mutual funds or annuities. No federal law mandated FDIC insurance for banks, though some states required their banks to be federally insured.

Further reforms followed rapidly. In his first 100 days in office, Roosevelt and Congress passed fifteen major laws, including the Agricultural Adjustment Act, the Home Owners' Loan Act, the Tennessee Valley Authority Act and the National Industrial Recovery Act, that fundamentally reshaped many aspects of the American economy. This decisive action also did much to restore Americans' confidence, as Roosevelt had declared in his inaugural address, "the only thing we have to fear is fear itself."

Regulation of Securities and Securities Markets Takes Root

Congress passed the Securities Act of 1933, which required public corporations to register their stock sales and to make regular financial disclosures to shareholders, and later the Securities Exchange Act of 1934 created the Securities and Exchange Commission (SEC) to regulate commerce in stocks, bonds, and other securities; to regulate exchanges, brokers, and over-the-counter markets; and to monitor the required financial disclosures.

The Investment Advisors Act of 1940 required delegation of investment responsibilities only to an adviser registered under the act or to a bank or an insurance company. There remained, however, a gap: creating a mechanism to regulate management of those pools of commingled funds known as mutual funds. Thus, after several years of study, Congress passed the Investment Company Act of 1940, which saw the first mandated use of disinterested directors to protect investors against conflicts of interest inherent in the intertwined structures of investment companies and their managers.

Safety Net Extended to Citizens as Social Security is Born

The Social Security Act was enacted on August 14, 1933 as an attempt to limit what were seen as dangers of the modern American life, including old age, poverty, unemployment, and the burdens of widows and fatherless children. The Act provided benefits to retirees and the unemployed, and a lump-sum benefit at death. Payments to current retirees are financed by a payroll tax on current workers' wages, half directly as a payroll tax and half paid by the employer. The act also gave money to states to provide assistance to aged individuals (Title I), for unemployment insurance (Title III), Aid to Families with Dependent Children (Title IV), Maternal and Child Welfare (Title V), public health services (Title VI), and the blind (Title X).

President Roosevelt's early efforts had begun to restore Americans' confidence, but they had not ended the Depression. In the spring of 1935, he launched a second, more aggressive set of federal programs, sometimes called the Second New Deal. The Works Progress Administration provided jobs for unemployed people and built new public works like bridges, post offices, schools, highways and parks.

The 1935 Public Utility Holding Company Act did away with holding companies more than twice removed from the utilities whose stocks they held, to end the use of holding companies to obscure the control of public utility companies. The National Labor Relations Act, passed in 1935 and also known as the Wagner Act, gave workers the right to form unions and bargain collectively for higher wages and fairer treatment.

The Federal National Mortgage Association (FNMA), commonly known as Fannie Mae, was founded in 1938 to support the policy goal of expanding home ownership by developing and supporting the secondary market for residential mortgages. This had the effect of allowing lenders to sell mortgage loans to FNMA and reinvest the proceeds into more lending. It also improved access to credit by smoothing regional differences in loan capacity of local savings and loan associations.

Frustration Sets in as Unemployment Persists

Still, the Depression dragged on. Workers grew more militant: In December 1936, for example, the United Auto Workers started a sit-down strike at a GM plant in Flint, Michigan that lasted for 44 days and spread to some 150,000 autoworkers in thirty-five cities. By 1937, some 8 million workers had joined unions and were loudly demanding their rights.

The economic performance of the 1930s showed a rapid upward trend. The country's real gross domestic product had fallen from $865 billion in 1929 to $635 billion in 1933 and rebounded to $1 trillion by 1940. But the percentage of jobless Americans remained high. In 1930, unemployment was at 8.7 percent, and climbed to 24 percent in 1932 before declining to 15 percent by 1940. Jim Powell, author of *FDR's Folly: How Roosevelt and His New Deal Prolonged the Great Depression*, asks, "There was expansion, but how come you still had average unemployment of 17 percent from 1933 to 1940?"

By the end of the 1930s, the New Deal had faded. The loss of the Democratic majority in 1938 and growing Congressional opposition made it difficult for President Roosevelt to introduce new programs. FDR's great experiments, then, didn't quite end the Great Depression. Only mobilization for a world war would bring an end to the most devastating economic crisis in United States history.

Government and Business Mobilize for World War II

Not exactly invoking neutrality in his decision to assist the Allied powers, President Roosevelt noted, "Even a neutral cannot be asked to close his mind or his conscience." When Japanese bombers attacked Pearl Harbor in December 1941, the United States joined in the war in earnest.

Despite warnings of war, the United States wasn't completely prepared. Many of the country's machine and tool industries had disappeared during the depression, the military was woefully under-supplied, and many soldiers found themselves drilling with toy guns and wooden tanks. The Depression, however, provided good preparation for wartime life: Americans had learned to scrimp and persevere.

Americans rose to the occasion. When FDR called for the production of 50,000 planes in a year, it was thought ridiculous. By 1944, the country was producing 96,000 a year. Technology blossomed. When metals became scarce, plastics were developed to take their place. Copper was taken out of pennies and replaced with steel; nickel was removed from nickels. Gasoline and tires were rationed, as were coffee, sugar, canned goods, butter, and shoes.

The federal government spent about $350 billion during World War II — or twice as much as it had spent in total since the formation of the United States. About 40 percent of that came from taxes; the rest came through government borrowing, much of that through the sale of bonds. Gross national product more than doubled between 1939 and 1945. Wages and corporate profits went up, as did prices.

Roosevelt and Business Create Formidable Alliance

In the early years of the war, Roosevelt consciously pursued a conversion program to shift industry to a wartime footing. Lingerie factories began making camouflage netting, baby carriages became field hospital food carts. Lipstick cases became bomb cases, beer cans went to hand grenades, adding machines to automatic pistols, and vacuum cleaners to gas mask parts.

Basically, Roosevelt made the decision that he had to mobilize the leaders of the mines, the factories, and the shops. He realized Congress could provide the money, but could not build the planes, design the tanks, or assemble the weapons. Without the cooperation of industry, massive production could not succeed, yet private business could not find all the capital required for the expansion of the plants nor take the risk that the end of the war would leave them with no orders and excess capacity.

Using the Reconstruction Finance Corporation, therefore, the federal government provided the funding needed to expand the factories, often leasing them to industry. The government also helped develop new sources of raw material supplies and created mass transportation to mobilize resources. It went into the business of producing synthetic rubber and aluminum, invested in other emerging industries, and helped stimulate new technologies.

Contrary to the stereotype of a wartime "command economy," a robust entrepreneurial spirit prevailed. Roosevelt brought in dozens of top business executives as "dollar-a-year" men to help run the government commissions and reduce the sentiment that government was telling business what to do. He used government to create markets and to help business set up new plants and equipment. The war created new technologies, industries, and associated skills.

Solidarity Works Miracles

Perhaps because mobilization included the ideological argument that the war was being fought for the interests of common men and women, social solidarity extended far beyond the foxholes. Public opinion held that our valorous veterans should not return jobless, without opportunity and education. That led to the GI Bill, which helped lay the foundation for the remarkable post-war expansion that followed. The stereotype of FDR as a regulation-lover flies in the face of the national experience in the 1940s. Wartime planning was far more business oriented than was New Deal planning, and with considerably less class warfare.

Air Corps aces would visit the factories; the pilot would tell the workers that it wasn't the pilots who were heroic, it was their planes. The war production posters emphasized that factories and GIs were one continuous front, a theme that Roosevelt also struck in his speeches. The people understood from the start that America's dominant contribution to the war would be its production. Productivity soared: the Kaiser shipyards, for example, were able to get production time for Liberty Ships down from 365 days to 92, 62, and, finally, to one day.

Roosevelt resisted the idea of compulsory service, believing that the momentum of democracy would be sufficient. If the jobs were out there, he believed that people would put their mattresses on top of their cars and go where the jobs were. He envisioned highways filled with people on the move; going south, going west. In one fireside chat, he advised people to get maps, and the Hammond company in New York sold out their entire stock of 2,000 maps in a single morning. Though mobilization was chaotic, it worked.

Wartime Success Reaches Far Beyond Battlefields

Word War II produced remarkable social gains. Eleanor Roosevelt, in particular, was successful in arguing that a fully productive work force requires everyone's talents, blacks and women alike; and if women are to work in the factories, their children require day care. She proved that absentee rates were high in the factories because worried women were going home to care for their children. She got restaurants to prepare hot meals, so women could bring home hot dinners. The productivity rates continued to soar as a result of these and other measures.

Government was viewed as a source of full employment, macroeconomic recovery, technological breakthrough, worker training, reindustrialization, and a good deal of incidental social progress. The alliance between large corporations and government had developed to the point where big business helped government develop and implement various certain economic and reconstruction programs.

The Committee for Economic Development, formed in 1942 by CEOs of our largest corporations to promote sustained economic progress, assisted with development and adoption of the Marshall Plan for post-war reconstruction as well as the Bretton Woods Agreement, an agreement among the world's industrial nations to a global monetary system designed to improve economic stability by promoting global trade. That system hashed out during July 1944 by forty-four nations in Bretton Woods, New Hampshire, provided for a fixed rate of exchange between the currencies of the world and the U.S. dollar, and the U.S. dollar was linked to gold.

Chapter 4
The Glow Following World War II

New expectations, new wages, and new options created by World War II mobilization and victory sparked a post-war economic boom. Through the 1950s and into the 1960s, the United States enjoyed the most prosperous period in its history. The new ideas and entitlements introduced during the war, however, also sowed the seeds of issues board members deal with today as we grapple with funding the social safety net and deal with both funding retirement plans and working with the resulting huge investment funds in their guise as institutional investors. It is remarkable to see both how well efforts to stabilize markets and rebuild confidence in our system worked given the enormous size of our capital markets today.

Corporate management and boards, buoyed by post-war optimism, did not yet pay much attention to the thinking so beautifully expressed by Adolf A. Berle and Gardiner C. Means in their 1932 masterpiece, *The Modern Corporation and Private Property*. Academics and policy makers, however, were looking at these issues as corporations grew larger:

> Over the enterprise and over the physical property—the instruments of production—in which he has an interest, the owner (of shares) has little control.

> At the same time, he bears no responsibility with respect to the enterprise or its physical property. It has often been said that the owner of a horse is responsible. If the horse lives he must feed it. If it dies he must bury it. No such responsibility attaches to a share of stock. The owner is practically powerless through his own efforts to affect the underlying property. . .

> Physical property capable of being shaped by its owner could bring to him direct satisfaction apart from the income it yielded in more concrete form. It represented an extension of his own personality. With the corporate revolution, this quality has been lost to the property owner much as it has been lost to the worker through the industrial revolution.

Here we have an excellent expression of the tension between ownership and control, which continues to fuel significant debate today as to whether shareholders do or do not own the companies in which they hold shares.

The 1950s Board Role

The prosperous 1950s were expressed in corporate governance terms as the peak of management dominance. Boards were seen largely as an extension of the CEO, chosen by him and unlikely to consider a challenge to his decisions or authority.

DOI 10.1515/9781547400270-004

Though current fashion is to be critical of such passivity, in the context of the time, balancing among multiple stakeholder interests was considered the priority, and boards had not yet received much scrutiny as entities with power unto themselves.

The war was waged and won by large organizations able to surmount logistical challenges. The senior management team, headed by the CEO, was likely perceived in similar fashion as providing centralized planning and production oversight and balancing the allocation of results among the various stakeholders.

The political climate favored such an approach, and the dominant economic position of the United States in the immediate post-war period supported it. The shared sacrifice of wartime seemed to produce a strong feeling that the fruits of post-war prosperity should be shared. Organized labor was strong, and the country was committed ideologically to providing a better life for workers, many of whom were veterans. It may be, too, that this view was driven to an extent by a desire to outperform the perceived competitive system of communism in terms of garnering worker loyalty.

A 1961 *Harvard Business Review* survey of 1700 executives showed that approximately 85 percent of respondents agreed that for corporate executives to act in the interests of shareholders alone, and not also in the interests of employees and consumers, would be unethical. Peter Drucker argued that board alignment with shareholder interests would undercut the desirable capacity of managers to manage in the public interest.

This view of the corporation logically, therefore, included seeing the role of the board as an advisory one. Key insiders and outsiders with important economic relationships with the company—its bankers, lawyers and suppliers—could serve as a useful sounding board for the CEO, consolidate valuable relationships, and provide expertise in the face of increasing complexity.

If the CEO was looking for trusted advisors who might help broaden his perspective, it followed that the CEO would select his directors. From that point of view, the more recently embraced concept of the board as overseer could be seen as injecting distrust. How could the CEO confide in directors whose ultimate mission was to hold him to account?

Stock Market Investing is Patriotic Duty

NYSE members watched with longing as post-war consumer income rose and households invested heavily in bonds, life insurance and homes. The memory of 1929 remained vivid, and safer investments were preferred to shares of stock, which still carried connotations of gambling.

As time passed, however, corporations flourished. Regulations introduced in the 1930s, a reorganized NYSE board, and the rising reputation of companies listed on the NYSE made investing begin to feel safer. Brokerage houses began marketing to the small investor and individual investors started to buy stocks.

Charles Merrill's brokerage firm enjoyed a conservative reputation stemming from his 1928 warnings to clients to reduce their stock market risk. In 1940, his firm began advertising directed toward smaller potential clients, explaining how a stock exchange encouraged the operation of a free market, an important national asset.

New York Stock Exchange members did not then want to fund similar marketing. When G. Keith Funston became its president in 1951, however, he made marketing a priority. Serving the NYSE until 1967, he promoted buying stocks listed on the NYSE as the patriotic duty of Americans and proclaimed the NYSE to represent the epitome of free enterprise.

The NYSE began a 14-year campaign called "Own Your Share of American Business." The slogan appeared in millions of newspaper and magazine advertisements, was posted on company bulletin boards and supermarket checkout counters and displayed prominently in department store windows.

In the mid-1950s, the NYSE established a department for public education. The department coordinated free speakers and produced brochures for consumers. According to a paper published in 1974 by the St. Louis Federal Reserve Bank, in 1940, less than 5% of the stock market's value was estimated to be held by individuals. By 1950, this percentage had risen to 8%. During the early 1960s the exchange provided thousands of lectures a year in libraries, service clubs and other venues that would attract the smaller investors. It worked. By 1965, ownership percentage had more than tripled to roughly 15% of the stock market's value being held by individuals.

The Nifty Fifty Catches On

In another effective marketing campaign, Morgan Guaranty Trust identified fifty stocks of high growth companies and christened them the "Nifty Fifty." Among them were fast-food pioneer McDonald's, early technology titans IBM, Texas Instruments and Digital Equipment Corp.; soft-drink maker Coca-Cola, and Wal-Mart, then in the early stages of becoming the world's largest retailer and private employer.

As we entered the 1960s, we were confident. We elected a young, charismatic president, we engaged in the challenges of the civil-rights movement, we were invested in the Space Race and it appeared that U.S. industry was becoming a juggernaut that would dominate the global economy. Unlike typical "buy-and-hold" stocks such as slow growing but generous dividend-paying utility company shares, a piece of the Nifty Fifty pie commanded high prices from investors. Their popularity drove a marked shift from "value" investing to a "growth at any price" mentality that resurfaced with a vengeance in the tech-stock bubble a quarter century later. The Nifty Fifty embodied a sense of economic manifest destiny.

Investor Relations Become a Corporate Function

To the extent that shareholders were activists such efforts were mostly confined to individual shareholders who owned one hundred or fewer shares to enable them to attend annual meetings. One well-known shareholder, Evelyn Y. Davis, particularly enjoyed needling International Telephone & Telegraph Corporation's CEO, Harold Geneen, loudly asking at annual meetings how executive compensation was determined and who counted the shareholder votes. Sometimes her microphone would fail for "unexplained technical reasons."

Corporate executives wanted these people to disappear. Not knowing how to deal with vocal shareholders, companies turned to outside public relations firms or proxy solicitors to handle annual reports and orchestrate friendly annual meetings that offered food and open bars. These third parties weren't always familiar with corporate matters, however, so some public relations efforts included overtly promotional material, which came perilously close to stock touting. Lawyers were getting nervous. Companies wanted more control.

In 1953 General Electric led the way and established an in-house investor relations department. Other companies followed suit, which created a mechanism to deal with individual shareholders as well as the growing number of intermediaries such as stock analysts, mutual funds and pension investors. Notably, there seems to have been no thought of including the board in this communication chain, as the board was generally seen as an adjunct of the CEO.

Read More

The Modern Corporation and Private Property, Adolf A. Berle and Gardiner C. Means, 1932

The New Society: The Anatomy of Industrial Order, Peter F. Drucker, 1950, Transaction Publishers; 2nd edition, 1993

"The Nifty-Fifty Re-Revisited", Fesenmaier, Jeff; Smith, Gary. Retrieved February, 2012

"The CEO's Worst Nightmare", Bennetts, Leslie, Vanity Fair Magazine, July 2002

"Investor Relations", Laskin, Alexander. Institute for Investor Relations, November, 2008

Chapter 5
Shifting Dynamics from 1970 to 2000

Coming as it did near the end of what had been a long period of optimism which allegedly included a spirit of sharing, Milton Friedman's much discussed 1970 *New York Times* essay, "The Social Responsibility of Business Is to Increase Its Profits," and its emphasis on shareholder value as virtually the sole criterion by which corporate performance should be judged seemed far out of the mainstream. He roundly denounces corporate "social responsibility" as a socialist doctrine and takes shareholders' ownership of the corporation as a given. He asserts that "the manager is the agent of the individuals who own the corporation" and, further, that the manager's primary "responsibility is to conduct the business in accordance with [the owners'] desires." He characterizes the executive as "an agent serving the interests of his principal."

Agency Theory is Born

The seeds of what has become known as agency theory, which has continued its relentless growth to this day, were further fertilized by the 1976 *Journal of Financial Economics* article "Theory of the Firm," in which Michael Jensen and William Meckling set forth the theory's basic premises:

- Shareholders own the corporation and are "principals" with original authority to manage the corporation's business and affairs.
- Managers are delegated decision-making authority by the corporation's shareholders and are thus "agents" of the shareholders.
- As agents of the shareholders, managers are obliged to conduct the corporation's business in accordance with shareholders' desires.
- Shareholders want business to be conducted in a way that maximizes their own economic returns. (The assumption that shareholders are unanimous in this objective is implicit throughout the article.)

Under this view, boards of directors are simply an organizational mechanism for controlling "agency costs"—the costs to shareholders associated with delegating authority to managers.

The impact of this view, which I am impudent enough to assert is dead wrong, has been pernicious, which we will explore in later chapters.

DOI 10.1515/9781547400270-005

The Stock Market Corrects

By 1972 the S&P 500 Index's price to earnings ratio (P/E) stood at 19, and the Nifty Fifty's average P/E was more than twice that at 42. Then came the stock market slump of 1973–74, in which the Dow Jones Industrial Average fell 45 percent in just two years, perhaps reflecting the end of the Bretton Woods monetary system and/or fixed stock trading commissions, concern over the Vietnam War, soaring inflation and the first of the 1970s oil crises.

Outrage over the Wreck of Penn Central Fuels New Focus on Board Role

The bankruptcy of the venerable Penn Central railroad resonated in its day as did the fall of Enron, and the questionable payments scandal revealed through the Watergate investigation at least as much rot as was found in the accounting abuses in the late 1990s. The result was to begin to push the board away from its then accepted advisory role toward the so-called oversight model, at least in aspiration. The forces put in motion in the 1970s did much to drive subsequent corporate governance reform forward. The decline of insiders and the rise of independent directors began then as did the formal role of audit committees.

The Penn Central story laid bare the weakness of the 1950s view of the board. The august members of that board appeared to have little to no inkling of the financial troubles facing the railroad. As working capital deteriorated and indebtedness escalated in the two years before the collapse, the board approved over $100 million in dividends. Suspicion of management escalated, as it was made brutally clear that the directors had been neither advisors nor monitors, but puppets.

Much as Enron's collapse foreshadowed financial frauds at many other firms, the Penn Central collapse was followed by other dramas such as the Equity Funding scandal and the failures of LTV, Ampex, and Memorex. Myles Mace's widely read 1971 book, *Directors: Myth and Reality*, exposed director passivity and the failure of the board concept as then understood. Based on decades of research, he declared that it was possible to conclude that the advising board had been no more than a way of giving managers the appearance of accountability.

Broad Corruption Revealed Leads to Focus on Governance Per Se

Meanwhile, the Special Prosecutor's investigation into the drama known as Watergate resulted in fifty public corporations being criminally prosecuted or subject to SEC enforcement action; another 400 voluntarily admitted having made illegal campaign contributions or paid bribes abroad and in the U.S. One result was adoption of the Foreign Corrupt Practices Act, which created enforcement powers and significant penalties for breaking the law.

In the aftermath it seemed that while senior corporate officers often knew of these payments, outside directors had not and were not otherwise in the loop of the corporation's internal controls. Inquiry that would lead to such knowledge was considered not decorous, and beyond the scope of the advising board. While that may seem remarkable today, it does offer some insight into why it seems that in later years intelligent and able directors often seemed asleep at the switch. Directors did not know there was a switch, did not recognize they were responsible for pulling it, and management typically did not see fit to inform them. Though expectations of the board may have changed, the legacy behavior of the advising board remained.

This view of the board's responsibility or lack of same was evident in the Delaware Supreme Court's 1963 ruling in Graham v. Allis-Chalmers Mfg. Co. that: *"absent cause for suspicion there is no duty upon the directors to install and operate a corporate system of espionage to ferret out wrongdoing which they have no reason to suspect exists."* This could certainly be interpreted to indicate that the board was not responsible for assuring themselves that disclosures were correct.

Additional pressure on the advising board model came from the corporate social responsibility movement fueled in the 1970s by concern about corporate involvement in the Vietnam War and their policies on the environment, employment, and other social issues. The corporation of the 1950s and 1960s considered the interests of employees and the communities in which they lived through charitable giving. Consistent with the temper of the times, the 1970s saw a push for deeper corporate engagement with social problems.

Other governance reform proposals were much further reaching and focused on the board. Nader, Green & Seligman famously proposed federal chartering, under rules that required full time directors nominated exclusively by shareholders and gave weight to board representation of various constituency groups.

The Board as Overseer Takes Root as Independent Directors Become Desirable

The cumulative effect of these pressures led, by the end of the 1970s, to a significant reconceptualization of the board's role and structure. The advising board model was replaced by recognition of the need for the oversight board, as presented in Mel Eisenberg's influential 1976 book, *The Structure of the Corporation: A Legal Analysis*. The new model of the board rapidly became conventional wisdom, endorsed by the Chairman of the SEC, the corporate bar, and even the Business Roundtable.

The staffing of the audit committee by independent directors came to be seen as essential. The SEC initially made the existence of an audit committee a matter of disclosure only, but in 1976 requested that the NYSE amend its listing requirements to include an audit committee composed of independent directors with access both to accounting information and to the outside auditors on a private basis. By the time the NYSE adopted the requirement, audit committees had become a widely accepted element of board structure, found in almost 95 percent of large public companies.

The term independent director entered the corporate governance arena as descriptive of the kind of director capable of fulfilling the oversight role. Until then, the board was divided into inside and outside directors, defined in a 1962 New York Stock Exchange statement that an outside director was simply one who is non-management. The composition of the board began to shift in favor of independent directors and pressure grew to increase the independence of the nominating committee.

The Definition of Independence Proves Elusive; We Know It When We See It

The question, however, was what constituted independence. The clear goal to my mind was to develop board members who were both seasoned and independent minded, willing as needed to challenge the thinking of management, possibly bring new points of view to the table, and act as needed, consistent with their actual legal responsibility.

But how can such qualities be defined and mandated? Unable to do that, definitions turned instead to trying to protect the exercise of independent judgment from the influence of economic and even social factors. Federal regulatory guidance, stock exchange listing standards, state fiduciary law, and best practice pronouncements have all played a role in line-drawing, and the results, while useful, are not consistent.

The 1978 Corporate Director's Guidebook, an influential product of prominent corporate lawyers, drew a two-level distinction, first distinguishing between management and non-management directors and then between affiliated and non-affiliated non-management directors. A former officer or employee was to be regarded as a management director. A director with other economic or personal ties which could be viewed as interfering with the exercise of independent judgment was an affiliated non-managerial director, such as commercial bankers, investment bankers, attorneys, and others who supply services or goods to the corporation.

In 1978 the SEC went so far as to propose proxy disclosure that would categorize outside directors as affiliated or independent. In response to corporate objections, the proposal was withdrawn. In its 1977 audit committee listing standard, the NYSE required staffing by directors independent of management.

It still permitted directors from organizations with customary commercial, industrial, banking, or underwriting relationships with the company to serve unless the board found that such relationships would interfere with the exercise of independent judgment as a committee member. That definition remained intact until 1999, when the criterion of audit committee independence was significantly tightened in response to the prodding of the Blue Ribbon Committee on Improving Audit Committee Effectiveness.

The 1980s Board Role: The Board Becomes Important

The adoption of the oversight board was not fully established by the end of the 1970s, since its acceptance by management was at least partially intended to forestall further reforms, such as the briefly popular idea of national chartering. By the end of the 1980s managements were, however, aggressively promoting the virtues of the monitoring board, since a robust board including a significant percentage of independent directors seemed to offer a safe harbor against the fear of hostile takeover, which became pervasive.

Although in total, hostile transactions accounted for only a small percentage of those completed, the idea of a possible hostile bid became a powerful threat. Nearly half of major U.S. corporations received an unwanted bid. Many friendly deals were negotiated in the shadow of a potential hostile bid. Even very large corporations came under attack from financial buyers whose access to the high yield bond market meant they could engineer a highly leveraged transaction that would ultimately be repaid through the sale of various corporate divisions and other assets.

A hostile bid was rationalized by some as a form of competition among management teams for control over the assets of a particular corporation. Theoretically, the team that could put the assets to highest and best use would be able to offer the highest price and would prevail, and a successful hostile bid would make those particular assets more productive. In addition, the background threat of a hostile bid would have a disciplining and stimulating effect on other managements. This would lead to more productive use of assets throughout the economy.

Mighty Institutional Investors Weigh In

The hostile takeover activity also reflected the increasing importance of institutional investors. By 1980 institutions held more than 40 percent of the value of U.S. equity markets, which arguably meant that more large shareholders were focused directly on shareholder value and delighted to sell to a bidder offering a significant market premium.

In part, this may have reflected investor sophistication about the target management's claims that the bid was too low were rarely proven true. They also may have understood what the general public did not: that many corporations, having experienced prolonged inflation, had assets on their books which were properly valued according to generally accepted accounting principles (GAAP) but had much greater value in the then prevailing market. Those undervalued assets provided significant impetus to deal makers who saw great opportunities that did not require much effort to realize.

Another important factor that influenced institutional investor behavior was the typical evaluation process of the investment management firm who was managing the institutional investor's money. Hire and fire decisions were made on the basis of performance track record. For example, a mutual fund marketed itself on the basis of annual performance; a money manager engaged to manage pension fund or endowment money was benchmarked against unmanaged broad market indices, or against peers, often on a quarterly basis.

Early in the takeover cycle, the return from such investments was spectacular as it was easy to capture value and pay down debt by selling the assets of the company acquired and realizing attractive returns quickly. These returns drew in more money. Many institutions became crucial funding sources for financial buyers. Some provided equity capital to buyout firms; others purchased the indebtedness that financed leveraged acquisitions. During this time, it was hard for pension fund and endowment executives and the investment managers who managed their money not to look like heroes, or at least like savvy investors.

The Courts Recognize Independent Judgment of the Board as Mission Critical

Many incumbent CEOs, unsurprisingly, did not agree with the efficiency-enhancing view of hostile takeovers, instead seeing such activity as driven by arbitrageurs looking for quick profits, able to secure funding due to the performance pressures on institutional investment managers cited above. Nevertheless, hostile bids were powerful phenomena that needed to be dealt with. In the face of fear, CEOs turned to the idea of the monitoring board and to independent directors for protection, despite the potential decrease in their autonomy. The concept of independent directors charged with independently evaluating the adequacy of the hostile bid compared to the value of the enterprise may have been difficult to swallow but offered valuable protection.

From a legal standpoint, independent directors also proved valuable regarding standards developing in Delaware defining fiduciary duty law. In a series of highly visible cases, the Delaware Supreme Court permitted a target board to just say no to a hostile bid. Boards were permitted to adopt a so-called poison pill, a corporate finance technique that imposed high costs on a successful hostile bidder. Judicial approval of such measures appeared to be tied not only to the existence of independent directors, but to their actively informed decision-making process.

The courts were faced with difficult choices. They could prohibit devices such as the poison pill and leave the outcome to shareholder action, which Delaware law otherwise strongly discouraged, or they could allow management the discretion to resist hostile bids, rife with conflict problems, or they could themselves decide on the reasonableness of takeover defenses in particular transactions which would transform courts into economic as opposed to legal standard setters.

Placing the onus on the board of directors, however, had a doctrinal foundation and could elegantly resolve the various conflicting agendas. Perhaps wanting not to alienate possible pro-takeover parties such as institutional investors or the federal government, the Delaware courts delved into not only board process but also director independence. The lesson was clear. The price of the power to just say no to a hostile bidder was a board that consisted of a majority of independent directors as well as a process that would rely on those directors to exercise their independent judgment.

The reliance on the business judgment of independent directors by the Delaware Supreme Court in the important decision of Zapata Corp. v. Maldonado held that even for a demand-excused shareholder derivative legal action, a special committee constituted of independent directors could nevertheless obtain dismissal of the action if it demonstrated this was in the best interests of the corporation. In its dismissal request, the special committee had the burden of demonstrating its independence. These developments increased the demand for directors and helped further define the independence standard.

Economic Uncertainty and Social Unrest Reduce American Confidence

The U.S. economy had not thrived in the 1970s, and for the first time it seemed that U.S. corporations were out-competed on the world stage. Chrysler, for example, in the early 1980s escaped bankruptcy only with a government bailout, and GM seemed to be losing out to Toyota as the world's premier automobile manufacturer. Inflation was having a significant impact, and general confidence in the American destiny was flagging.

The role of institutional investors including both mutual funds and pension investors has only become more critical since then and we will explore both shortly in greater detail. We will also look at how their return requirements and undervalued corporate assets powered the birth of the private equity and leveraged buyout markets. We will explore the role of the brokerage firm Drexel Burnham in building the high yield bond market and financing various acquisitions. Finally, we will spend some time dwelling on the development of the swap markets and the techniques and impact of securitization. These markets, still largely invisible to board members, are part of the now enormous world of derivative products, all of which took root in the remarkable decade of the 1980s.

Market Crashes on Black Monday

On October 19, 1987, the markets dropped a stomach-wrenching 23 percent giving rise to the label Black Monday, echoing the first day of the 1929 crash. Continuing a decline that began the prior week, sell orders overwhelmed the system at the opening bell Monday morning, and floor specialists couldn't open for an hour.

Confusion and panic spread through cash and futures markets. This, the biggest percentage drop in stock market history, prompted a rare two-column *Wall Street Journal* headline: "The Crash of '87: Stocks Plunge 508 Amid Panicky Selling." The market rebounded the next day, posting a record gain of 102.27 points on the Dow. Confidence appeared restored when another rally followed on Wednesday, and so began the bull market that would last another decade.

Behind the scenes, however, the repercussions of such a plunge received much study. The New York Stock Exchange seriously considered closing, a step that would have sent a profoundly troubling signal to the world's markets. In the end, only a flood of liquidity from the Federal Reserve and a concerted effort by big companies, prompted by frantic calls from their investment bankers, to buy back their stock combined with an odd but fortuitous spike in futures on the Major Market Index brought the markets back from the brink.

Changing Market Forces Become Visible

Though they did not cause the crash, two relatively new elements of market structure contributed to the volatility: program trading and portfolio insurance. Program trades are large-volume transactions that are typically executed automatically when index prices rise or fall to predetermined levels. Portfolio insurance is a hedging technique used by institutional investors to mitigate market risk by short-selling stock index futures. Both are unpredictable and trigger volatility.

The 1987 panic roused investors' worst fears and sent a sobering message to the managers of the corporations whose combined market valuations shed a stunning $500 billion that day. The complexities of a vastly changed capital market environment were at work. This environment relied not on thoughtful assessments of the soundness of corporate fundamentals, but rather on automated trading algorithms and an unsettling concentration of ownership by institutional investor intermediaries, whose own priorities often clashed with those of primary investors seeking long-term capital appreciation. The unsuspecting public was left behind.

NYSE Establishes Safeguards

As a response to the market crash of October 1987, the NYSE established a circuit breaker system in October 1988, halting trading temporarily if prices fall steeply in a short period of time. The system was devised based on the federal Brady Commission report, which suggested that rapidly falling prices could intensify panic among investors and cause limit orders to become stale. The report also suggested that broad price swings could create uncertainty about order execution, which would prompt investors to refrain from trading.

The theory was that by creating a required a pause in trading, investors would have some time to assimilate new information and thus make informed choices during periods of high volatility.

Initially, the exchange set the triggers to suspend trading for up to 15 minutes following point declines in the Dow Jones Industrial Average of approximately 10, 20 and 30 percent. In 2013, the exchange altered the rule to establish circuit breaker triggers for declines of 7, 13 and 20 percent in the S&P 500. Also, under the rules modification, if the market declined by 20 percent, trading is halted for the remainder of the trading session.

The 1990s Board: Independence Criteria Tighten as Equity Linked Compensation Grows

The anemic results or failure of many highly leveraged late-1980s contested transactions damaged the credibility of hostile bids generally. Easy financing for buyers was gone with the 1990 demise of Drexel Burnham. The post-1980s conventional wisdom was that the hostile bid was a high cost mechanism to achieve an acquisition, and their use declined.

The trend toward increasing the role of independent directors, defining that meaning, and supporting the ability to behave independently, however, continued. In 1989, Jay W. Lorsch and Elizabeth MacIver in their book *Pawns or Potentates: The Reality of America's Corporate Boards* argued that the independent directors and boards were acting more like pawns and not so much as the potentates they were legally intended to be. Various mechanisms, many first adopted during the 1970s corporate governance reform, developed to define and enhance the independence of directors.

These included continuing tightening of the standards and rules of disqualifying relationships of independent directors as well as increasing of both negative and positive reinforcement of vigilance, such as legal liability for fiduciary duty breach, reputational sanctions, and stock-based compensation. At the board level, further development of internal board structures continued, such as more mandated committees and the designation of a lead director. Finally, there was a clear move beginning to reduce CEO influence in director selection and retention by the creation of a nominating committee staffed solely by independent directors.

Various panels and blue ribbon commissions developed somewhat influential best practice guidelines for relationship tests. The most important version, in the American Law Institute's 1992 Principles of Corporate Governance, recommended that the board of a public corporation should have a majority of directors who are free of any significant relationship with the corporation's senior executives.

Significant relationship was defined in a way to disqualify many affiliated directors, both through categorical exclusions relating to the firm's principal outside law firm or investment bank, and through attention to customer/supplier relationships crossing a relatively low ($200,000) materiality threshold. The Principles also called for the corporation's nominating committee to engage in a more individualized review of factors that could undermine the independence of particular directors.

Further federal regulatory tightening of the independence standard came through the 1996 establishment in Section 162(m) of the Internal Revenue Code of criteria for directors eligible to approve exceptions to the $1 million deductibility cap on executive compensation. Those criteria disqualified a former officer of the corporation and a director who receives remuneration from the corporation either directly or indirectly, in any capacity other than as a director, and define acceptable limits of director ownership interest in or employment by an entity that received payments from the corporation.

These IRS regulations influenced the SEC's 1996 rules specifying independent director approval of certain stock-related transactions as a condition of exemption from the short swing profit recapture provisions of section 16(b) of the 1934 Securities Exchange Act. The definition of an independent director with such approval power followed the substance of the IRS regulation. The tests of economic distance for director independence established by these two important federal regulatory agencies became important benchmarks in other realms evaluating independence.

True Independence Grows in Value

The shift toward independent directors is reflected not just in the numbers or percentages but also in the likelihood of independence in fact. The legal resolution of the hostile takeover battles of the 1980s made clear not only that the firm is not always up for sale, but that the ultimate decision maker was not management but instead had to be the less conflicted board. The growing focus on director independence was stimulated by the desire to enhance the credibility of such decision making to the relevant audiences, including the courts and increasingly active institutional investors.

With hostile takeovers defanged, a major force driving the alliance between management and the board was gone, and the board sought ways to align management behavior with the interests of shareholders. Some 1990s boards sought to bring stock price-linked incentives into executive compensation contracts, termination decisions, and severance packages. This marks another important turning point in governance thinking: a continuing movement toward serving the shareholder as distinct from the stakeholders more prevalent in prior decades.

These compensation contracts typically involved the use of stock options. Both tax and accounting rules favored the use of plain vanilla stock options, meaning immediately exercisable, at-the-money options on the company's stock.

Such options were taxable to the executive only when exercised, not when issued and grants of such options were not expensed so did not reduce the corporation's net income. Their popularity is suggested by the shift in composition of S&P 500 CEO compensation over the 1992–2000 period from 27 percent to 51 percent in stock options.

Equity Linked Compensation Creates Moral Hazard

Stock option packages can create a significant moral hazard, which can easily be seen in hindsight, especially given subsequent developments. Managers with large option grants may be strongly tempted to produce results the market expects by manipulation of financial results, not difficult to do by overstating earnings. Several recent studies find that the probability of accounting fraud, though small, nevertheless increases with the amount of stock-based compensation and increases as well with the fraction of total compensation that is stock-based.

It might appear that achieving financial results through manipulation would not be a serious threat, as the corporation's true condition will eventually come to light. The stock price will fall, the executive's options become worthless, and legal sanctions for fraud may ensue. Before such revelations occur, however, the executive may already have exercised his options and effected a prompt sale of the underlying stock at the inflated price; the corporation might reprice the worthless options or grant some new ones; the necessary earnings restatement may be buried with some other extraordinary adjustment; or a positive shift in market conditions may overtake the earlier misrepresentation. And so on.

In short, executives receiving large grants of options had major incentives to pursue the highest possible share price, with foreseeable moral hazard problems, as well as potential threats to earnings quality. Appropriate operation of the contracts critically depended upon the quality of the corporation's disclosure. The necessary link had to be the deliberate and focused oversight by the board of financial disclosure, which was, in many cases, just plain missing. Many boards had simply failed to appreciate and protect against the special temptations created by stock-based compensation to misreport financial results.

Independence of Mind Needs Help from Independence of Process

Observers have debated whether boards generally failed in their obligation to establish arm's length bargaining with senior managers. Regardless of the board's independence in other matters, it seems clear that independence in the setting of compensation was compromised in many situations. In some cases, the CEO or other members of the management team participated in compensation committee activities.

Conspicuously, boards often rely on consulting firms to assist them in developing and evaluating compensation packages, which can be extremely complex, as can the definition of appropriate peer groups. Likely a holdover habit from previous periods, the board then typically used the same consulting firm that management used for broader employee compensation framework development. Clearly, that firm may have difficulty realizing that it needs to work for two separate clients. The knowledge of the company and its people cannot help but permeate the recommendations made to the board, historically more remote and less familiar.

Revolving CEOs

Another trend developing in the 1990s was the increasing board tendency to evaluate CEO performance with respect to shareholder returns and to terminate more quickly, borne out by a study by Booz Allen Hamilton of CEO turnover in the 1995–2001 period for the 2500 largest companies. The CEO turnover rate worldwide nearly doubled in the 1995 vs. 2000 period, and the rate of explicitly performance-related turnovers increased three times, from 25 in 1995 to 80 in 2000. The result was to shorten average CEO tenure from 9.5 years in 1995 to 7.3 years in 2001.

The first and most obvious conclusion is that CEOs must deliver acceptable and recognizable total returns to shareholders. Shareholder returns clearly moved higher on the management and board agenda than in years past, when net income and return on assets were the measures by which a corporation's managers were judged. In those bygone days, management focused on effective stewardship; the relevant benchmarks were competitors in the same industry. Focus on shareholder return, however, broadens those benchmarks as shareholders are judging each company against all others. This shift continued the pressure for fundamental change in management behavior and board perspective.

Another element of the 1990s board focus was the use of the equity linked golden parachute, a generous severance package, often based on approximately three times salary/bonus of prior years. In a change in control transaction the accelerated vesting of stock options granted but not yet vested was often added. The severance payments were nice, but the option acceleration provisions could make the CEO genuinely rich. This was a significant consolation prize for the terminated CEO, which presumably reduced resistance, and made it easier for the board to attract a replacement CEO under similarly demanding performance expectations.

In the case of an uninvited takeover bid, such packages often converted CEOs from opposition to acquiescence. One consequence was that despite the availability of the nearly bullet-proof anti-takeover defense of a poison pill, takeover activity in the United States reached new heights in the 1990s. In particular, in the 1996–2000 period, fewer than 100 (of 40,000 total) acquisitions were reported as hostile.

Read More

"The Social Responsibility of Business Is to Increase Its Profits", Milton Friedman, *New York Times*, 1970

"Theory of the Firm: Managerial Behavior, Agency Costs and Ownership Structure", Jensen, Michael C. and Meckling, William H., University of Rochester, 1976

The Wreck of the Penn Central, Daughen, Peter, & Binzen, Joseph, 1971

The Structure of the Corporation: A Legal Analysis, Eisenberg, Melvin, 1976; Beard Books 2006

Taming the Giant Corporation, Nader, Ralph; Green, Mark, and Seligman, Joel; W. W. Norton & Company, 1977

The Foreign Corrupt Practices Act of 1977, published by Department of Justice, Criminal Division

Mergers and Acquisitions, Auerbach, Alan J., ed. University of Chicago Press, 1987

The Cycles of Corporate Social Responsibility: An Historical Retrospective for the Twenty-first Century, Wells, C.A. Harwell, 2002

Pawns or Potentates: The Reality of America's Corporate Boards, Lorsch, Jay W. & MacIver, Elizabeth, 1989

Principles of Corporate Governance, edited and published by American Law Institute, 1992

"Executive Compensation: A New View from a Long-Term Perspective, 1936–2005", Frydman, Carola, MIT Sloan School of Management and NBER, & Saks, Raven, Federal Reserve Board of Governors, Oxford University Press 2010.

"CEO Incentives: It's Not How Much You Pay, But How", Jensen, Michael C. & Murphy, Kevin J., Harvard Business Review, 1990

Chapter 6
Post 2000 Intensification of Focus on the Board

In another set of transactions that resulted in headlines, scandal, numerous court cases, and some major fines and board reorganizations, we look at the issue of options back dating. A number of companies found themselves caught up in this drama in the early 2000s, having liberally used options as compensation in prior years.

In 1972, a revision (APB 25) in accounting rules resulted in the ability of a company to avoid having to report executive incomes as an expense to their shareholders if the income resulted from an issuance of "at-the-money" stock options. In essence, the revision enabled companies to increase executive compensation without informing their shareholders if the compensation was in the form of stock options contracts that would only become valuable if the underlying stock price were to increase at a later time.

In 1994, a new tax code (162 M) provision declared all executive income levels over one million dollars to be "unreasonable" in order to increase taxes on such compensation by ending their previous tax-deductible status. To avoid those taxes, many companies adopted the policy described above of issuing "at-the-money" stock options in lieu of additional income.

When company executives discovered that they had the ability to backdate stock option grants, thus making them both tax deductible and "in-the-money" on the date of actual issuance, the common practice of stock option backdating for financial gain began on a widespread level. The problem with this practice, according to the SEC, was that stock option backdating, while difficult to prove, could be considered a criminal act.

For the many companies that had problems with backdating, consequences fell along a broad spectrum. Where management was guilty of conscious wrongdoing in backdating and attempted, for example, to conceal the backdating by falsifying documents, and the backdating resulted in a substantial overstatement of earnings, SEC enforcement actions and even criminal charges resulted. Where the backdating was a result of informal internal procedures or even just delays in finalizing the paperwork documenting options grants, there may have been no formal sanction. The company, however, faced public humiliation and loss of confidence as a result of having to restate its financial statements, which was not an insignificant penalty.

It is likely that most of the criminal actions the government intended to bring regarding serious cases of backdating were brought in 2007. The Sarbanes-Oxley Act of 2002, which we will review shortly, defined a five-year statute of limita-

DOI 10.1515/9781547400270-006

tions for securities fraud, and requires option grants to senior management to be reported within two days of the grant date. This all but eliminated the opportunity for options backdating.

Corruption Eruption Leads to Sarbanes Oxley and Growing Focus on Board

Enron Corporation was a Houston-based energy, commodities, and services company, the result of a 1985 merger between Houston Natural Gas and Inter-North, both relatively small regional companies. By the end of 2000, Enron employed approximately 20,000 and was one of the world's major electricity, natural gas, communications and pulp and paper companies, with claimed revenues of nearly $101 billion during 2000. Fortune named Enron «America's Most Innovative Company» for six consecutive years.

By the end of 2001, it was revealed that its reported financial condition was sustained by institutionalized and systematic accounting fraud. Enron has since become a well-known example of willful corporate fraud and corruption. Massive insider trading and intentionally deceitful accounting practices were revealed along with top executives ignoring conflicts of interest that siphoned significant money out of the corporation. Enron filed for bankruptcy in the Southern District of New York in late 2001. It emerged from bankruptcy in November 2004, pursuant to a court-approved plan of reorganization, as Enron Creditors Recovery Corp., liquidating remaining operations and assets.

One of Enron's predecessors was the Northern Natural Gas Company, formed in 1930, in Omaha, Nebraska. The low cost of natural gas and cheap labor supply during the Great Depression helped the company double in size by 1932 and bring the first natural gas to Minnesota. Over the next 50 years, Northern acquired many energy companies. It was reorganized in 1979 as the main subsidiary of a holding company, InterNorth, which was a diversified energy and energy-related products company. By the 1980s, InterNorth had become a major force for natural gas production, transmission and marketing as well as for natural gas liquids, and was an innovator in the plastics industry. In 1983, InterNorth merged with the Belco Petroleum Company, a Fortune 500 oil exploration and development company founded by Arthur Belfer.

Houston Natural Gas (HNG) corporation was formed from the Houston Oil Co. in 1925 to provide gas to customers in the Houston market through the building of gas pipelines. Under CEO Robert Herring, the company became a dominant force with a large pipeline network. In the late 1970s rising gas prices and new regulation made it more difficult to turn a profit in the Texas market. In 1984,

Kenneth Lay became CEO and inherited the troubled but large diversified energy conglomerate.

InterNorth became a target for corporate raider Irwin Jacobs. CEO Sam Segnar, searching for a company to merge with to fend off Jacobs, discovered HNG. In May 1985, InterNorth acquired HNG for $2.3 billion, 40 percent higher than the current market price, and created the second largest gas pipeline system in the United States. InterNorth's north-south pipelines complemented HNG's east-west pipelines well.

Lay succeeded Segnar as CEO, and had to find a way to pay Jacobs, still a threat, over $350 million. Lay consolidated the gas pipeline efforts and began to ramp up its electric power and natural gas efforts. In 1989, Jeffrey Skilling, then a consultant at McKinsey & Co., came up with the idea Enron adopted to link natural gas to consumers more directly, called the "Gas Bank." The division's success prompted Skilling to join Enron as its head in 1991. Enron also began expansion overseas.

In the early 1980s, most contracts between natural gas producers and pipelines were "take-or-pay" contracts, where pipelines agreed to pay for a minimum volume of gas in the future at prearranged prices, and pipelines, in turn, had similar long-term contracts with their suppliers. Changes in natural gas regulation in the mid-1980s permitted more flexible arrangements and led to increased use of spot market transactions. By 1990, 75 percent of gas sales were spot transactions. Enron benefited from the increased flexibility resulting from the regulatory changes.

In an attempt to achieve further growth, Enron pursued diversification by reaching beyond its pipeline business to natural gas trading, and then became a financial trader and market maker in electric power, coal, steel, paper and pulp, water, and broadband fiber optic cable capacity. By 2001, Enron had become a conglomerate that owned and operated gas pipelines, electricity plants, pulp and paper plants, broadband assets, and water plants internationally, and traded extensively in financial markets for the same products and services.

In August 2000, Enron's stock price peaked at $90.56, and Enron executives began selling. The general public and Enron's investor base were told by Ken Lay to buy because the stock price would rebound during the near future. By August 15, 2001, Enron's stock price had decreased to $42, and by October 2001, had decreased to $15. With the October announcements of accounting irregularities and business failures, the market response crippled the company immediately, dependent as it was on short term funding for its trading businesses. On November 8, Enron agreed to being acquired by a smaller competitor, Dynergy. On November 28, Enron's public debt was downgraded to junk bond status, however, and Dynergy withdrew its proposal. With its stock price at $0.26, Enron filed for bankruptcy protection on December 2, 2001.

The fallout resulted in both Lay and Skilling being convicted for conspiracy, fraud, and insider trading. Lay died before sentencing, Skilling was sentenced to 24 years and 4 months in prison and a $45 million penalty, later reduced. Others received jail sentences and/or significant fines. Arthur Andersen, then one of the "Big Five" accounting firms, was dissolved as in 2002, the company was found guilty of obstruction of justice for destroying documents related to the Enron audit. Andersen was forced to stop auditing public companies, as the SEC is not allowed to accept audits completed by convicted felons. Although the conviction was dismissed in 2005 by the Supreme Court, the damage to the Andersen name precluded its revival even on a limited scale.

The Functioning of the Board of Directors Gains Attention

This extraordinary bad acting resulted in Congressional hearings into the Enron matter, including a focus on the role of the board of directors in the drama. A delightfully cogent and concise summary of the findings appears below.

UNITED STATES SENATE COMMITTEE ON GOVERNMENTAL AFFAIRS
THE ROLE OF THE BOARD OF DIRECTORS IN ENRON'S COLLAPSE
July 8, 2002
R E P O R T prepared by the PERMANENT SUBCOMMITTEE ON INVESTIGATIONS

"On December 2, 2001, Enron Corporation, then the seventh largest publicly traded corporation in the United States, declared bankruptcy. That bankruptcy sent shock waves throughout the country, on both Wall Street and Main Street where over half of American families now invest directly or indirectly in the stock market. Thousands of Enron employees lost not only their jobs but a significant part of their retirement savings; Enron shareholders saw the value of their investments plummet; and hundreds, if not thousands of businesses around the world, were turned into Enron creditors in bankruptcy court likely to receive only pennies on the dollars owed to them. . . ."

SUBCOMMITTEE FINDINGS Based upon the evidence before it, including over one million pages of subpoenaed documents, interviews of 13 Enron Board members, and the Subcommittee hearing on May 7, 2002, the U.S. Senate Permanent Subcommittee on Investigations makes the following findings with respect to the role of the Enron Board of Directors in Enron's collapse and bankruptcy.

1. *Fiduciary Failure.* The Enron Board of Directors failed to safeguard Enron shareholders and contributed to the collapse of the seventh largest public company in the United States, by allowing Enron to engage in high risk accounting, inappropriate conflict of interest transactions, extensive undisclosed off-the-books activities, and excessive executive compensation. The Board witnessed numerous indications of questionable practices by Enron management over several years, but chose to ignore them to the detriment of Enron shareholders, employees and business associates.

2. *High Risk Accounting.* The Enron Board of Directors knowingly allowed Enron to engage in high risk accounting practices.
3. *Inappropriate Conflicts of Interest.* Despite clear conflicts of interest, the Enron Board of Directors approved an unprecedented arrangement allowing Enron's Chief Financial Officer to establish and operate the LJM private equity funds which transacted business with Enron and profited at Enron's expense. The Board exercised inadequate oversight of LJM transaction and compensation controls and failed to protect Enron shareholders from unfair dealing.
4. *Extensive Undisclosed Off-The-Books Activity.* The Enron Board of Directors knowingly allowed Enron to conduct billions of dollars in off-the-books activity to make its financial condition appear better than it was and failed to ensure adequate public disclosure of material off-the-books liabilities that contributed to Enron's collapse.
5. *Excessive Compensation.* The Enron Board of Directors approved excessive compensation for company executives, failed to monitor the cumulative cash drain caused by Enron's 2000 annual bonus and performance unit plans, and failed to monitor or halt abuse by Board Chairman and Chief Executive Officer Kenneth Lay of a company-financed, multi-million dollar personal credit line.
6. *Lack of Independence.* The independence of the Enron Board of Directors was compromised by financial ties between the company and certain Board members. The Board also failed to ensure the independence of the company's auditor, allowing Andersen to provide internal audit and consulting services while serving as Enron's outside auditor.

Much has been written about the remarkable failure of the board, which was comprised of a number of people with excellent credentials, to see what was happening and to call a halt. It seems inexplicable that smart and seasoned professionals did not understand the key issues, especially when two of their number appear to have resigned stating their reason as concern over the direction in which the business was moving.

While I do not believe their passivity is defensible, it is very difficult to stop practices that appear to be enormously profitable, no matter how hard it is to believe them. The accounting may in fact be hard to decipher, but highly skilled directors are supposed to address that by being sure that the arcane is presented clearly. The conflicts of interest are impossible to explain away. What happened? It is merely conjecture on my part, but the concept of the board rather than the CEO being responsible may not have fully caught up with them. Perhaps they came of age in a different era. If true, it is a pretty weak excuse.

The outcry following Enron's collapse was deafening. As post-Enron reform pressure mounted, the New York Stock Exchange initiated a significant revision of its board composition standards in an effort to restore public confidence and to show that private regulation could address the governance failures that Enron revealed without further federal legislation.

A majority of directors of listed companies were required to be independent, and stringent independence criteria applied to all such directors, not just audit committee members. The compensation committees, not just the audit committee, were required to include only these more stringently defined independents. The Business Roundtable emphasized the importance of independent directors and importance of the board's role in focusing on the integrity and clarity of the corporate financial statements and financial reporting.

Just as it seemed that forestalling legislative action might succeed, the WorldCom scandal broke in the spring of 2002, which again raised the saliency of corporate governance problems and created unstoppable momentum for the legislation that became the Sarbanes-Oxley Act. Ironically, then, some of the emphasis on director independence in the post-Enron environment is the byproduct of a failed effort to offer up stronger board monitoring to forestall legislative change.

Sarbanes-Oxley Act

The number and scale of corporate scandals, including Enron, WorldCom, Adelphia, Parmalat and others had finally reached a tipping point where the U.S. government felt it had to act. The resulting Public Company Accounting Reform and Investor Protection Act of 2002 (Sarbanes-Oxley) invaded the inner sanctum of the boardroom with far reaching regulation. To my eye, it took 400 years from the date of the formation of VOC for the functions of the board to be explicitly codified, and for the board as a force unto itself it had long held to be fully recognized, with both explicit responsibility, and consequences for failure.

The private sector had been preparing for this moment, issuing numerous reports on suggested best practices following previous scandals. The primary reports that SOX reforms drew upon include the Cadbury Report, developed following a raft of governance failures in the United Kingdom and released in 1992, and the Organization for Economic Co-Operation and Development (OECD) Corporate Governance Principles first released in 1999, and since updated several times. (OECD is becoming an increasingly influential entity in governance, about which we will learn more shortly.)

Also of note are the National Association of Corporate Directors Blue Ribbon Commission reports since 1993 on various governance topics. Rounding out the governance triangle were management groups (Business Roundtable, Institute of Internal Auditors) and investor groups (Council of Institutional Investors), which helped guide policy makers in Congress and in the stock exchanges. Certain attorneys including Marty Lipton of Wachtell Lipton and Ira Millstein of Weil Gotshal also carried weight with stock exchange officials and other policymakers.

Sarbanes-Oxley, and later simply SOX, was quickly developed and passed, and a little more than a year later the major stock exchanges had a raft of new listing rules for public company boards, modeled largely on existing "best practices." SOX would have a profound impact on corporate reporting, create a new regime of rules and regulations for publicly traded corporations, and it and the scandals that prompted it would accelerate the consideration of corporate governance by governments and corporations around the globe. SOX, like the Cadbury Report and the OECD Principles, has influenced similar laws in many other countries.

The law requires, along with many other elements, that:
- The Public Company Accounting Oversight Board (PCAOB) be established to regulate the auditing profession, which had been self-regulated prior to the law. Auditors are responsible for reviewing the financial statements of corporations and issuing an opinion as to their reliability.
- The Chief Executive Officer (CEO) and Chief Financial Officer (CFO) attest to the financial statements. Prior to the law, CEO's had been bold enough to claim in court they hadn't reviewed the information as part of their defense.
- Board audit committees have members that are independent and disclose whether or not at least one is a financial expert, or reasons why no such expert is on the audit committee.
- External audit firms cannot provide certain types of consulting services and must rotate their lead partner every five years. Further, an audit firm cannot audit a company if those in specified senior management roles worked for the auditor in the past year. Prior to the law, there was the real or perceived conflict of interest between providing an independent opinion on the accuracy and reliability of financial statements when the same firm was also providing lucrative consulting services.

SOX has been called the "broadest sweeping legislation to affect corporations and public accounting since the 1993 and 1934 securities acts." It made considerable changes to the regulatory environment, focusing on addressing the "systematic and structural weaknesses affecting the U.S. capital markets which were revealed by repeated failures of audit effectiveness and corporate financial and broker-dealer responsibility." While compliance, especially with Section 404 on internal control requirements, in the early years following enactment of SOX was burdensome for many companies, most, including the major accounting firms who saw their businesses changed overnight, have now adapted.

SOX also introduced new standards of accountability for boards of U.S. companies or companies listed on U.S. stock exchanges. Directors now risk large fines and prison sentences in the case of accounting crimes. The vast majority of companies covered have hired internal auditors to ensure that the company adheres to required standards of internal control. The internal auditors are required by law to report directly to an audit committee, consisting of directors more than half of whom are independent directors, and at least one of whom is a "financial expert."

The law requires companies listed on NYSE and NASDAQ to field a majority of independent directors not employed by the corporation or in a business relationship with it.

In an op-ed piece in *The New York Times* on April 2012, called "Sarbanes-Oxley Changed Corporate America," Michael W. Peregrine, a partner at the law firm McDermott Will & Emery, observed cogently that *"The impact of Sarbanes-Oxley isn't necessarily found in the collective impact of its substantive provisions. Rather, it is found in the profound way the law has reshaped attitudes toward corporate governance. . . Sarbanes-Oxley seized the center of corporate direction from the corner office and returned it to the boardroom, where it belonged. Moreover, the law encouraged the identification of "best practices" to guide boardroom conduct. It has helped to shape the focus of state courts and regulators on the proper application of other fiduciary duty laws. It has raised the public consciousness of corporate governance."*

The post-Enron reforms lay the groundwork for a revised model of corporate governance. The model operates at many different levels. It ratchets up the liability for primary wrong-doers, particularly corporate officers. It imposes new duties, new liabilities, and a new regulatory structure on certain gatekeepers, accountants in particular but also, lawyers and, in a fashion, securities analysts.

The collapse of Enron, WorldCom, and similar but less catastrophic disclosure failures vividly demonstrated weaknesses in the board governance system produced by the 1990s and pointed the way toward clearer roles for independent directors and standards of independence. Both the federal securities law and the stock exchange listing requirements imposed more rigorous standards of director independence.

The principal objective of the Sarbanes-Oxley Act of 2002, then, was the protection of the integrity of financial disclosure, both through extensive new regulation of accountants and through specific disclosure responsibilities imposed on directors. It also took giant steps, some welcome and some not, toward making clear the expected functions of the corporate board of directors.

Read More

The Role of the Board of Directors in Enron's Collapse, Permanent Subcommittee on Investigations, United States Senate Committee on Governmental Affairs, 2002

The Smartest Guys in the Room, The Amazing Rise and Scandalous Fall of Enron, McLean, Bethany, & Eklind, Peter, Penguin, 2003 & 2013

A Conspiracy of Fools: A True Story, Eichenwald, Kurt, Broadway Books & Random House, 2005

"A Guide to The Sarbanes-Oxley Act of 2002", http://www.soxlaw.com, maintained by AICPA

Part II: **The Players and Capital Market Forces**

Stakes are high as boards are now significantly comprised of independent directors who must manage the challenges inherent in having less information than management while also playing defense in the face of pressure from short-term activists, longer-term investors, and increasingly active regulators. Huge shifts in our capital markets compound the challenges as institutional investors dominate as never before, activist investors boldly assert rights they may or may not have and pursue various aggressive tactics seen and unseen, and "innovation" in capital market instruments has led not only to a huge private equity sector but also to a complex intertwined network of largely obscure derivative instruments.

We will return to the profound impact of SOX in the U.S. and abroad, but first let us spend some time looking squarely at the extraordinary rise of independent directors. We will then consider the profound changes in the composition of capital markets during the period in which independent directors as a concept achieved dominance, and then look at the forces that led us into the 2008 abyss. With that background we can better understand the changes in corporate governance that have and will continue to occur since the 2008 financial crisis.

The effect of the changes on the board's role is not only to make the role of independent directors more important than ever, which had already been established as a trend during our walk-through history. For the first time, the independent directors have explicit, rather than implicit, power. Boards, particularly the audit committee, are given a specific mandate to supervise the firm's relationship with the accountants and to oversee the corporation's internal financial controls and financial disclosure.

Read More

The Role of the Board of Directors in Enron's Collapse, Permanent Subcommittee on Investigations, United States Senate Committee on Governmental Affairs, 2002

The Smartest Guys in the Room, The Amazing Rise and Scandalous Fall of Enron, McLean, Bethany, & Eklind, Peter, Penguin, 2003 & 2013

A Conspiracy of Fools: A True Story, Eichenwald, Kurt, Broadway Books & Random House, 2005

"A Guide to The Sarbanes-Oxley Act of 2002", http://www.soxlaw.com, maintained by AICPA

Chapter 7
The Rise of Independent/Disinterested Directors

The dramatic shift in board composition toward independent directors and away from insiders and affiliated directors is one of the most important developments in U.S. corporate governance. It may also be among the least understood. In addition to the numerical shift, the independence-in-fact of directors has been buttressed by adoption of various rule-based and structural mechanisms.

By 2004, under the influence of Sarbanes-Oxley and the stock exchange listing rules, the shift was virtually complete: 91 percent of U.S. public companies reported two or fewer insiders; 9 percent reported three insiders. Large public firms have moved to a pattern of one, perhaps two inside directors and an increasing number of independent directors. In 2013, in U.S. public companies, 85 percent of directors were independent, and 60 percent of boards had so-called "super-majority boards" with only one non-independent director—the Chief Executive Officer. Over the last few decades, the primary legislative and judicial response to almost every major corporate scandal in the U.S. has been to increase reliance on independent directors.

Considering Independent Director Effectiveness

The evidence of effectiveness is mixed, which is not surprising given the reasoning that brought independent directors to the forefront. Although boards with a predominance of independent directors may do a better job in certain defensive roles such as firing the CEO, avoiding overpayment in a takeover, avoiding distracting acquisitions, there is little evidence of impact on the upside.

Anecdotally, independent directors have not had a great track record protecting the companies in their charge. Failed investment banks Lehman Brothers and Bear Stearns had boards with a supermajority of independent directors. Earlier, the SEC cast much of the blame for the 1970 collapse of the Penn Central Company on passive non-management directors. Enron had a fully functional audit committee operating under the SEC's expanded rules on audit committee disclosure.

While anecdotal examples of failure do not prove the absence of success, and there may be many, more to the point are the results of several studies of the effect of independent directors on corporate performance in the United States. The overall weight of the findings is that there is no solid evidence suggesting that independent directors improve corporate performance or reduce the likelihood

DOI 10.1515/9781547400270-007

of failure. To me, this is hardly surprising, as the concepts that brought independence to the fore were legal ones, and not economic ones.

Dueling Definitions

The term "independent director" may be intended to describe hoped for independent mindedness as much as anything. In various descriptions, the term "independent in fact" seems to be growing in use, as the many definitions of independence applied can be confusing. The terms "independent," "outside," "non-management," "non-executive," and "disinterested" are often used as if they are interchangeable, but they are not. Each implies a different role for the director described and is defined by state and federal laws as well as stock exchange regulations. Not surprisingly, the result is an inconsistent set of rules across jurisdictions.

New York Stock Exchange Listing Requirements Stress Independence of Directors

In response to the requirements of SOX, corporate governance standards that require listed company boards to have a majority of independent directors were introduced in 2003. These standards further require that audit, compensation, and nomination committees must all be composed entirely of independent directors.

The NYSE Listed Company Manual requires, for example:
- Independent directors: "Listed companies must have a majority of independent directors...Effective boards of directors exercise independent judgment in carrying out their responsibilities. Requiring a majority of independent directors will increase the quality of board oversight and lessen the possibility of damaging conflicts of interest" (Section 303A.01.) An independent director is not part of management and has no "material financial relationship" with the company.
- Regular meetings that exclude management: "To empower non-management directors to serve as a more effective check on management, the non-management directors of each listed company must meet at regularly scheduled executive sessions without management" (Section 303A.03).

No director qualifies as "independent" unless the board of directors affirmatively determines that the director has no material relationship with the listed company (either directly or as a partner, shareholder or officer of an organization that has a relationship with the company). Companies must disclose which directors are independent and disclose the basis for that determination.

Unlike SOX, the NYSE rules do not contemplate specific mandatory powers for independent directors. In addition to an audit committee, listed companies must have a nominating committee and a compensation committee, each composed solely of independent directors. Unlike the audit committee, however, these committees need not have exclusive power in their respective field and could be limited simply to making recommendations to the board as a whole. On the other hand, independent directors must constitute a majority of the board.

The NASDAQ rules give more power to independent directors. As in NYSE-listed companies, audit committees have the exclusive power to hire and fire the outside auditor. Unlike in NYSE-listed companies, however, the compensation of officers is to be decided by a majority of independent directors or by a compensation committee consisting solely of independent directors (subject to minor exceptions), and board nominations are to be decided in a similar fashion. Although both NYSE-listed and NASDAQ-listed company boards must have a majority of independent directors, the board as a whole in an NYSE-listed company could override committee recommendations in matters of compensation and nomination, but not in a NASDAQ-listed company.

We dwell on this to illustrate first that apparently small differences in definition can have a huge impact on corporate activity, and second that if the regulators and stock exchanges are neither clear nor consistent in the roles expected from independent directors, it is hardly surprising that independent directors often do not understand the expectations placed on them, and where they come from. I have spared you a recitation of the many and varied theories expressed in academic and legal precincts as to what independent directors are intended to do but suffice it to say that there are many possible useful functions and little agreement. This leaves the independent director to pick and choose, or simply to take the path of least resistance and follow the leader.

Here is an example: substantial disagreement exists regarding stock ownership by the putatively independent director. Those who see the independent director primarily as a defender of shareholder interests against management will naturally see more share ownership as better, because it will more closely align the interests of the director with the shareholders. Those who view the independent director as someone whose judgment should be untainted by any financial interest in the company are suspicious of share ownership. And adherents of each view roundly disdain the other.

The two exchanges, for their part, differ from federal law and from each other. The NYSE simply incorporates by reference the requirements of federal law as far as audit committee members are concerned. But where its own requirement for a majority of independent directors is concerned, it imposes no limits on shareholding whatsoever. In proposing its rule change, the NYSE specifically noted the views of commentators that share ownership should be viewed as desirable and stated that "as the concern is independence from management, the exchange does not view ownership of even a significant amount of stock, by itself, as a bar to an independence finding."

NASDAQ takes a different view. It sets a limit on audit committee director shareholding of the lower of (1) whatever the SEC prescribes under the SOX, and (2) 20 percent. As we have seen, the SEC has not in fact prescribed any per se upper limit on director shareholding (although it has established a safe harbor of under 10 percent). Thus, NASDAQ may end up forbidding what the SEC, which defines affiliation via a concept of control, might allow.

There is an is important fundamental difference in approach between the SEC and both the exchanges. Both exchanges require company boards to have a majority of independent directors except when the company is a "controlled company," i.e., when a single person, group, or company controls more than 50 percent of the voting power. In other words, they see independent directors as a protection for shareholders against management, not against other shareholders. A shareholder who controls a company does not need an external rule maker to protect him from the management team that he can appoint. Minority shareholders may need protection from controlling shareholders, but the exchanges are apparently willing to leave this task to other bodies of law, such as federal securities law requiring disclosures, and state corporate law mandating certain fiduciary duties.

The SEC's approach, however, is different. As we have seen, an "affiliated person" cannot be "independent," and the SEC defines affiliation, among other things, in terms of control. Under the SEC's principle, when stock ownership is significant enough to lead to control, affiliation exists, and independence disappears. The NYSE's approach implies that when stock ownership is enough to lead to control, the director is super-independent of management, so the need for protection by a rule disappears. Thus, the SEC's view of the proper role of independent directors seems consistent with the view that they should have ties neither with management nor with the fortunes of the company itself.

More important than federal law for purposes of corporate governance is state law, under which corporations are organized. United States corporation law at the state level does not generally provide for the institution of independent directors as such or define them. Instead, state corporate statutes, which typically reference Delaware law as the bellwether, focus on conflict-of-interest transactions. Using this lens, certain consequences will follow depending on whether or not those with both a conflict of interest and decision-making power recuse themselves from decision-making on that matter.

For context, it is important to understand how common law would operate if state statutes did not deal with conflict-of-interest transactions. The common law rule in many states in the late 19th century was quite absolute: many conflict-of-interest transactions could be set aside at the instance of any stockholder. State statutes, then, typically operate by specifically displacing the common law rule on conflict-of-interest transactions and permitting them provided certain conditions are met. These conditions usually pertain to disclosure of the conflict of interest and approval of the transaction by disinterested decision-makers, whether directors or shareholders.

The Delaware General Corporation Law (DGCL) states in section 144 that a transaction in which a director or officer stands on both sides "shall not be voidable by reason of a conflict of interest if one of the following conditions are met: (1) the relevant facts are known to the board and a majority of disinterested directors approve; or (if, for example, the entire board has a conflict of interest) (2) the relevant facts are known to the shareholders, and the shareholders approve; or (if for any reason neither of the first two occurs) (3) the terms of the transaction are, as of the time it is authorized by the directors or the shareholders, fair to the corporation."

In short, the Delaware concept of independence is specific to disinterestedness in a particular conflict-of-interest transaction, which is different from abstract independence. It is not assumed that such directors will always be the same person, and do not require the institution of abstractly independent directors. Instead, they take a transaction-by-transaction approach, and ask in each case whether there was approval by decision-makers who were disinterested in the transaction in question.

The Delaware judiciary has on several occasions stressed the preferability of a case-by-case analysis over the application of abstract definitions. When asked how a court would determine whether a board had acted independently, E. Norman Veasey, the former chief justice of the Delaware Supreme Court, replied,

> We can't set down rules for independence. In Delaware, we're a judicial body, not a legislative one.... But we didn't just fall off the turnip truck, you know. We can tell whether somebody is acting independently or not. I don't think, for instance, that lawyers who get substantial fees from a corporation can be considered independent directors for most purposes, although they might be for some.

The Delaware approach has the advantage of dealing directly with the problem as it arises. A company's management often does, and sometimes must (for example, in the case of compensation), engage in transactions that either are or look very much like self-dealing or in some other way create a conflict of interest. In such cases the blessing of directors, who are both disinterested in the transaction in question and independent of management, can be invaluable. As noted above, corporate statutes in the United States do not prohibit self-dealing transactions outright but instead provide a safe harbor for transactions that are approved by directors who are disinterested in the transaction in question. The good-faith use by management of such directors is recognized by courts and extremely valuable.

But the difficult problem remains: Independence is more a disposition, a state of mind, rather than a concrete fact. The relationship rules, the negative and positive incentives, the board structures, and the nomination procedures all draw on our imperfect knowledge of human nature and behavior, which itself is influenced by the shifting social and cultural environment.

Independent director requirements in other major jurisdictions have grown in importance as well but are less exacting. In the United Kingdom, for example, there is no independent director requirement at all. Instead, companies listed on the London Stock Exchange are required by its listing rules to disclose, in their annual report and accounts, a statement of how they have applied the principles in Section 1 of the Combined Code, which provide that except in smaller companies, at least half the board (excluding the chairman) should consist of non-executive directors determined by the board to be independent.

As of 2016, most Member States of the European Union (EU) and virtually all major Asian jurisdictions have rules requiring the appointment of at least some independent directors to their companies' boards. The OECD Principles of Corporate Governance of 2015 recommend assigning important tasks to independent board members. The regulatory basis for this obligation is found either in the pertinent company laws, the listings rules and/or the corporate governance codes. Independent directors have obviously become global players.

Independent Directors Fill a Structural and Legal Need

Though there are many studies that purport to analyze the effectiveness of independent directors of public companies, to me most of them miss what seems to me to be an obvious point. If as we have seen every jurisdiction in the world requires that corporations must be supervised by a board of directors, who can perform that task?

The CEO as the top corporate officer clearly has a supervisory role, but if company employees or affiliated persons who do business with the company also serve on the board, how can these folks, who all depend in various ways on the company and the CEO, supervise the company, the CEO and even themselves? Thus, in order for the board to be able to acquit itself of its supervisory responsibilities and its fiduciary duties to the corporation, at least a majority of the directors of the corporation must be independent. This is a simple concept, based on the notion of arm's length fair dealing. This is true regardless of whether the independent directors improve performance or not.

As an historical note, the concept of the independent director as a required party on any board was, to the best of my knowledge, introduced by the Investment Company Act of 1940, which was grappling with the tightly intertwined roles involved in the fund investment vehicle, the investment management company, and the distributor of fund shares. Funds typically have no employees, and their affairs are managed by the investment management company that organizes the fund, pursuant to a contract. Often the same people are overseeing all of the entities, which gives rise to a situation rife with conflicts of interest. What the 40 Act did was insert the concept if the independent directors as arbiters of those conflicts, with a specific mandate to watch out for the affairs of the fund vehicle. In effect, they were providing daylight, as a proxy for regulatory involvement.

Read More

"Director Independence Standards Chart", Thomson Reuters Practical Law Corporate & Securities

NYSE: Corporate Governance Guide, Consulting Editors Rosenblum, Steven A., Cain, Karessa L., & Niles Sabastian V., 2014

NYSE Listed Company Manual, New York Stock Exchange

Governance Clearing House, Listing Center Reference Library, NASDAQ

Chapter 8
The Rise of Institutional Investors

Several different types of institutional investors have come to dominate our capital markets. Here we loosely break them into their legal forms, and then the investment types in which they participate, to try to make them and the pressures they face understandable.

Mutual Fund Development

To trace the origin of the pooled investment vehicle we call the mutual fund we again look to the Dutch Republic. The first known such fund was formed in 1773, by Amsterdam-based businessman Abraham van Ketwich who created a trust named Eendragt Maakt Magt ("unity creates strength"). His aim was to provide small investors with an opportunity to diversify, which continues to be an important advantage provided by mutual funds today.

Mutual funds were introduced to the United States in the booming 1890s, as closed-end funds with a fixed number of shares, in which the value of the shares traded above, at, or below the funds' net asset values. The first open-end mutual fund with redeemable shares was established in 1924 as the Massachusetts Investors Trust and is still in existence today. In 1928, Scudder, Stevens and Clark launched the first no-load fund, a fund which did not charge a commission to the buyer. The Wellington Fund, the first mutual fund to include stocks and bonds, as opposed to direct investments in business and trade, was also launched in 1928.

By 1929, the industry claimed $27 billion in total assets according to Investment Company Institute data. As a point of reference, by 1970, there were approximately 360 funds with $48 billion in assets. At the end of 2016, mutual fund assets worldwide totaled $40.4 trillion, according to the Investment Company Institute, and the largest pool of such funds is based in the United States, with $18.9 trillion in assets.

The Investment Company Act of 1940, a Depression era piece of legislation that was delayed by several years of study, was enacted to define coved investment companies and detail the process required to govern them. Mutual funds are simple enough: they typically take the form of a trust with perpetual life. Because their shares are offered to the public, they must be registered with the SEC just like a public company. The complexity comes in because the fund does not typically have its own employees. It contracts for services from its investment

DOI 10.1515/9781547400270-008

manager, often the creator of the fund, and from administrators and transfer agents and underwriters, who sell the shares.

The interest of the investment manager is generally in increasing its own profits, which may not always be consistent with the best interests of the fund shareholders. To protect shareholders from this conflict, the '40 Act spells out the requirements for the fund's board, and mandated that a certain percentage of directors, then 40 percent, needed to be disinterested.

This was important as investment manager employees could also be fund directors as well as administrators, transfer agents, and underwriters. These people wearing many hats needed an impartial voice responsible only for the health and wealth of the fund. To the best of my knowledge this was not only the first instance of independent directors being specified but also the first clear directive setting forth the processes board members were responsible for undertaking.

In 1971, Wells Fargo Bank established the first index fund, a concept that fund luminary John Bogle used as a foundation on which to build The Vanguard Group, renowned for its low-cost index funds. Index funds hold portfolios built to match the components of a specified market index, such as the Standard & Poor's 500 Index (S&P 500). Its attractions include broad market exposure, low operating expenses, low portfolio turnover, and the ability to avoid the cost of active management, which rarely achieves consistent results that match or exceed the index.

The 1970s also saw the rise of the no-load fund, funds that charge no upfront commission to investors. This new way of doing business had an enormous impact on the way mutual funds were sold and would make a major contribution to the industry's success. With the 1980s and 1990s growth of assets, previously obscure fund managers became superstars; Max Heine, Michael Price and Peter Lynch, the mutual fund industry's top gunslingers, became household names and money poured into the retail fund industry at a stunning pace.

In 1993 I was building a no load mutual fund complex. While credited by Lipper Analytical Services with growing assets to $1 billion faster than any non-bank complex in history, I confess to having had considerable help from what was to me an unexpected source. One Thursday afternoon, we received a call from a radio station warning us that their Sunday show would be highlighting our funds and to plan for extra help answering the phones.

Mystified, I made contingency plans just in case. Lo and behold, during the show our phones started to ring and by the time the flood was over we had substantially increased the size of our fund complex. And this happened again and again. Thankfully our funds continued to perform during that crazy year, even with that huge influx of new money.

Comments from Mutual Fund Leader John C. Bogle

John Bogle offers valuable insight in the Reflections column in the *Financial Analysts Journal* in 2005. I include most of his commentary below, as I find it compelling, and his authority in making such observations is difficult to dispute.

> The staggering increase in the size of the industry and the huge expansion in the number and types of funds are but the obvious manifestations of the radical changes in the mutual fund industry. It has also undergone a multifaceted change in character. In 1945, it was an industry engaged primarily in the profession of serving investors and striving to meet the standards of the recently enacted Investment Company Act of 1940, which established the policy that funds must be "organized, operated, and managed" in the interests of their share-holders rather than in the interests of their managers and distributors. It was an industry that focused primarily on stewardship. Today, in contrast, the industry is a vast and highly successful marketing business, an industry focused primarily on salesmanship. As countless independent commentators have observed, asset gathering has become the fund industry's driving force. . .
>
> The vast changes in fund objectives and policies have been accompanied by equally vast changes in how mutual funds are managed. In 1945, the major funds were managed almost entirely by investment committees. But the demonstrated wisdom of the collective was soon overwhelmed by the perceived brilliance of the individual. The Go-Go Era of the mid-1960s and the recent so-called New Economy bubble brought us hundreds of ferociously aggressive "performance funds," and the new game seemed to call for free-wheeling individual talent. The term "investment committee" virtually vanished, and the "portfolio manager" gradually became the industry standard. . .
>
> Together, the coming of more aggressive funds, the burgeoning emphasis on short-term performance, and the move from investment committee to portfolio manager had a profound impact on mutual fund investment strategies, most obviously in soaring portfolio turnover. . . In 1945, mutual fund managers did not talk about long-term investing; they simply did it. That's what trusteeship is all about. But over the next 60 years, that basic tenet was turned on its head and short-term speculation became the order of the day.
>
> Not that the long-term focus did not resist change. Indeed, between 1945 and 1965, annual portfolio turnover averaged a steady 17 percent, suggesting that the average fund held its average stock for about six years. But turnover then rose steadily; fund managers now turn their portfolios over at an average rate of 110 percent annually. Result: Compared with the six-year standard that prevailed for some two decades, the average stock is now held by the average fund for an average of only 11 months.
>
> Moreover, turnover rates do not tell the full story of the role of mutual funds in the financial markets. The dollars involved are enormous. For example, at a 100 percent rate, today's managers of $4 trillion in equity assets would sell $4 trillion of stocks in a single year and then reinvest that $4 trillion in other stocks, $8 trillion in all. Even though more competitive (and increasingly electronic) markets have slashed unit transaction costs, it is difficult to imagine that such turnover levels, in which trades often take place between two competing funds, can result in a net gain to fund shareholders collectively.
>
> If a six-year holding period can be characterized as long-term investment, and if an 11-month holding period can be characterized as short-term speculation, mutual fund man-

agers today are not investors. They are speculators. I do not use the word "speculation" lightly. Nearly 70 years ago, John Maynard Keynes contrasted speculation ("forecasting the psychology of the market") with enterprise ("forecasting the prospective yield of an asset") and predicted that the influence of speculation among professional investors would rise as they emulated the uninformed public—that is, seeking to anticipate changes in public opinion rather than focusing on earnings, dividends, and book values.

In my 1951 thesis on the mutual fund industry, I was bold enough to disagree with Keynes' baleful prediction. As funds grew, I opined, they would move away from speculation and move toward enterprise by focusing, not on the momentary, short-term price of the share, but on the long-term intrinsic value of the corporation. As a result, I concluded, fund managers would supply the stock market "with a demand for securities that is steady, sophisticated, enlightened, and analytic." I could not have been more wrong. Mutual funds, once stock owners, became stock traders and moved far away from what Warren Buffett describes as his favorite holding period: Forever.

In 1945, funds owned only slightly more than 1 percent of the shares of all U.S. corporations. Today, they own nearly 25 percent. They could wield a potent "big stick" but, with a few exceptions, have failed to do so. With their long record of passivity and lassitude about corporate governance issues, fund managers must accept a large share of the responsibility for the ethical failures in corporate governance.

. . . long term didn't seem to be relevant. By 2002, the redemption rate had soared to 41 percent of assets, an average holding period of slightly more than three years. The time horizon for the typical fund investor had tumbled by fully 80 percent.

Part of the astonishing telescoping of holding periods can be traced to opportunistic, gullible, and emotional fund investors as well as the change in the character of our financial markets (especially in the boom and bust of the stock market bubble during 1997–2002). But by departing from the industry's time-honored tenet of "we sell what we make" and jumping on the "we make what will sell" bandwagon—that is, creating new funds to match the market fads of the moment—this industry must also assume much responsibility for the soaring investment activity of fund investors.

In 1945, the average expense ratio (total management fees and operating expenses as a percentage of fund assets) for the largest 25 funds, with aggregate assets of but $700 million, was 0.76 percent, generating aggregate costs of $4.7 million for fund investors. Six decades later, in 2004, the assets of the equity funds managed by the 25 largest fund complexes had soared to $2.5 trillion, but the average expense ratio had soared by 105 percent to 1.56 percent, generating costs of $31 billion. In other words, while their assets were rising 3,600-fold, costs were rising 6,600-fold. (The dollar amount of direct fund expenses borne by shareholders of all equity funds has risen from an estimated $5 million annually in the 1940s to something like $35 billion in 2004, or 7,000-fold.) Despite the substantial economies of scale that exist in mutual fund management, fund investors have not only not shared in these economies, they have actually incurred higher costs of ownership.

Sixty years ago, the mutual fund industry placed its emphasis on fund management as a profession— the trusteeship of other people's money. Today, there is much evidence that salesmanship has superseded trusteeship as our industry's prime focus. What was it that caused this sea change? Perhaps trusteeship was essential for an industry whose birth in 1924 was quickly followed by tough times— the Depression and then World War II. Perhaps salesmanship became the winning strategy in the easy times thereafter, an era of almost unremitting economic prosperity. Probably, however, the most powerful force behind the change was that mutual fund management emerged as one of the most profitable businesses in our nation. Entrepreneurs could make big money managing mutual funds.

In 1958, the whole dynamic of entrepreneurship in the fund industry changed. Until then, a trustee could make a tidy profit by managing money but could not capitalize that profit by selling shares of the management company to outside investors. The SEC held that the sale of a management company represented payment for the sale of a fiduciary office, an illegal appropriation of fund assets. If such sales were allowed, the SEC feared, it would lead to "trafficking" in advisory contracts, a gross abuse of the trust of fund shareholders. But a California management company challenged the regulatory agency's position. The SEC went to court—and lost.

Thus, as 1958 ended, the gates that had prevented public ownership since the industry began 34 years earlier came tumbling down. A rush of initial public offerings followed, with the shares of a dozen management companies quickly brought to market. Investors bought management company shares for the same reasons that they bought shares of Microsoft Corporation and IBM Corporation and, for that matter, Enron: Because they thought their earnings would grow and their stock prices would rise accordingly.

The IPOs were just the beginning. Publicly held and even privately held management companies were acquired by giant banks and insurance companies that were eager to take the new opportunity to buy into the burgeoning fund business at a healthy premium (averaging ten times book value or more). The term "trafficking" was not far off the mark; there have been at least forty such acquisitions during the past decade alone, and the ownership of some fund firms has been transferred numerous times. Today, among the fifty largest fund managers, only eight remain privately held (plus mutually owned Vanguard). Six firms are publicly held, and the remaining thirty-five management companies are owned by giant financial conglomerates— twenty-two by banks and insurance companies, six by major brokerage firms, and seven by foreign financial institutions.

It would be surprising if this shift in control of the mutual fund industry from private to public hands, largely those of giant financial conglomerates, had not accelerated the industry's change from profession to business. Such staggering aggregations of managed assets—often hundreds of billions of dollars under a single roof—surely serves both to facilitate the marketing of a fund complex's brand name in the consumer goods market and to build its market share. Conglomeration does not seem likely to make the money management process more effective, however, nor to drive investor costs down, nor to enhance the industry's original notion of stewardship and service.

For 78 years—from its start back in 1924 through 2002—the mutual fund industry was free of major taint or scandal. But as asset gathering became the name of the game, as return on managers' capital challenged return on fund shareholders' capital as the preeminent goal, as conglomeration became the dominant structure, and as stewardship took a back-seat to salesmanship, many fund managers were not only all too willing to accept substantial investments from short-term investors and allow those investors to capitalize on price differentials in international time zones (as well as engage in other unrelated but profitable activities), they were also willing to abet and even institutionalize these practices.

To improve their own earnings, managers put their own interests ahead of the interests of their fund shareholders. They allowed short-term traders in their funds to earn illicit higher returns at a direct, dollar-for-dollar cost to their fellow investors holding for the long term. Brought to light by New York Attorney General Eliot L. Spitzer in September 2003, the industry's first major scandal went well beyond a few bad apples. More than a score of firms, managing a total $1.6 trillion of fund assets, including some of the oldest, largest, and once most respected firms in the industry, have been implicated in wrongdoing. This scandal exemplifies the extent to which salesmanship has triumphed over stewardship.

Clearly, the mutual fund industry of 2005 is different not only in degree but in kind from the industry of 60 years earlier—infinitely larger and more diverse, with more speculative funds focused on ever-shorter investment horizons. It is less aware of its responsibility for corporate citizenship; its funds are held by investors for shorter time periods; and it is far more focused on asset gathering and marketing. The fund industry is increasingly operated as a business rather than a profession and, despite the awesome increase in its asset base, has far higher unit costs. The culmination of these changes is a scandal that crystallizes the extent to which the interest of the managers have superseded the interest of fund shareholders.

* * *

The Growth of Passive Investing

Following that beautifully articulated discussion of the development of the mutual fund industry from Mr. Bogle, we need to explore the tremendous growth since he wrote that article in the use of ETFs, an acronym for electronically traded funds. ETFs currently account for nearly a quarter of U.S. stock-market trading volume. ETFs have attracted more than $2 trillion in net new inflows globally over the past 8 years, and worldwide ETF assets have grown to $3.4 trillion over the same period, according to ETFGI, a London-based consultancy.

Looked at another way, Vanguard, the firm Mr. Bogle built, now owns 5 percent or more of 491 of the 500 companies listed in the Fortune 500 due in large part to its ETF assets. This reach is extraordinary, and Vanguard is not the largest ETF sponsor. At a July 2015 conference, according to the *Financial Times*, billionaire activist investor Carl Icahn called BlackRock a "very dangerous company" while sitting next to Larry Fink, co-founder and chief executive of what has become, in large part due to its dominance in the ETF sector, the world's largest asset manager. (Mr. Bogle, by the way, has publicly stated that he is not a fan of ETFs.)

While Mr. Fink dismissed his comment as "flat out wrong," several weeks later, ETFs were at the center of one of the wildest days of trading in U.S. stock market history. More than 20 percent of all U.S.-listed ETFs were forced to stop trading on August 24 after the Dow Jones Industrial Average dropped nearly 1,100 points in the first few minutes of the day and then rebounded by almost 600 points minutes later. Many ETFs traded well below their net asset value, which prompted concern that investors in them were unprotected. While the long-term impact on ETF growth has not seemed significant, this ETF "flash crash" drew attention from exchanges, regulators, and academics as to the potential unforeseen risks that such large market participation by ETFs might entail.

Itzhak Ben-David, finance professor at Ohio State University, sees the additional liquidity provided by ETFs as a "double-edged sword" since it can disappear so easily, and says ETFs can increase volatility in the pricing of the stocks they own. He believes they raise volatility at an overall market level. In 2015, SEC commissioner Luis Aguilar, raised concerns among providers when he asked: "Should we consider curtailing the growth of ETFs?"

While the jury is out on how ETFs, passively managed in accordance with the composition of identified market indices, will perform in adverse market conditions, their presence as competitors for mutual funds cannot be ignored since they are so large and growing.

The Defined Benefit Pension Plan Grows

No book on corporate governance is complete without delving into the topic of retirement compensation and its progeny, pension funds. Directors oversee retirement compensation, and they represent their company's shareholders, including any pension funds that have invested in them. Therefore, the history of pension plans and pension funds is highly relevant to directors today.

In 1875, American Express Company started the first corporate pension fund for its employees, perhaps inspired by promises made by the government to Civil War veterans. By 1929, 397 private-sector plans were in operation in the United States and Canada including plans organized by Standard Oil of New Jersey (1903); U.S. Steel Corp. (1911); General Electric Co. (1912); American Telephone and Telegraph Co. (1913); Goodyear Tire and Rubber Co., (1915); Bethlehem Steel Co. (1923); American Can Co. (1924); and Eastman Kodak Co. (1929).

The Internal Revenue Service undertook various rulings to clarify tax related aspects of such funds, improving attractiveness to both employer and employee. In 1938, pension plans were ruled irrevocable. By 1940, 4.1 million private-sector workers (15 percent of all private-sector workers) were covered by a pension plan.

In 1946, the United Steelworkers of America made pensions an issue in their strike against Inland Steel. At that time, the National Labor Relations Act did not cover pensions. Steelworkers Local 1010 in Indiana Harbor took the issue to the National Labor Relations Board. In 1947, the Labor-Management Relations Act of 1947 (LMRA or "Taft-Hartley" Act) provided fundamental guidelines for the establishment and operation of pension plans administered jointly by an employer and a union.

In 1950, General Motors (GM) established a pension plan for its employees. GM wanted to invest in stocks, but many state laws prohibited fiduciaries, including insurance companies and pension plans as well as trusts, from investing in stocks. Their interest and the burgeoning bull market may have moved state legislatures to consider adopting the Prudent Man Rule, discussed below. By 1950, 9.8 million private-sector workers (25 percent) of all private-sector workers) were covered by a pension plan.

The Welfare and Pension Plan Disclosure Act of 1958 established disclosure requirements to limit fiduciary abuse. By 1960, 18.7 million private-sector workers (41 percent of all private-sector workers) were covered by a pension plan. The Welfare and Pension Plan Disclosure Act Amendments of 1962 shifted responsibility for protection of plan assets from participants to the federal government to prevent fraud and poor administration. Also, in 1962, the Self-Employed Individual Retirement Act of 1962, also known as the Keogh Act, made qualified pension plans available to self-employed persons, unincorporated small businesses, farmers, professionals, and their employees.

Employee Retirement Income Security Act of 1974 (ERISA) Strengthens Pension Rules

By 1970, 26.3 million private-sector workers (45 percent of all private-sector workers) were covered by a pension plan. The Employee Retirement Income Security Act of 1974 (ERISA) was enacted in 1974 to secure the benefits of participants in private pension plans through participation, vesting, funding, reporting, and disclosure rules. It established the Pension Benefit Guaranty Corporation (PBGC) to provide a safety net for participants in private-sector defined-benefit pension plans by insuring the participants' benefits under the plan; to give participants in plans covered by the PBGC guaranteed "basic" benefits in the event that their employer-sponsored defined benefit plans become insolvent. ERISA provided added pension incentives for the self-employed through changes in Keogh plans and for persons not covered by pensions through individual retirement accounts (IRAs). It established legal status of employee stock ownership plans (ESOPs) as an employee benefit and codified stock bonus plans under the Internal Revenue Code. It also established requirements for plan implementation and operation. The Revenue Act of 1978 established qualified deferred compensation plans (sec. 401(k)) under which employees are not taxed on the portion of income they elect to receive as deferred compensation rather than direct cash payments. The act created simplified employee pensions (SEPs) and further refined IRA rules.

In 1980, 35.9 million private-sector workers (46 percent of all private-sector workers) were covered by a pension plan. In 1987, we see the Omnibus Budget Reconciliation Act of 1987 changing funding rules to address underfunded and overfunded pension plans and PBGC premium levels and structure. It established maximum funding limit of 150 percent of current liability, beyond which employer contributions are not deductible and tightened minimum funding requirements for underfunded plans and required a quarterly premium payment for single-employer plans.

The Defined Benefit Pension Plan Declines

In 1990, we see the first percentage decrease in covered employees, with 39.5 million (43 percent) of all private sector workers) covered by a pension plan. In 1994, the Uruguay Round Agreements Act of 1994 included provisions from the Retirement Protection Act of 1993 that require greater contributions to underfunded plans. It limited the range of interest rate and mortality assumptions used to establish funding targets, phased out the variable rate premium cap, modified certain rules relating to participant protections, and required private companies with underfunded pension plans to notify PBGC before engaging in a large corporate transaction.

Thereafter, we see a continuing decline in private sector employees covered by plans as corporations grappled with costs in general and funding costs in particular, and more and more turned from defined benefit plans, administered by the employer, to defined contribution (DC) plans, in which employees under Section 401(k) could deduct contributions to the plan, employers could match, and employees chose from a menu of eligible investments, typically a group of mutual funds. Thus, we have another source of mutual fund growth as defined benefit pension plans continue to decline in popularity.

The percentage of workers covered by a traditional defined benefit pension plan declined steadily from 43% in 1990 to 20% in 2008. From 1980 through 2008, the proportion of private wage and salary workers participating in only DC plans increased from 8% to 31%.

Some experts expect that remaining private-sector plans will be frozen in the next few years and eventually terminated. Under the typical DB plan freeze, current participants will receive retirement benefits based on their accruals up to the date of the freeze but will not accumulate any additional benefits; new employees will not be covered. Instead, employers will either establish new DC plans or increase contributions to existing DC plans.

Retirement Assets Shift into Mutual Funds

Economist Paul Krugman wrote in November 2013: "Today, however, workers who have any retirement plan at all generally have defined-contribution plans—basically, 401(k)'s—in which employers put money into a tax-sheltered account that's supposed to end up big enough to retire on. The trouble is that at this point it's clear that the shift to 401(k)'s was a gigantic failure. Employers took advantage of the switch to surreptitiously cut benefits; investment returns have been far lower than workers were told to expect; and, to be fair, many people haven't managed their money wisely. As a result, we're looking at a looming retirement crisis, with tens of millions of Americans facing a sharp decline in living standards at the end of their working lives. For many, the only thing protecting them from abject penury will be Social Security."

A 2014 Gallup poll indicated that 21 percent of investors had either taken an early withdrawal of their 401(k) defined contribution retirement plan or a loan against it over the previous five years; while both options are possible, they are not the intended purpose of 401k plans and can have substantial costs in taxes, fees and a smaller retirement fund.

Public Sector Pension Plans

Public pension plans got their start with various promises, informal and legislated, made to veterans of the Revolutionary War and, more extensively, the Civil War. They expanded and began to be offered by a number of state and local governments during the late 19th century. Unlike the private sector, in the public sector once an employee is hired their pension benefit terms cannot be changed. Retirement age in the public sector is usually lower than in the private sector.

Public sector pensions are offered by federal, state and local levels of government. Like private plans, employer contributions to these plans typically vest after some period of time. These plans may be defined-benefit or defined-contribution pension plans, but the former have been most widely used by public agencies in the U.S. throughout the late twentieth century.

Federal civilian pensions were offered under the Civil Service Retirement System (CSRS), formed in 1920. CSRS provided retirement, disability and survivor benefits for most civilian employees in the federal government, until the creation of a new federal agency, the Federal Employees Retirement System (FERS), in 1987.

Some have grown to be extremely large, led by the California Public Employees Retirement System, aka CalPERS, holds over $300 billion as of December 31, 2016, and California State Teachers Retirement System holds just under $200 billion. The only larger U.S. plan is the Federal Retirement Thrift Plan at $485 billion. The world's largest pension fund is the Government Pension Investment Fund in Japan, at $1.2 trillion, followed by the Government Pension Fund in Norway, at $893 billion.

These figures are drawn from the Pensions & Investments/Willis Towers Watson 300 Analysis for the year 2016, which offers the further, somewhat daunting observation that the capital is becoming even more concentrated at the very top, with the largest twenty funds in the world accounting for 40.3 percent of the assets of the Willis Towers Watson 300 ranking.

The Growing Pension Crisis

Both private sector and public-sector plans are governed by identified plan fiduciaries, who oversee the investment of the corpus that is managed on behalf of plan beneficiaries. Annual hurdle rates are established based on the demographics of the covered population, the amount available to invest and a projected return, and the amount projected to be needed to fund obligations to beneficiaries. Though these assumptions are not simple and depend on actuarial tables to calculate them, many plans have had difficulty funding their plans at a rate sufficient to meet projected payouts, and thus are considered underfunded. This is conspicuously the case with some public pension funds.

It is not simple to develop agreement on the amount by which pension plans may be under or overfunded, as there are many assumptions that may differ from one analyst to the next. If a higher investment return is assumed, for example, relatively lower contributions may be required of those paying into the system. Critics have argued that investment return assumptions are artificially inflated, to reduce the required contribution amounts by individuals and governments paying into the pension system.

For example, bond yields (the return on guaranteed investments) in the U.S. and elsewhere are low (and the U.S. and other stock markets did not consistently beat inflation between 2000 and 2010). But many pensions have annual investment return assumptions in the 7–8% p.a. range, which are closer to the pre-2000 average return. If these rates were lowered by 1–2 percentage points, the required pension contributions taken from salaries or via taxation would increase dramatically. By one estimate, each 1 percent reduction means 10 percent more in contributions. For example, if a pension program reduced its investment return rate assumption from 8% p.a. to 7% p.a., a person contributing $100 per month to their pension would be required to contribute $110.

In addition, the International Monetary Fund reported in April 2012 that developed countries may be underestimating the impact of longevity on their public and private pension calculations. The IMF estimated that if individuals live three years longer than expected, the incremental costs could approach 50 percent of 2010 GDP in advanced economies and 25 percent in emerging economies. In the United States, this would represent a 9 percent increase in pension obligations. The IMF recommendations included raising the retirement age commensurate with life expectancy.

Whatever the estimated shortfall, economists in general agree there is a looming pension crisis as we face the predicted difficulty in paying for corporate, state, and federal pensions in the world, due to a difference between pension obligations and the resources set aside to fund them. There is significant debate regarding the magnitude and importance of the problem, as well as the solutions.

For example, as of 2008, the estimates for the underfunding of the United States state pension programs ranged from $1 trillion using a discount rate of 8 percent to $3.23 trillion using U.S. Treasury bond yields as the discount rate. The ratio of workers to pensioners (the "support ratio") is declining in much of the developed world. This is due to two demographic factors: increased life expectancy coupled with a fixed retirement age, and a decrease in the fertility rate. Increased life expectancy (with fixed retirement age) increases the number of retirees at any time, since individuals are retired for a longer fraction of their lives, while decreases in the fertility rate decrease the number of workers.

Investing by Public and Private Plan Fiduciaries

Why dwell on retirement funding in this book? All board members need a general understanding of current and prior methods of providing for the future of corporate workers. More crucially, however, this background on the situation of existing public and private employers may help give context to how and why pension investors have invested as they have, and to the demands they may make as investors in company stock. In particular, these pressures help to explain the growth in their investment in strategies such as private equity and hedge funds, which are presented as strategies that not only offer attractive returns, but tout that their returns are uncorrelated with the broad market indices.

Looking back at how fiduciary investing standards evolved, English law got off to a bad start with respect to investing by trusts. With spectacularly bad timing, in 1719 Parliament authorized trustees, also known as fiduciaries, to invest in shares of the South Sea Company. Some of them did, and when the South Sea "Bubble" burst the next year, share prices declined by 90 percent.

Parliament reacted in fright and developed a restricted list of presumably proper trust investments: initially government bonds, and later well-secured first mortgages. Lord St. Leonard's Act in 1859 added English East India stock, and across the decades, some dribbles of legislation approved various other issues. Only in 1961 was the English statute amended to allow trustees to invest in equities more generally, and even then, the investment was subject to a ceiling of half of the trust fund.

Developments in American law led away from legal lists, however, and were forged in Massachusetts. In 1830, in the celebrated case of Harvard College v. Amory, the Supreme Judicial Court adopted what came to be known as the prudent man rule. Trustees, said the Massachusetts court, should "observe how men of prudence... manage their own affairs, not in regard to speculation, but in regard to the permanent disposition of their funds, considering the probable income, as well as the probable safety of the capital to be invested."

The Massachusetts rule represented a great advance by abandoning the attempt to specify approved types of investment. Prudence is another word for reasonableness, and the prudent man rule echoed the contemporaneously developed reasonable man rule in the law of negligence. The standard of prudent investing was the standard of industry practice or what other trustees similarly situated were doing.

By 1950, twenty-two American states had adopted by statute a version of the Massachusetts rule. The prudent man rule, as applied by the courts, came to be encrusted with a strong emphasis on avoiding so-called "speculation," as well as varying interpretations of its meaning. Investment practice nevertheless under the prudent man rule led rapidly to judicial approval of the use of corporate securities, both equities and bonds, in trust accounts. The GM pension plan, mentioned above, was thence free to invest in stocks.

As late as the 1959 restatement of the prudent man rule, we find the assertion that "the purchase of shares of stock on margin or purchase of bonds selling at a great discount because of uncertainty whether they will be paid on maturity" is speculative and imprudent. In some jurisdictions, investing in junior mortgages, no matter how well secured, was per se imprudent. The view crystallized that an investment in a "new and untried enterprise" was inherently speculative and imprudent.

Widely varying and occasionally ludicrous judicial applications of the notion of speculation continued in some jurisdictions into recent times. Trustees in the first half of the twentieth century, preoccupied with avoiding speculation and preserving capital, were inclined to emphasize long-term government and corporate bonds as the characteristic trust investment.

Experience with inflation during the 1960s and 1970s, which we will discuss shortly, taught, however, that holding bonds placed significant inflation risk on the bondholder. Investments in debt could therefore experience declines in real value as severe as in equities. We now know that, in inflation-adjusted terms, the long-term real rate of return on equities has greatly exceeded that of bonds. The Ibbotson studies estimate the inflation-adjusted rate of return on stocks since the 1920s at about 9 percent per year, as compared to about 3 percent for bonds.

The prudent man rule requires that each investment be judged on its own merits and that speculative or risky investments must be avoided. Margin accounts and short selling of uncovered securities are also prohibited. Its modern interpretation goes beyond the assessment of each asset individually to include the concept of due diligence and diversification. The logic is this: an asset may be too risky on its own, thus failing the prudent man rule, but may still be beneficial as a small proportion of the total portfolio. The prudent man rule implies that the fiduciary should perform enough due diligence to ensure that the portfolio meets the investment needs of its beneficial owners.

Shifting Patterns of Share Ownership in United States

In his 2016 book *The Activist Director*, attorney Ira Millstein estimates that pension funds at that time controlled more than $20 trillion in assets worldwide, and mutual fund holdings totaled over $16 trillion. Institutions like these own at least 60 percent of the largest one thousand U.S. corporations. Thus, even though the beneficial owners of the invested dollars are widely dispersed, the control of substantial investments in the majority of U.S. corporations is concentrated in the hands of a fairly small number of investment managers. He estimates the numbers to be fewer than a dozen intermediaries—firms like Blackrock, State Street, Fidelity, and Vanguard, and the largest pension fund managers.

The following comments from SEC Commissioner Luis Aguilar made on *Institutional Investors: Power and Responsibility* at Robinson College of Business, Georgia State University on April 19, 2013 offer some useful insight and estimated magnitude of the shift in our capital markets:

> The proportion of U.S. public equities managed by institutions has risen steadily over the past six decades, from about 7 or 8% of market capitalization in 1950, to about 67% in 2010. The shift has come as more American families participate in the capital markets through pooled-investment vehicles, such as mutual funds and exchange traded funds (ETFs). Institutional investor ownership is an even more significant factor in the largest corporations: In 2009, institutional investors owned in the aggregate 73% of the outstanding equity in the 1,000 largest U.S. corporations.

The growth in the proportion of assets managed by institutional investors has been accompanied by a dramatic growth in the market capitalization of U.S. listed companies. For example, in 1950, the combined market value of all stocks listed on the New York Stock Exchange (NYSE) was about $94 billion. By 2012, however, the domestic market capitalization of the NYSE was more than $14 trillion, an increase of nearly 1,500%. This growth is even more impressive if you add the $4.5 trillion in market capitalization on the NASDAQ market, which did not exist until 1971. The bottom line is, that as a whole, institutional investors own a larger share of a larger market.

Of course, institutional investors are not all the same. They come in many different forms and with many different characteristics. Among other things, institutional investors have different organizational and governance structures, and are subject to different regulatory requirements. The universe of institutional investors includes mutual funds and ETFs regulated by the SEC, as well as pension funds, insurance companies, and a wide variety of hedge funds and managed accounts, many of which are unregulated.

The growth in assets managed by institutions has also affected, and been affected by, the significant changes in market structure and trading technologies over the past few decades, including the development of the national market system, the proliferation of trading venues —including both dark pools and electronic trading platforms —and the advent of algorithmic and high-speed trading. These changes —largely driven by the trading of institutional investors —have resulted in huge increases in trading volumes. For example, in 1990, the average daily volume on the NYSE was 162 million shares. Today, just 23 years later, that average daily volume is approximately 2.6 billion shares - an increase of about 1,600%.

* * *

The Perils and Possibilities of Concentrated Share Ownership

As Commissioner Aguilar observes, over the past few decades, the ownership of public corporations has been turned on its head. While private individuals owned approximately two-thirds of U.S. equities in 1970, today it is institutional investors like Blackrock, Vanguard, and State Street that control two-thirds of such shares. This increase in institutional assets, often referred to as fiduciary capitalism or mutual fund capitalism, came with the rise of pension funds and mutual funds. More recently, the popularity of a form of index fund, Exchange Traded Funds (ETFs) has accelerated the shift of assets from active to passive investment strategies.

The concentration of ownership and the growth of passive assets are now so great that corporate engagement is far more practical than divestment for the largest institutional investors. The size of investor positions create increased liquidity constraints which raise the cost of exit while the relative cost of engagement has fallen, as it is spread across a larger asset base. As a result, institutional investors are compelled to be more involved in corporate affairs.

Large-scale corporate engagement, or fiduciary capitalism, is still a relatively new phenomenon for many institutional investors. A study by Ernst & Young found that as recently as 2010 just 6 percent of S&P 500 companies reported any investor engagement. As of June 2016 the figure had increased to 66 percent.

There is also a regulatory reason for engagement. Even absent a change in the law, the definition of best practices in corporate governance continues to evolve, as does our understanding of fiduciary duty. In 2005, a report by law firm Freshfields stated that "integrating ESG considerations into an investment analysis . . . is clearly permissible and is arguably required in all jurisdictions." By the time the 2015 United Nations report, "Fiduciary Duty in the 21st Century," was released, thinking had gone much further. "Failing to consider long-term investment value drivers, which include environmental, social and governance issues, in investment practice is a failure of fiduciary duty."

Although the investment horizons of passively managed mutual funds are in theory infinite, the investment behavior of their investors is not. As long as retail investors' investment horizons remain short, daily pricing and liquidity are offered, and the performance of active managers is benchmarked daily, it is unlikely that institutional investors can become truly patient providers of capital.

The Rise of Proxy Advisor Power

These pressures on institutional investors to engage with managements of the companies in which they must invest as well as the increase in the size of global capital markets and in the speed at which money moves has seen ever greater standards of care develop since the end of World War II on the part of regulators, companies, and investors alike. Efforts to clarify understanding of the parties' responsibilities and their role in driving increased value for their various beneficiaries are ongoing.

Capital markets came to be dominated by the professional institutional investor, investing on behalf others as discussed above. At each level, beneficial interest holders, the underlying investors, need explanations as to why certain actions, and thus gains or losses, occurred. Structured communication procedures such as annual reports, proxy statements, and filings with the SEC and other regulators evolved to help investors compare various investments on an apples-to-apples basis.

Managing this torrent of money and interpreting these communications and the growing body of related regulations has fueled the growth of professional investment advisors, trust companies, mutual funds, pension and investment consultants, attorneys, actuaries, accountants, and a fairly recent addition: the proxy advisor. Proxy advisors help institutional investors decide how to vote on the matters that require approval from shareholders of the public companies in which they hold investments.

Proxy Advisors Helped Interpret High Volume of Information

Boards of directors of public companies must consult their shareholders before taking certain actions. Their shareholders, often large institutions in turn in charge of other people's money, need to understand the issues involved in order to vote. These annual shareholder votes, collected through the solicitation of voting "proxies," have long been in use.

Shareholders, however, often ignored the voting opportunity. In 1974, however, the Employee Retirement Income Security Act became law, and required fiduciaries responsible for corporate pension investment portfolios not only to vote, but to vote responsibly. Fiduciaries for other large pools of money followed suit, and institutional investors began to scrutinize corporate board candidates, shareholder proposals, and other corporate matters for their portfolio companies.

Analyzing governance matters required a different set of skills and a great deal of time. And presented an opportunity for a new kind of professional service provider. The principals Institutional Shareholder Services (ISS), the first proxy advisor, saw an opportunity and formed ISS in 1985 as an organization able to focus full time on governance matters and help fiduciaries decide on their positions.

Responsible Voting of Proxies in Best Interests of Clients Required

In 2003, the U.S. Securities & Exchange Commission tightened voting standards further. Those voting client proxies were not only to vote responsibly but to ensure that their votes were in the best interests of their clients. Legal liability for fulfilling their obligation to vote became a serious worry, which increased investors' reliance on the "professional" proxy advisor as a way to reduce litigation risk. The result was a huge increase in reliance on proxy advisors ISS and their smaller counterpart Glass Lewis, who now together control 97 percent of the market for proxy advice. Together they affect 38 percent of votes cast at U.S. public company shareholder meetings.

Proxy Advisors Take Heed: Physician, Heal Thyself

Decades of regulation intended to support free and open markets has now inadvertently put power over the policies, and thus the fortunes, of many United States listed corporations and their beneficial owners into the hands of two firms who are not subject to market or regulatory scrutiny, and for whom no level of the now intricate system has voted. The SEC has created an exemption from its proxy rules for proxy advisory firms, so they are not governed by the disclosure rules that apply to other participants in proxy voting.

Their processes are secret, their information sources not clear, their reports not publicly available and reportedly often not available to the companies on whose voting matters they are advising shareholders unless the company purchases them. Their concentration of market power is high, and they may often be conflicted, serving corporate clients with advice on positioning, investor clients on voting, and even recommending action on initiatives brought by their own clients. Disclosure of such conflicts is not required. Finally, the information they rely on may or may not be correct, and there is no consistent mechanism available to the companies involved to review the proxy advisors' positions in advance of a position being taken.

★ ★ ★

Harvey Pitt, former chairman of the SEC, summed up the issues clearly in representing the U.S. Chamber of Commerce before the House Subcommittee on Capital Markets and Government Sponsored Enterprises on Examining the Market Power and Impact of Proxy Advisory Firms on June 5, 2013:

> As you have requested, I will not repeat the Chamber's detailed written statement. Instead, I would like to briefly highlight 5 points for your consideration.
>
> First, effective and transparent corporate governance systems that encourage meaningful shareholder communications are critical if public companies are to thrive. Informed and transparent proxy advice can promote effective corporate governance, but only if transparency exists throughout the proxy advisory process, and the advice provided directly correlates to and is solely motivated by advancing investors' economic interests. Sadly, these two essential components of proxy advice have been lacking for some time.
>
> Second, as has already been observed, two firms—ISS and Glass Lewis—control 97 percent of the proxy advisory business and dominate the industry. Together, they effectively can influence nearly 40 percent of the votes cast on corporate proxy issues, making them de facto arbiters of U.S. corporate governance.
>
> Third, these firms advocate governance standards to U.S. public companies, but they do not practice what they preach. Serious conflicts permeate their activities, posing glaring hazards to shareholder interests. They are powerful but unregulated and they cavalierly

refuse to formulate and follow ethical standards of their own, render their advice transparently, accept accountability for advocated standards, and assume responsibility to avoid factual errors and shoulder the burden to rectify the mistakes that they make.

This lack of an operable framework for those exercising such a significant impact on our economic growth is wholly unprecedented in our society. Indeed, 2 weeks ago ISS settled serious SEC charges stemming from its failure to establish and enforce appropriate written policies.

Fourth, significant economic consequences flow from proxy advisory firms' unfettered power and lack of fidelity to important ethical and fiduciary precepts, something that has been recognized both here and abroad. Although U.S. regulators have not fulfilled promises to address these issues, Canadian and European regulators, among others, are speaking out.

Fifth, the answer to these concerns is not more regulation, but rather a collaborative public-private effort to identify core principles and best practices for the proxy advisory industry. In March, the Chamber published best practices and core principles which provides a crucial foundation for successfully delineating standards for the industry to embrace and follow.

What is essential is for responsible voices—this subcommittee, the SEC, institutional investors, public companies, and proxy advisory firms—to lend support to the effort to promulgate and apply effective standards.

Mr. Chairman, members of the subcommittee, it is my hope and strong recommendation that these hearings result in a serious commitment to achieve those goals. Thank you.

* * *

Various bills to tighten regulation of proxy advisory firms have been introduced in Congress. These would require proxy advisory firms to (1) register with the SEC; (2) employ an ombudsman to receive complaints about voting information accuracy; (3) disclose potential conflicts of interest; (4) disclose procedures for formulating proxy recommendations and analyses; and (5) in essence, provide companies with an opportunity to review and comment on a proposed recommendation by a proxy advisory firm before the recommendation is provided to investors.

Given the broad sweep of events that brought these two to such remarkable power, we can likely count on the fact that such dominance is not sustainable. Large investors and corporations will find ways to correct the balance, and regulatory change will ultimately occur. Until then, as the saying goes, power corrupts, and absolute power corrupts absolutely.

Read More

Fidelity's World: The Secret Life and Public Power of the Mutual Fund Giant, Henriques, Diana B., Scribner & Sons, 1995

Global Financial Stability Survey, International Monetary Fund, 2012

"US Proxy Advisory Industry Draws Regulatory Scrutiny", Financial Times, March 2018

Chapter 9
The Impact of The Great Inflation

We have now traced the changing composition of the universe of owners of public companies, and the pressures they face. Now we return to the post World War II period to consider the development and impact of economic policy. We address economic policy because it has a strong effect on the fates of companies overseen by directors. Corporate board members who ignore policy do so at their peril.

Most notable among the laws that emerged post–World War II was the Employment Act of 1946, which continues to have lively impact today. Among other things, the act declared it a responsibility of the federal government for the first time "to promote maximum employment, production, and purchasing power" and provided for greater coordination between fiscal and monetary policies.

This act is the basis for the Federal Reserve's continuing dual mandate "to maintain long run growth of the monetary and credit aggregates...so as to promote effectively the goals of maximum employment, stable prices and moderate long-term interest rates". Its passage appears motivated in large part by both the painful memory of the unprecedented high unemployment in the United States during the 1930s, and by the desire to provide employment for the hordes of returning veterans.

These policies, Keynesian based, worked on the management of aggregate demand by way of the spending and taxation policies of the fiscal authority and the monetary policies of the central bank. The idea that monetary policy can and should be used to manage aggregate spending and stabilize economic activity is a generally accepted tenet that continues to guide the policies of the Federal Reserve and other central banks.

The Seeds of the Great Inflation Are Sown by the Fateful Phillips Curve

Keynesian policies led, however, according to one prominent economist, to "the greatest failure of American macroeconomic policy in the post-war period." The Great Inflation was the defining macroeconomic event of the second half of the twentieth century and continues to have significant repercussions.

Over the nearly two decades it lasted, the global monetary system established during World War II was abandoned, there were four economic recessions, two severe energy shortages, and the unprecedented peacetime implementation of wage and price controls. But that failure also brought a transformative change in

DOI 10.1515/9781547400270-009

macroeconomic theory and, ultimately, the rules that today guide the monetary policies of the Federal Reserve and other central banks around the world. If the Great Inflation was a consequence of a great failure of American macroeconomic policy, its conquest should be counted as a triumph.

The basis of the policy was the belief that permanently lower rates of unemployment could be provided if modestly higher rates of inflation were tolerated. The idea that the "Phillips curve" represented a longer-term trade-off between unemployment, which was very damaging to economic well-being, and inflation, which was sometimes thought of as more of an inconvenience, was an attractive assumption for policymakers who hoped to forcefully pursue the dictates of the Employment Act.

The stability of the Phillips curve was a fateful assumption, however; one that economists Edmund Phelps (1967) and Milton Friedman (1968) warned against, arguing that the trade-off between lower unemployment and more inflation that policymakers believed they could make would likely be a false bargain, requiring ever higher inflation to maintain.

Chasing the Phillips curve in pursuit of lower unemployment could not have occurred if the policies of the Federal Reserve were well-anchored. And in the 1960s, the U.S. dollar was anchored, if tenuously, to gold through the Bretton Woods agreement. The story of the Great Inflation is in part also about the collapse of the Bretton Woods system and the separation of the U.S. dollar from its last link to gold.

Among the flaws of the Bretton Woods system was the attempt to maintain fixed parity between global currencies. Many nations, it turned out, were also pursuing monetary policies that promised to march up the Phillips curve for a more favorable unemployment–inflation nexus. As the world's reserve currency, the U.S. dollar had an additional problem. As global trade grew, so too did the demand for U.S. dollar reserves.

For a time, the demand for U.S. dollars was satisfied by an increasing balance of payments shortfall, and foreign central banks accumulated more and more dollar reserves. Eventually, the supply of dollar reserves held abroad exceeded the U.S. stock of gold, implying that the United States could not maintain complete convertibility at the existing price of gold—a fact that would not go unnoticed by foreign governments and currency speculators.

As inflation drifted higher during the latter half of the 1960s, U.S. dollars were increasingly converted to gold, and in the summer of 1971, President Nixon halted the exchange of dollars for gold by foreign central banks. The post-war global monetary system was finished. With the last link to gold severed, most of the world's currencies, including the U.S. dollar, were now unanchored. Except during periods of global crisis, this was the first time in history that most of the monies of the industrialized world were on an irredeemable paper money standard.

Our Economy Fights Another War, on Several Fronts

The late 1960s and the early 1970s were a turbulent time for the U.S. economy. President Johnson's Great Society legislation brought about major spending programs across a broad array of social initiatives at a time when the U.S. fiscal situation was already being strained by the Vietnam War.

To that tension was added the repeated energy crises that increased oil costs and sapped U.S. growth. The first crisis was an Arab oil embargo that began in October 1973 and lasted about five months. During this period, crude oil prices quadrupled to a plateau that held until the Iranian revolution brought a second energy crisis in 1979. The second crisis tripled the cost of oil.

From the perspective of the central bank, the inflation being caused by the rising price of oil was largely beyond the control of monetary policy. But the rise in unemployment that was occurring in response to the jump in oil prices was not. Motivated by a mandate to create full employment with little or no anchor for the management of reserves, the Federal Reserve accommodated large and rising fiscal imbalances and leaned against the headwinds produced by energy costs. These policies accelerated the expansion of the money supply and raised overall prices without reducing unemployment.

Looking back at the information policymakers had in hand during the period leading up to and during the Great Inflation, economist Athanasios Orphanides has shown that the real-time estimate of potential output was significantly overstated, and the estimate of the rate of unemployment consistent with full employment was significantly understated. Thus, the effect of flawed policy was compounded by flawed data. The stable trade-off between inflation and unemployment that policymakers had hoped to exploit did not exist.

Employment v. Inflation

As businesses and households came to anticipate rising prices, any trade-off between inflation and unemployment became a less favorable exchange until both inflation and unemployment became unacceptably high. This, then, became the era of "stagflation." In 1964, when this story began, inflation was 1 percent and unemployment was 5 percent. Ten years later, inflation would be over 12 percent and unemployment above 7 percent. By the summer of 1980, inflation was near 14.5 percent, and unemployment was over 7.5 percent.

The Fed continued to struggle to achieve its dual mandate set forth by the Employment Act of 1946, re-codified in 1978 by the Full Employment and Balanced Growth Act, more commonly known as the Humphrey-Hawkins Act after the bill's authors. Humphrey-Hawkins explicitly charged the Federal Reserve to pursue full employment and price stability, required that the central bank establish targets for the growth of various monetary aggregates, and provide a semiannual Monetary Policy Report to Congress.

Nevertheless, likely for reasons based on the employment history referenced above, the employment half of the mandate appears to have had the upper hand when full employment and inflation came into conflict. As Fed Chairman Arthur Burns would later claim, full employment was the first priority in the minds of the public and the government, if not also at the Federal Reserve.

By the late 1970s, the public had come to expect an inflationary bias to monetary policy. Survey after survey showed a deteriorating public confidence over the economy and government policy in the latter half of the 1970s. During this time, business investment slowed, productivity faltered, and the nation's trade balance with the rest of the world worsened. Inflation was widely viewed as either a significant contributing factor to the economic malaise or its primary basis.

Federal Reserve Chairman Volcker Toughs It Out

But once in the position of having unacceptably high inflation and high unemployment, policymakers faced a dilemma. Fighting high unemployment would almost certainly drive inflation higher still, while fighting inflation would just as certainly cause unemployment to spike even higher. In 1979, Paul Volcker, formerly the president of the Federal Reserve Bank of New York, became chairman of the Federal Reserve Board. When he took office in August, year-over-year inflation was running above 11 percent, and national joblessness was just a shade under 6 percent.

Fighting inflation was now seen as necessary to achieve both objectives of the dual mandate, even if it temporarily caused a disruption to economic activity and, for a time, a higher rate of joblessness. In early 1980, Volcker said, *"[M]y basic philosophy is over time we have no choice but to deal with the inflationary situation because over time inflation and the unemployment rate go together.... Isn't that the lesson of the 1970s?"*

Volcker believed that fighting mounting inflation should be the primary concern for the Fed: *"In terms of economic stability in the future, [inflation] is what is likely to give us the most problems and create the biggest recession"* (FOMC transcript 1979, 16). He also believed that the Fed faced a credibility problem when it came to keeping inflation in check. During the previous decade, the Fed had demonstrated that it did not place much emphasis on maintaining low inflation, and public expectation of such continued behavior would make it increasingly difficult for the Fed to bring inflation down. *"[F]ailure to carry through now in the fight on inflation will only make any subsequent effort more difficult,"* he remarked.

Over time, greater control of reserve and money growth, while less than perfect, produced a desired slowing in inflation. This tighter reserve management was augmented by the introduction of credit controls in early 1980 with the Monetary Control Act. Over the course of 1980, interest rates spiked, fell briefly, and then spiked again. Lending activity fell, unemployment rose, and the economy entered a brief recession between January and July. Inflation fell but was still high even as the economy recovered in the second half of 1980.

But the Volcker Fed continued to press the fight against high inflation with a combination of higher interest rates and even slower reserve growth. The economy entered recession again in July 1981, and this proved to be more severe and protracted, lasting until November 1982. Unemployment peaked at nearly 11 percent, the highest level experienced since the Great Depression, but inflation continued to move lower and by recession's end, year-over-year inflation was back under 5 percent. In time, as the Fed's commitment to low inflation gained credibility, unemployment retreated, and the economy entered a period of sustained growth and stability. The Great Inflation was over.

Read More

"The Role of Monetary Policy," Friedman, Milton, American Economic Review 58, no. 1 (March 1968).

"Alternative Responses of Policy to External Supply Shocks," Gordon, Robert J., Brookings Papers on Economic Activity 6, no. 1 (1975).

"Origins of the Great Inflation," Meltzer, Allan H., Federal Reserve Bank of St. Louis Review 87, no. 2, part 2 (March/April 2005).

A History of the Federal Reserve, Volume 2, Book 2, 1970–1986, Meltzer, Allan H., Chicago: University of Chicago Press, 2009.

"Monetary Policy Rules Based on Real-Time Data," Orphanides, Athanasios, Finance and Economics Discussion Series 1998–03, Federal Reserve Board, Washington, DC, 1997.

"Monetary Policy Rules and the Great Inflation," Orphanides, Athanasios, Finance and Economics Discussion Series 2002–08, Federal Reserve Board, Washington, DC, 2002.

"Phillips Curves, Expectations of Inflation and Optimal Unemployment Over Time," Phelps, E.S., Economica 34, no. 135 (August 1967): 254–81.

"The Relationship between Unemployment and the Rate of Change of Money Wages in the United Kingdom 1861–1957," Phillips, A.W., Economica 25, no. 100 (1958)

Stocks for the Long Run: A Guide to Selecting Markets for Long-Term Growth, 2nd ed., Siegel,

Jeremy J., New York: McGraw-Hill, 1994.
"The Federal Reserve's 'Dual Mandate': The Evolution of an Idea," Steelman, Aaron, Federal Reserve Bank of Richmond Economic Brief no. 11–12 (December 2011).

Impact of Prolonged Inflation on Capital Market Innovation

That inflationary environment had a long-term effect, however, on U.S. capital markets. The high inflation in the U.S. and differing returns available in different markets ushered in the era of "financial innovation" on Wall Street. While each new technique provided an ingenious solution to a real client problem, the aggregate effect was to fundamentally change the way our markets function. And lest you think I have neglected the focus of this book, it is my view that the ramifications of prolonged inflation are what finally brought focus to the role not just of the corporation, but of its board of directors. What follows is an explanation of that view.

Our capital markets are not just exponentially larger than they were in the mid 20th century but have been fundamentally changed not just by the dominance today of institutional investors, but by the advent of the leveraged buyout and development of private equity as well as by financial derivatives and securitization. The effects of prolonged inflation are inextricably bound up in these developments and have brought the distinct role of the board into much greater focus. Boards and directors have been as a result faced with ever more complex situations to parse through and act upon and are often unaware of the underlying forces at work. This increasing complexity shows no sign of slowing down, and directors need to be aware of these changes.

Securitization Solves a Genuine Problem, and Turns the World Upside Down

To understand the phenomenon called securitization that has had such profound impact on the world and the boardroom as we know it, we need to again look back. In 1970, the first money market fund was established as a mutual fund, creating what was seen to be a safe place to earn interest outside of a bank. As interest rates rose in the era of high inflation, money moved rapidly out of banks and into the new money market accounts. Concerned about deposit flight from thrift institutions, then a protected species given their special role in making home mortgage loans due to the belief that home ownership promoted stability, Congress allowed the first interest bearing deposit accounts to be offered by thrifts and savings banks in the late 1970s.

To help the thrifts who now had to pay depositors high interest but could afford neither to sell their current low coupon fixed rate loans nor fund new ones at high rates, Congress allowed them to write off sale-related losses as "goodwill" over a long period of time to preserve the impression they were solvent. In doing so, however, Congress all but wrote the death knell for the thrift industry. With the huge new influx of secondary product sold to the Street by the thrifts, the secondary mortgage market per se finally took off in the early 1980s. Ironically, the thrift industry, no longer uniquely useful, was quickly made irrelevant.

Suddenly, the Street's bond trading floors, historically sleepy backwaters controlled by a tight knit group of local guys who maintained discipline through tried and true, often unwritten, rules, became places where huge amounts of money could be made due to the volatility of interest rates.

Not Your Daddy's Trading Floor

Trading in mortgages became the hottest game in town, as the analytical complexities of valuing mortgages could be used to advantage by a savvy trader dealing with less sophisticated sellers and buyers. Pools could be purchased from the thrift institution assuming one rate of prepayment and sold at a radically different assumed prepayment rate. They were making a killing, as no one was in position to know what a realistic price actually was. Traders were in heaven, and they seemed to have, as delightfully and accurately detailed in Michael Lewis's book *Liars Poker*, protected positions. They were seen as kings.

In a powerful example of the shifting of the trader from employee concerned about protecting his employer's balance sheet, earning his keep through building the enterprise, to the direct pursuit of personal benefit, one legendary trader managed to get himself into a loss position of $25 million. Let's call him Richie. He is alleged to have told the head of fixed income trading that the loss left him unmotivated, and he was thinking of leaving the job. In deep alarm, as he did not know how to get out of the loss position, the boss asked what could be done.

After some thought, Richie responded that he needed an incentive to get him going. He proposed that if he cut the loss in half, he would receive $1 million. If he got the position to flat before year end, he needed $2 million. Anything above zero would need to include payment to Richie of half the profits. The boss took the deal, Richie traded back to the plus side, and everyone was happy. Kind of.

Trading floors attracted MBAs drawn by the earning potential, and rocket scientists by the great puzzle of valuing pools in which each mortgage included 360 possible prepayment dates, and each pool of mortgage backed securities traded included thousands of mortgages. Option valuation thinking bloomed, and the MBAs, the quant jockey rocket scientist Ph.D.'s, the long-time traders from the neighborhood, and the gamblers who arrived from Las Vegas struggled to learn new vocabularies. Almost overnight, the old hand signals to traders disappeared, along with the once strictly upheld convention that a trader's word was his bond.

As an aside, when Adolph Berle's widow, a long-time family friend, asked me what I did when I was starting the derivatives function at Drexel Burnham in 1984, words failed me and I told her I was an anthropologist on Wall Street. Some time later, at dinner at her Gramercy Park brownstone (always a black-tie affair that started at 8:00 pm and ended at 10:00), she introduced me to my dinner companions as an anthropologist on Wall Street and asked me to offer some of my observations. Who was in attendance? Henry Kissinger and Arthur Schlesinger.

Interest Rate Arbitrage Comes of Age with the Swap Market

Moving along, in another response to inflation related volatility, the swap (derivatives) markets were born, allowing borrowers and issuers to separate principal repayment risk from interest rate or currency risk. A simple contract entered into by two or more counterparties, the swap contract was private and invisible, free of any regulatory involvement.

The swap contract allowed a borrower who could borrow in one market at attractive fixed rates but preferred floating rate payments to agree to make floating rate payments to another borrower, who preferred fixed rate payments but could not access such financing directly but had attractively priced floating rate cost of funds. The contract therefore called for the second borrower to make fixed rate payments. The contract netted the payments, so the parties paid the resulting differences to each other periodically. The principal repayment was not involved. At the outset, the broker in the middle received a several month mandate by telex to source the counter party and took a hefty, risk free fee for putting them together.

It was a very secretive market at the outset in the early 1980s, and only a few dealers participated. As volume grew, these dealers started to inventory attractive swaps by becoming the counter party themselves, hedging the position in the government bond market, and then laying off the other side of the trade as counter parties were found. I was a participant in this process, which initially was quite home grown, and developed for the most part out of finance departments, not trading areas. One Monday morning, we in the swap group discovered that all of our hedges were gone. Upon investigation, it was discovered that the government bond traders in London, responsible for the positions while U.S. markets were closed, had not recognized our bonds as hedges, and sold them in the face of attractive bids.

In another anecdote showing the shift in culture from enterprise balance sheet to individual, I joined Drexel Burnham from Bankers Trust Company, hired to start the interest rate swap function under the guidance of an academic sort of guy who had previously traded in futures, not very successfully, if memory serves. I could not figure out why in the first year of our operation he consistently wanted to overprice our trades, which seemed to me shortsighted as it would reduce much needed deal flow and repeat business.

At the end of the year, the light dawned. He had made a deal pursuant to which he personally received 35% of the discounted value of the income from the swap transactions. I imagine he knew that his superiors, once they understood the arcane world he had refused to explain clearly to them, would never renew that deal, so he did as many swaps as he could at high spreads during that one year. He also, I later learned, changed my initials on the trade blotters so it looked as if I was much less productive than I was, so that, once he had learned everything he could from me, he could easily terminate my employment.

That ploy did not work, and he left for greener pastures. He developed a joint venture with a AAA rated insurance company with whom he cut an even better deal. The insurance company provided the AAA rating and the money to pay for office space far from headquarters, and he provided the intellectual capital needed to create a swap business. He was to be compensated on the basis of 50% of the discounted value of the profits, aka the swap spread.

On paper this may look benign, or at least not unfair. In fact, though, since the swap profit or spread is collected over the life of the swap contract, this was a disastrous deal for the insurance company, who was required to pay that compensation in current cash, cash it had not yet collected. Of course, he wrote as many swaps as he could, and offered longer swaps than anyone else in the market. And that insurance company would pay the price, over and over again, until the music finally stopped in 2008.

The swap market continued to develop and be used in an ever-increasing range of situations, from currency swaps to swaps on hurricane risk to credit default swaps and beyond. Once a very quiet market, the interest rate swap curve joined the other reference curves for all traders; while at inception it solved genuine problems for genuine customers, its replication as a model for transferring all kinds of risk became overpowering.

Read More

Liar's Poker, Rising Through the Wreckage on Wall Street, Lewis, Michael, W.W. Norton & Company, 1989

Interest Rate & Currency Swaps: The Markets, Products and Applications, Dattatreya, Ravi, Probus Professional Publications, 1993

Credit Default Swap Markets in the Global Economy: An Empirical Analysis, Tamakoshi, Go & Hamori, Shigeyuki, Routledge Studies in the Modern World Economy, 2018

Chapter 10
Mortgage Backed Securities and Structured Products Conundrums

As the supply of both new and seasoned mortgages continued strong, the teeming hordes on Wall Street continued to seek ways to build a broader market for the product. While there was a long-established bank to bank market for pools of whole mortgage loans, the selling process was cumbersome as the loans were small and buyers generally wanted to reunderwrite a good- sized sample to test the quality of each pool.

Further, the loans were small and required servicing, which meant that each month the principal and interest needed to be collected and accounted for. While other mortgage lenders could do this, investment funds and insurance companies could not. Finally, the right to prepay at any time meant that even if an investor went to the trouble of buying and figuring how to provide servicing for a pool of whole loans, the investor would have little idea how long the loans would be outstanding and thus what sort of return would be forthcoming,

The growing ability to analyze options, developed by those rocket scientist Ph.D.'s, and to rearrange cash flows as demonstrated by the swap departments led in 1984 to the first large Collateralized Mortgage Obligation, or CMO, using roughly $1 billion in residential mortgage collateral, underwritten in conformance with Freddie Mac standards and sold by Freddie Mac into the special purpose vehicle as described below.

As a side note, mortgages originated to meet FHLMC and FNMA and GNMA criteria were called conventional or conforming product and labeled by coupon and agency. Thus, conventional mortgages backed by FNMA (called mortgage backed securities or MBS) and FHLMC (called PCs or participation certificates) and those backed by Government National Mortgage Assurance or GNMA or Ginnie Mae (MBS) were referred to as Agency product. These conventions had been in effect for decades, and the Agency market was huge.

The CMO allowed institutional investors unable to accept the prepayment risk associated with mortgage backed securities to participate in the mortgage market with greater predictability of return by stratifying mortgage pools sold into a special purpose vehicle (SPV) into "tranches" of SPV debt with various expected payment speeds. The earliest prepayment proceeds would go to the shortest life tranche, and so on. As an added benefit, because of the broad diversification of individual borrowers in each pool, the credit quality of the CMO was seen to be quite high.

DOI 10.1515/9781547400270-010

To repeat this concept, which came to be pivotal in later years, securitization enables loan originators to sell assets to a dealer, a Wall Street firm for the most part. The dealer creates a pool of loans with similar underlying collateral and documentation and a similar payment pattern such as MBSs or home mortgages and sells them into an off-balance sheet vehicle (SPV) that issues various tranches of debt to be serviced by the vehicle's collection of the individual payments of mortgage principal and interest. The payments and prepayments go to service the debt in accordance with rules laid out in the securitization offering document, which defines the "waterfall" of entitlements.

Eligible MBS pools were stress tested against borrower performance data collected since FNMA and the FHA/VA were formed in the 1930s to estimate their likely performance in various interest rate and credit environments. When the subprime market began to develop, the borrower payment histories kept by FHA/VA and FNMA were referred to as "prime" or high-quality borrower data. Rating agencies determined how much over collateralization or credit insurance would be required to achieve high ratings for each tranche.

The leftover cash flows, the cash expected after all tranches were paid off, was the estimated equity in the deal, called the residual, and if certain conditions were met, the seller could keep the residual without having to carry the loans on the balance sheet, having achieved a "true sale" in the eyes of accounting and law. The estimated value of the residual was required by accounting rules to be recognized as income at the time of the securitization, using assumptions as to expected defaults and prepayments despite the fact that collection will not occur until the debt is paid.

Using Securitization Techniques, the Sky Was the Limit—Or Maybe Not

With this structure available, thrifts, banks, and others such as investment funds could originate mortgage loans and sell into such a vehicle, and, more importantly, anyone who followed the rules for off balance sheet vehicles and true sale opinions could use them. Securitization was here to stay. While it greatly expanded the funds available for homebuyers, attractive from the point of view of public policy as declared when FNMA was formed in the New Deal, the model it created would come back to haunt corporations, banks, directors, and the public again and again as the securitization model was used on new and different types of collateral, with less understanding of the underlying borrowers' likely behavior in different environments. In 1987, securitization techniques were applied to automobile and credit card loans, and in 1991 to commercial mortgages. In 1994 subprime mortgages began to be securitized.

Having deferred recognition of the thrift problem for nearly a decade, Congress finally acted with the passing of FIRREA (Financial Institutions Reform Recovery and Enhancement Act) in 1989 and the creation of Resolution Trust Corporation (RTC). Banking regulators defined risk-based capital standards for commercial banks, to specify the level of capital required to support specified asset types. One byproduct of this initiative was an increased propensity of commercial banks to sell loans in order to manage their capital, which increased reliance on securitization. RTC took on a huge number of mortgages of many types and slowly liquidated them by using independent loan sales advisors, of which my firm was one. We were able to securitize some of the mortgages and secure an attractive gain for RTC.

The Mortgage Derivative Market Implodes

In 1994, when the Federal Reserve Bank raised the Federal Funds rate unexpectedly, the downside of the mortgage related product believed to have such high credit quality became real. Many institutional buyers, focused on credit risk, had not understood the interest rate risk they were incurring, and we saw the first wave of derivatives driven scandals as the market value of these instruments simply disappeared. In short, estimates of the expected life of the instrument were in many cases proven badly wrong as investors had not applied the concept of duration, the expected amount by which portfolio value would change given a 1% change in interest rates, holding the shape of the yield curved constant.

My firm, Solon Asset Management Corporation, an institutional investment management firm working with fixed income portfolios including specifically mortgage related product, suddenly had many new hedge fund, pension fund and municipality clients. We moved with sleeping bags into our offices to be near both market data and the fax machine as margin calls were both received and delivered. This is likely the first time that derivatives became visible to the general public, as Orange County sought bankruptcy protection and many other wealthy areas were aghast to find their money gone.

Hark, Securitization of Sub Prime Mortgages Begins

Meanwhile, in 1994 the market for securitized subprime mortgages began to grow rapidly. The basic argument used was that if borrowers with poor credit history were offered credit, the price they would pay would outweigh the possibly greater risk of default, similar to the argument made regarding the return on high yield bonds. Additionally, difficulty gaining credit was thought likely to inhibit borrower prepayment. Loans were small and if bundled together offered the benefits of diversification.

Demand was strong, and origination swelled. The subprime market had historically been a fairly local one, and the originators mostly local companies operating in a niche business, knowing a good deal about their borrowers and selling their product as whole mortgage loans to banks with careful underwriting criteria. Securitization, however, gave such companies an attractively low cost of funds, and the opportunity to originate larger volumes, selling to the Street to securitize. This appeared to be a compelling opportunity for growth.

Independent loan originator operations have typically been cash flow negative, though this was often disguised by their recognizing as a gain on sale, required under accounting rules, the expected residual or equity value associated with the loans sold. The value of these future cash flows was dependent on a number of assumptions rarely supported by historical experience and was in turn discounted to present value.

Earnings as Defined by Generally Accepted Accounting Principles May Not Create Cash

Many board members of issuers as well as Wall Street underwriters and investors were confused by this as the Street rushed to take these companies, with their demonstrated growth in declared earnings (the "earnings" declared as a result of the gain on sale described above), public. Oops, those earnings and the resulting assets were not cash, and not easily salable. While acting as restructuring advisor to a subprime originator in 2007, we managed what we believed to be the first sale of a securitized residual interest.

As more subprime originators got involved, borrower prepayments escalated well beyond expected levels. Subprime borrowers could now refinance without difficulty. In 1997, the first massive write downs on residual values occurred. The originators, many of them now public, shuddered and were scrutinized. The assumptions made on the data used to establish ratings for securitizations, data that was not based on subprime payment histories but was instead based on assumed variations from the prime borrower data described above, were adjusted and the market moved on to its next and near fatal test.

Sub Prime Industry Almost Died in 1998

The events of 1998 almost stopped the subprime sector in its tracks, as in the wake of the international debt crisis and the collapse of Long Term Capital Management, liquidity dried up overnight. Absent liquidity, these companies cannot function. They typically have no borrowing power of their own as their balance sheets have few assets other than mortgage loans, which are financed by other lenders in advance of the next securitization.

Suddenly unable to borrow as the securitization market closed, many originators had no choice but to liquidate overnight. The quality of their loans was discovered to be much lower than expected. Whole loan buyers, for example, would not buy much of the product that had been originated for securitization, because as described above they evaluated every loan on its merits, whereas securitizations were based on aggregate loan pool parameters with little to no reunderwriting of individual loan files.

Many companies had gotten stuck on a vicious treadmill: they had to originate in ever greater volumes to keep their perceived earnings momentum high, and for the same reason they were aggressive in valuing residuals held on their books. Their underwriting standards became more and more generous as competition increased, and borrowers, knowing they could easily find alternative financing, ignored collection efforts. And then the music stopped.

While serving as emergency CEO of the oldest and strongest of these subprime originator and servicer companies, I knew that efforts had been made to sell the company before my arrival. Only one commercial bank had expressed any interest at all, as commercial banks then were worried about reputation risk and most did not want to be associated with the taint of lending to lower credit quality buyers.

I took the company apart and sold it in pieces, only to discover that in securitizing $6 billion in almost forty transactions, the issuer had never had their own issuer's securitization counsel, instead relying entirely on underwriter's counsel. I also found myself signing papers to pay for the removal of hundreds of pounds of canine fecal matter from houses, some with only three walls. On balance I was not displeased that subprime originators were disappearing.

Public Policy Starts the Subprime Cycle Again

And then, in 1999, the cycle started again. Under Secretary Andrew Cuomo, the Department of Housing and Urban Development (HUD) directed the mortgage agencies FNMA and FHLMC to increase their purchase of mortgages made to low-

and moderate-income borrowers from 42% to 50%. HUD also raised two other Congressionally mandated goals: a special affordable housing goal for families with very low incomes jumped from 14% to 20%, a 43 percent increase, and raised a geographically targeted goal for underserved areas (central cities, rural areas, and underserved communities based on income and minority concentration) from 24% to 31%, a 29% increase. A huge influx of new money flooded into the subprime market, and banks were required to originate under various community reinvestment mandates.

Note that, according to the press release announcing these new targets, America's homeownership rate hit a record high in 1998, with 66.3 percent of all households owning their own homes. Secretary Cuomo was quoted as saying that these higher affordable housing goals would disproportionately benefit minorities and city residents, helping to close the homeownership gap. Regrettably, the subprime lending market was alive again, and FNMA and FHLMC needed to buy hundreds of millions of products or face stiff daily fines for every day they missed their quota.

Repeal of Glass Steagall Act Allows Commercial Banks and Investment Banks to Compete

Also, in 1999, Congress repealed the Glass Steagall Act, enacted in 1933 to separate investment banking functions such as underwriting securities from commercial banking activities such as accepting deposits and extending loans. The basic argument, based on pre-1929 experience, had been that consumer deposits must be protected and should not be subjected to the risks that investment banks, operating with capital deployed explicitly to make money for accepting risk, wanted to take. By 1999, it was hoped, such depositor protections were no longer needed, and the public would benefit from the ensuing increased competition.

U.S. commercial banks could now trade on a level playing field with investment banks. Perhaps facing pressure to diversify, banks increasingly began seeking to free up the capital required to do so by originating loans and syndicating them or selling them into CDOs (Collateralized Debt Obligations) and CLOs (Collateralized Loan Obligations), a variation of the securitization vehicles used in the mortgage markets.

Investment banks, wanting to compete with banks' lending power had also been originating loans and syndicating them to others or creating CDO's, to allow both sets of institutions to originate in volume, use their capital efficiently, and create new fee income to boost returns on capital. As discussed above, these vehicles were designed to be off balance sheet, in accordance with

GAAP and the law. Many different types of collateral, including subprime mortgages, were fair game.

And We Pushed Ourselves into the Abyss

Following the terror attacks on September 11, 2001, fear of further attacks roiled an already-struggling economy, one that was just beginning to come out of the recession that followed the bursting of the tech bubble of the late 1990s. In response, the Federal Reserve began cutting rates dramatically to encourage borrowing, and related spending and investing. From the White House down to the local parent-teacher association, efforts were made to encourage the public to see spending as a form of patriotism.

As lower interest rates worked their way into the economy, the real estate market reacted. Both the number of homes sold and the prices they sold for increased dramatically beginning in 2002. The interest rate on a 30-year fixed-rate mortgage was at the lowest levels seen in nearly 40 years. Record low interest rates combined with ever-loosening lending standards to push real estate prices to record highs across most of the United States.

Low Interest Rates Fuel Frenzies in Multiple Arenas

Existing homeowners were refinancing in record numbers, tapping into recently earned equity that could be had with a few hundred dollars spent on a home appraisal. In the huge volume that ensued, even basic requirements like proof of income were being overlooked by mortgage lenders; 125% loan-to-value mortgages were being originated again, based on the faulty logic that rising real estate prices would translate to a 125% LTV mortgage being below the value of the house in two years or less.

A market literally as close to home as real estate becomes impossible to ignore when in the space of five years, home prices in many areas had doubled. Many of those who hadn't purchased a home or refinanced considered themselves behind in the race to make money in that market. Mortgage lenders knew this and pushed ever more aggressively. New homes couldn't be built fast enough, and homebuilders' stocks soared.

Collateralized Debt Obligations Explode, In More Ways Than One

In 2002, originators introduced asset backed securities, including mortgage related securities, to CDOs as they were regarded as being less risky, better diversified, and more liquid than the corporate debt used theretofore. The CDO market, then estimated at about half a trillion dollars in size, mushroomed to an estimated size of over $2 trillion by the end of 2006. The CDO had become what some skeptics call an investment landfill, much like the subprime securitizations of the mid-1990s. While initially intended for corporate debt obligations, the structures were also useful for commercial real estate loans, for residential mortgage related product, and even for hedge fund collateral.

By 2006, according to a Deutsche Bank research report by Anthony Thompson et al., over half of the CDOs issued were based on structured finance collateral, and the great majority of that is estimated to be subprime collateral. It appears that many more difficult to place, lower rated tranches went into CDOs, making it much easier to place the senior tranches and keep originating more new deals, again with ever weaker collateral. Unfunded, synthetic CDOs were introduced, with derivative contracts used to replicate the cash flows expected by various pools of collateral. CDOs were introduced that invested in other CDOs: CDOs squared.

The Abyss Itself

With Wall Street, Main Street and everyone in between at least appearing to profit from the activity, who was going to put on the brakes? By the middle of 2006, however, cracks began to appear. New home sales stalled, and median sale prices halted their climb. Interest rates, while still low historically, were on the rise, with inflation fears threatening to raise them higher. Default rates began to rise sharply. Suddenly, the CDO didn't look so attractive to investors in search of yield. Many of the CDOs had been re-packaged so many times that it was difficult to tell how much subprime exposure was actually in them.

Scores of mortgage lenders, with no more eager secondary markets or investment banks to sell their loans into, were cut off from what had become a main funding source. Late in 2006, dozens of mortgage lenders began to seek bankruptcy protection. The real estate markets plummeted after years of record highs. Foreclosure rates doubled in twelve months, by the end of 2007.

Many institutional funds were faced with margin and collateral calls from nervous banks, which forced them to sell other assets, such as stocks and bonds, to raise cash. The increased selling pressure took hold of the stock markets, as major equity averages worldwide were hit with sharp declines in a matter of weeks, which effectively stalled the strong market that had taken the Dow Jones Industrial Average to all-time highs in July of 2007.

In 2008 the turmoil driven by developments in the subprime mortgage markets had ripple effects throughout the world. What made it more intense this time is a function of the policies described above that supported the movement of money out of the banking system and thus out of regulatory oversight, for over 30 years. Large financial institutions bought and sold credit default swaps on assets they didn't own. By 2008, these derivative contracts had grown to an estimated $62 trillion from $900 billion in 2001. Warren Buffett called them "financial weapons of mass destruction."

Multiple Financial Institutions Fail

Lehman Brothers Holdings, Inc., the fourth largest investment bank in the United States, also filed for bankruptcy protection in September 2008, the largest investment banking bankruptcy since the 1990 filing of Drexel Burnham Lambert Group, Inc. Bear Stearns, long a tough trading- oriented investment bank, ran out of money and was bought out by J.P. Morgan. The initial deal was $2 a share. Tense negotiations upped it to $10, valuing the company at less than the market price of the Bear's Manhattan flagship office. Venerable Merrill Lynch, known for its large retail investor activities, failed and was taken over by Bank of America in that same month.

Government-sponsored enterprises (GSEs) Federal National Mortgage Association (Fannie Mae) and Federal Home Loan Mortgage Corporation (Freddie Mac) having struggled despite huge injections of government cash to support the housing market over the course of 2008, were placed into conservatorship by the U.S. Treasury in September 2008 to allow the government to continue to use them to provide emergency support to the housing market.

American International Group (AIG), that insurance company that started the joint venture in 1986 to create a swap business was pushed to the brink of insolvency when a credit rating downgrade triggered the rights of swap counterparties to demand collateral AIG didn't have. Policymakers however, chose to rescue AIG with a September 16, 2008 agreement with the Federal Reserve Bank for a U.S. $85 billion secured loan facility, in exchange for warrants for 79.9% of the equity of AIG.

In the panic that followed the Lehman Brothers' bankruptcy and the AIG bailout in September 2008, investors rushed to quality, moving funds from corporate investments to the safety of government securities. Safety at this point was far more important than yield.

Investors began selling money market funds on Friday, September 12th, ahead of Lehman Brothers' bankruptcy on Monday, September 15 and continued to do so on Monday, September 15. On September 16, one money market fund, the Reserve Primary Fund, announced that it anticipated sufficient losses on its holdings of Lehman commercial paper that it might not be able to redeem all its shares at $1 per share. In mutual fund parlance, it "broke the buck," a very rare occurrence.

This does not mean that its investors suffered substantial losses, but only that fund managers did not believe it could support its $1 constant share price. Reserve Primary Fund's shareholders did not lose more than 1 or 2 percent of the value of their shares, far less than the 7 percent that stock market investors lost on a single day, September 29, 2008, during the financial crisis.

Nevertheless, the idea that there was some connection between the losses at the Reserve Primary Fund and the instability in the financial system that occurred after the Lehman bankruptcy and the AIG bailout took root. The withdrawal of funds from the Reserve Primary Fund was somewhat dramatically called a "run," although in substantial part it was the result of a general investor move to the perceived safety of government money market funds. The fact that the RPF "broke the buck" added to the drama but was not of material significance in light of the fund's eventual investor losses of less than 2 percent.

And WaMu, Too, Bites the Dust

In related developments, Washington Mutual Savings Bank (WaMu) became the largest failed bank in U.S. history. At year-end 2007, WaMu had more than 43,000 employees, offices in 15 states and $188.3 billion in deposits. Its net loss for the year was $67 billion (source: WaMu 2007 Annual Report). In the second half of September 2008, panicked WaMu depositors withdrew $16.7 billion, 9 percent of its deposits, out of their savings and checking accounts. The Federal Deposit Insurance Corporation said the bank had insufficient funds to conduct day-to-day business, seized control and started looking for buyers, ultimately striking a deal with JP Morgan.

Read More

The Handbook of Mortgage-Backed Securities, 7th Edition, Fabozzi, Frank J., Oxford University Press; 7th Edition, 2016

When Genius Failed: The Rise and Fall of Long-Term Capital Management, Lowenstein, Roger, Random House, 2000

The Big Short: Inside the Doomsday Machine, Lewis, Michael; WW Norton & Company, 2010

Fatal Risk: A Cautionary Tale of AIG's Corporate Suicide, Boyd, Roddy; Wiley & Sons, 2011

Crash of the Titans: Greed, Hubris, the Fall of Merrill Lynch, and the Near-Collapse of Bank of America, Farrell, Greg; Crown Books & Random House LLC, 2010

Greed and Glory on Wall Street: The Fall of the House of Lehman, Auletta, Ken; Open Road Media 2015

"Four Ways Washington Mutual Still Matters," Forbes, February 22, 2012.

Chapter 11
The Aftermath of the Abyss

The climb out of the abyss, exacerbated by a new and complex capital market, left an unsuspecting public feeling victimized. With echoes of the early 1930s in his ears, President Obama created the Troubled Asset Relief Program (TARP), which bought not only assets but equity stakes in the banks, a temporary "nationalization" that unsettled Wall Street. In 2011, President Obama signed into law the Dodd-Frank Wall Street Reform and Consumer Protection Act. Among many other provisions, Dodd-Frank permanently raised the FDIC deposit insurance limit to $250,000 per account and expanded the FDIC's responsibilities to include regular risk assessments of all FDIC-insured institutions.

These actions, though helpful, may exacerbate the problem. Banks as corporate lenders play a greatly reduced role compared to banks as deal originators. Loans are less often, therefore, made by entities that have to live with whether they get repaid or not. Commercial banks, looking to boost fee income, reduce regulatory capital required, and avoid the onerous regulatory requirements, now live, as did the thrifts before them, in a world in which they can be bypassed.

Banks can be and often are replaced by independent vehicles with no dedicated capital required that can greatly increase the availability of financing but are not organized to work with a borrower to revise credit terms or to manage a workout or foreclosure and learn from the experience. The independent vehicles are supported by investments from institutional investors struggling to earn sufficient returns to fund their obligations to beneficiaries

Low interest rates for the first few years of the decade fueled both demand for loans, especially mortgage loans, as consumers sought to own their home, and investor demand for low duration, higher yield investments. Securitization of mortgage loans made it easy to meet this demand on both sides, and more and more paper was originated to feed the investor market. As the events of the late 1990s in the subprime market showed us, the volume of loans far outpaced the underlying credit or actual asset quality, and overwhelmed the systems apparently analyzing the risk. No amount of risk diversification will protect against weak underwriting that often accompanies easy access to money.

Securitization markets and derivative markets are not self-limiting but are limited only by the ingenuity of the creator and the willingness of the counter party. There are no brakes built into the system until defaults occur. Little capital is required to create these vehicles; only willing buyers. The supply of derivatives contracts and special purpose vehicles can go on proliferating as long as the parties will sign contracts.

DOI 10.1515/9781547400270-011

Much of the ensuing activity does not fall under any regulator's responsibility, and regulatory bodies are largely based on older business models and not based on understanding securitization and derivative instruments and their global proliferation. No one entity can see what is happening in national markets, let alone international markets.

Important to recognize, especially for board members, is that every cog in the system is doing his job as he knows it. Originators originate loans that can be sold. If buyers buy what they originate, they have been trained by that act to originate more of it regardless of whether the underwriting was good or bad and the asset value actually there. The Street is doing its job as an intermediary, originating product and structuring it into forms that meet the needs of the investors. The rating agencies, roundly criticized for falling down on the job, are also in business, and have long been paid by the issuer, which clearly presents a bit of a conflict. The buyers are putting money to work in structures they believe sound though their ability to do due diligence on the underlying collateral is limited. Everyone is getting paid. Many compensation models emphasize fee income over overall results. Personal accountability is reduced as players increasingly look to "get theirs" and the variety of ways to achieve that proliferate.

As the complexity of instruments and derivatives of derivatives continue to grow, ever more specialized skills are required to think about them. Specialists may be deeply immersed in a particular aspect of a securitization without understanding the whole structure. Each player in a specialized area may be thinking that someone else understands the "why" of what he is doing; he is just doing the "what" part as well as he can. Silos form.

The complexity of some of these instruments may well be beyond the ability of any human being to understand, and the market may basically run on momentum until a shock occurs. Complexity forces reliance on machines and models and removes the necessary ability to make judgment calls. The off-balance sheet special purpose vehicles represent a huge global market, and no one can have an integrated view of the whole. The complexity of many of the instruments, or derivatives of derivatives, causes humans to default to machines, models, and the mythical guy in the next office who gets it.

Read More

Crash and Beyond: Causes and Consequences of the Global Financial Crisis, Farlow, Andrew, Oxford University Press, 2013

Financial Fiasco: How America's Infatuation with Home Ownership and Easy Money Created the Economic Crisis, Norberg, Johan, Cato Institute, 2009

Chapter 12
The Rise of Leveraged Buyouts, High Yield Bonds, and Private Equity Investment

Before we can move forward to actually defining and executing the job of the corporate board and its members, we need to explore several more critically important developments in the capital markets: the developments in the market for corporate control, both byproducts of inflation just as securitization was. Specifically, we look at the intertwined development of leveraged buyouts, the high yield bond market and hostile takeovers, as well as the now respectable private equity market and the development of hedge funds, including their aggressive activism.

Why do we dwell on these? Because unless board members have grown up in the dynamic capital markets, it is difficult to understand the motivations of the various parties that may be knocking on the board room door. Understanding how they have come to exist and the forces that are driving them may be critical to helping the corporation work effectively with people who see the world through a different lens.

No Longer Your Granddaddy's Way to Buy a Company

Investors have been acquiring businesses and making minority investments in privately held companies since the dawn of the industrial revolution and probably before. Andrew Carnegie sold his steel company to J.P. Morgan in 1901 in arguably the first true modern buyout. Later, J. Pierpont Morgan's J.P. Morgan & Co. would finance railroads and other industrial companies throughout the United States, President Teddy Roosevelt's actions against his holdings notwithstanding.

With few exceptions, private equity investment in the first half of the 20th century was the domain of wealthy individuals and families. In 1938, Laurance S. Rockefeller helped finance the creation of both Eastern Air Lines and Douglas Aircraft and the Rockefeller family had vast holdings in a variety of companies. Eric M. Warburg founded E.M. Warburg & Co. in 1938, which would ultimately become Warburg Pincus, with investments in both leveraged buyouts and venture capital.

DOI 10.1515/9781547400270-012

The Venture Capital Firm is Born

In 1946 the first two venture capital firms American Research and Development Corporation. (ARDC) and J.H. Whitney & Company were formed. ARDC was founded by Georges Doriot, the "father of venture capitalism," founder of INSEAD and former dean of Harvard Business School, with Ralph Flanders and Karl Compton, former president of MIT, to encourage private sector investments in businesses run by soldiers who were returning from World War II.

ARDC was the first institutional private equity investment firm that raised capital from sources other than wealthy families. ARDC is credited with the first major venture capital success story when its 1957 investment of $70,000 in Digital Equipment Corporation (DEC) would be valued at over $35.5 million after the company's initial public offering in 1968, representing a return of over 500 times on its investment and an annualized rate of return of 101%. In 1972, Doriot merged ARDC with Textron after having invested in over 150 companies.

During the 1960s and 1970s, venture capital firms focused their investment activity primarily on starting and expanding companies. More often than not, these companies were exploiting breakthroughs in electronic, medical or data-processing technology. As a result, venture capital came to be almost synonymous with technology finance.

The Private Equity Fund is Born

It was also in the 1960s that the common form of private equity fund, still in use today, emerged. Private equity firms organized limited partnerships to hold investments in which the investment professionals served as general partner and the investors, who were passive limited partners, put up the capital. The compensation structure, still in use today, also emerged, with limited partners paying an annual management fee of 1–2% and a carried interest typically representing up to 20% of the net profits of the partnership. Such vehicles had limited lives, of typically seven years, which drove private equity behavior in managing the companies they purchased. They were not organized to be buy and hold investors.

Warren Buffett, often described as a stock market investor rather than a private equity investor, employed many of the same techniques in the creation on his Berkshire Hathaway conglomerate. In 1965, Buffett assumed control of Berkshire Hathaway, then a textile company. Buffett, however, used the Berkshire Hathaway corporation as an investment vehicle to make acquisitions and minority investments in dozens of insurance and reinsurance industries such as GEICO and other companies including American Express, The Buffalo News, the Coca-Cola Company, Fruit of the Loom, Nebraska Furniture Mart, and See's Candies.

Buffett's value investing approach and focus on earnings and cash flows are characteristic of later private equity investors, though he generally does not face the same pressure they do to harvest the fruits of their investment by selling the company in a finite period of time. Buffett would distinguish himself relative to more typical leveraged buyout practitioners through his reluctance to use leverage and hostile techniques in his investments.

Importantly, the structure he developed using Berkshire Hathaway allowed him the latitude to indulge in his frequently quoted favorite holding period should the investment merit it: forever. Private equity funds typically need to harvest their investments and return the proceeds to investors after some investment horizon, spelled out in the fund documents, concludes. Using a corporation as his investment vehicle gave Buffett great flexibility.

In the years following the end of World War II, the Great Depression was still relatively fresh in the minds of America's corporate leaders, who considered it wise to keep corporate debt ratios low. As a result, for the first three decades following World War II, very few American companies relied on debt as a significant source of funding. Companies and empires called conglomerates grew, and middle management swelled. Corporate profitability began to slide.

The Leveraged Buy Out Arrives

It was in this environment that the modern leveraged buyout, known until then as a bootstrap acquisition, was born. In the late 1970s and early 1980s, newly formed firms such as Kohlberg Kravis Roberts and Thomas H. Lee Company saw an opportunity to profit from inefficient and undervalued corporate assets. Many public companies were trading at a discount to net asset value, and many early leveraged buyouts were motivated by profits available from buying entire companies, breaking them up and selling off the pieces. This "bust-up" approach combined with the power of debt to finance these acquisitions eventually led to the media backlash against the greed of so-called "corporate raiders" caricatured by books such as *The Rain on Macy's Parade* and *Barbarians at the Gate*.

The acquisition of Orkin Exterminating Company in 1964 by Henry Kravis, Jerome Kohlberg, and George Roberts, investment bankers at Bear Stearns, is among the first significant leveraged buyout transactions. In the following years, the three bankers would complete a series of buyouts including Stern Metals (1965), Incom (a division of Rockwood International, (1971), Cobblers Industries (1971) and Boren Clay (1973). Unable to convince Bear Stearns to develop a dedicated fund to pursue these investments in house, the trio left Bear in 1976 to start KKR, their own firm. By 1978, the nascent KKR was successful in raising its first institutional fund with approximately $30 million of investor commitments.

Pension Plans Buy in to Private Equity Investing

The boom in leveraged buyouts in the 1980s was supported by three major legal and regulatory events. The failure of the Carter tax plan of 1977 that would have, among other results, reduced the disparity in tax treatment regarding interest paid to bondholders and dividends paid to stockholders made the continued use of leverage to reduce taxes available. Debt continued to be the most tax efficient way to finance acquisitions.

With the passage of ERISA in 1974, corporate pension funds were prohibited from holding certain risky investments including many investments in private equity related companies. In 1978, certain parts of ERISA restrictions were relaxed under the "prudent man rule," thus allowing corporate pension funds to invest in private equity, and a major new source of capital to invest in private equity became available.

On August 15, 1981, Ronald Reagan signed into law the Economic Recovery Tax Act of 1981, lowering the top capital gains tax rate from 28 percent to 20 percent, and making potentially high return investments even more attractive for taxable investors such as corporate treasuries, and insurance companies.

Why did pension plan investors, historically conservative, invest in these vehicles and/or the related high yield debt offerings? As described above, they have hurdle rates of return to meet to keep their corpus growing sufficiently to fund their obligations to their pensioners. The volatility of the publicly traded market returns made predictions there difficult. Many felt they needed to catch up by investing in asset classes that might offer both greater return and greater certainty of return. Growth in private equity surged as institutional investors such as the Shell Pension Plan, the Oregon State Pension Plan, the Ford Foundation and the Harvard Endowment Fund started investing a small part of their massive portfolios into what came to be called alternative investments. And others followed these leaders.

These investments were considered attractive because they offered an alternative to investing in real estate and investments that moved with the broad market, stocks and bonds. These investments, mainly in venture capital and leveraged buyout funds, were believed to offer a return pattern independent of market movements. Another term used to describe them is investments with absolute return, which does not vary as the public securities markets move up and down.

The Hostile Takeover Epidemic

The leveraged buyout became notorious as the public became aware of the ability of private equity to affect mainstream companies and "corporate raiders" and "hostile takeovers" entered the public consciousness. Additionally, the threat of the corporate raid could lead to the practice of "greenmail," where a corporate raider or other party would acquire a significant stake in the stock of a company and receive an incentive payment (effectively a bribe) from the company to convince the acquirer to avoid pursuing a hostile takeover of the company.

The decade saw a large boom in private equity activity culminating in the 1989 leveraged buyout of RJR Nabisco, which would remain the largest leveraged buyout transaction for nearly 17 years. In 1980, the private equity industry would raise approximately $2.4 billion of investor commitments and by the end of the decade in 1989 that figure stood at $21.9 billion.

The Role of Michael Milken

Michael R. Milken, born in 1946 in California, became well known during the 1980s. While a student at Berkeley in the late 1960s, Mr. Milken came across support for his hypothesis that a portfolio of high-yield bonds would outperform an investment-grade portfolio, even taking into account the higher likelihood of default. A study by Braddock Hickman, a central banker and student of corporate finance, showed that even during the Depression there was a high rate of return on non-investment-grade bonds. The interest-rate spread over supposedly safer bonds was more than enough compensation for the higher expected losses.

In the 1970s the market for high yield bonds was tiny, comprised of "fallen angels," the former investment-grade securities of companies that had fallen on hard times, which changed hands infrequently and at big discounts to face value. While studying at the Wharton School Mr. Milken accepted employment at Drexel Firestone, a venerable Philadelphia investment firm, and began trading in fallen angels, handily proving the thesis correct.

In the early 1970s, Drexel Firestone merged with Burnham Securities. Though the firms operated under the august Drexel name, scrappy trading firm Burnham was the dominant firm, and operations moved to New York. Milken's influence and resources available grew. In April 1974, Drexel underwrote its first original high yield bond issue when it raised $30 million for Texas International, a small oil-exploration company. The argument made to them as to why to issue high yield, expensive debt rather equity to finance their goals was based on two main points: debt was not dilutive, and the cost of the debt was partially offset by the ability to deduct interest paid from taxes. In short, they were a cheaper form of capital.

Milken helped his customers make money. If they did well, they came back for more and in time a number built entire businesses on the supply of securities from Drexel. He offered investors an exit when needed, at a price. That liquidity attracted mutual funds into the arena. Mr. Milken's skill as a market maker was rooted in his knowledge of the bonds issued, and his extraordinary recollection of his clients' holdings, which helped him find buyers for product that others wanted to unload. He also, of course, expected certain sellers to buy more bonds when he needed them to. He is alleged to have read prospectuses for pleasure non-stop and constantly to focus on discerning new trends.

Milken Flexes His Funding Muscles

Drexel's ability to underwrite new high yield bond issues became an important tool for the leveraged-buy-out (LBO) firms of the 1980s. Milken's ability quickly to raise hundreds of millions of dollars in debt for favored clients made the threat of buy-outs credible. Its dominance of the high-yield corporate bond market turned once obscure Drexel into a powerhouse. By 1986, Drexel, which in its long history had never threatened to join the financial elite, was Wall Street's most profitable firm, in part due to its refusal to allow syndication of its bond issues, which would have allowed other firms to share in the spoils.

Such was Milken's control of the high yield market and his clients' confidence in him that Drexel could issue what came to be called a highly confident letter indicating that the client of the moment could produce the funds needed to close a deal, without needing to raise the money in advance. Remarkably, these were accepted by many counterparties, and provided a new source of funds for many small but growing firms, which had not been able to attract support from traditional commercial or investment banks. The entrepreneurial owners of these companies saw the growth potential in their respective industries. These entrepreneurs were the bread and butter business of Milken's High Yield Department.

Corporate Titans Are Shaken by an Upstart

Management of many large publicly traded corporations reacted negatively to the threat of a potential hostile takeover and boards pursued defensive measures including poison pills, golden parachutes and increasing debt on the company's balance sheet. Drexel was seen as an upstart firm, greatly to be feared as well as denounced by established corporate leaders. Many of the court decisions allowing the defenses to stand relied on decision making by independent directors, as the best available embodiment of the less conflicted true stewards of the corporation. These court decisions appear to have depended in large part on not only the presence of independent directors but also on the process those directors who were disinterested in the transaction went through to consider the transaction.

Drexel raised capital for small firms which had enough cash flow to meet interest payments to grow bigger, thus the focus on earnings before interest, taxes, depreciation, and amortization, or EBITDA, a concept developed at Drexel. Some industries were not well-suited for debt finance: the mobile-phone business did not generate much upfront cash and cable TV firms had big start-up costs before subscription revenue flowed. One solution was to "over-fund" firms, to raise more capital than they needed so that they could make their initial interest payments with the additional proceeds. Another approach was to use zero-coupon bonds, on which interest payments were deferred until the principal came due.

Drexel's fees on high yield bond issues were much higher than was typical for investment-grade bonds. The typical Drexel client, however, was not eligible for investment grade financing, and as entrepreneurs growing businesses they were generally much more interested in the availability of the funds than concerned about its cost. Drexel was able to charge an enviable fee for access to Milken's abilities and scarce investor base.

As part of Drexel fees, the Milken team often demanded equity warrants for the high yield and corporate finance teams involved, as well as for their buyers to sweeten the deal. Of questionable legality, these deals came to be known as the warrant strip or the infamous investment partnerships, and further enhanced the loyalty of those included in the club who received them. In my view, this structure influenced the structure of the partnerships later infamously created by Enron and Ken Lay, a Drexel client and a beneficiary of the warrant strip.

The Government Fights Back—For Real

We will never know exactly what triggered the long running SEC investigation into Milken and Drexel, but there were some likely apocryphal stories that major corporate executives, frightened of takeover, approached senior government officials to get them to act to stop him. What seems likely to me, a Drexel employee and shareholder at the time and later leader of the shareholders who forced the restructuring of its board, is that regulators believed that too much power was concentrated in one man's hands.

To the best of my knowledge, there was no such thing as illegal insider trading in the bond market, as the notion that bonds could determine the ownership of a company had not been contemplated by lawmakers. Instead, it was possible to argue that Milken actually created inside information by his ability to finance takeovers of big companies by fast moving entrepreneurs.

Nevertheless, rather than do the difficult work of addressing what might have been a gap in the securities laws, regulators likely thought Milken and Drexel would be easy targets. They could likely more easily curb Milken's influence by pursuing him for securities law violations than by clarifying the law. To my mind, Milken had not only amassed too much power, but had done so outside the fabric of the accepted system. Quite simply, his power, brains, reach, and outsider status made him a very frightening force.

Drexel Burnham Lambert was first publicly rocked by scandal on May 12, 1986, when Dennis Levine, a Drexel investment banker, was charged with insider trading. Levine pleaded guilty to four felonies, and implicated one of his recent partners, arbitrageur Ivan Boesky. Largely based on Boesky's promises to provide information about his dealings with Milken, the SEC formally initiated an investigation of Drexel on November 17, 1986. Two days later, Rudy Giuliani, then United States Attorney for the Southern District of New York, launched his own criminal investigation.

For two years, Drexel steadfastly denied any wrongdoing, claiming that the criminal and SEC cases were based almost entirely on the statements of an admitted felon looking to reduce his sentence. Their assertions were, however, not enough to keep the SEC from suing Drexel in September 1988 for insider trading, stock manipulation, defrauding its clients and stock parking. All of the allegedly improper transactions involved Milken and his department.

Giuliani Plays Hardball with RICO Threat

Giuliani began threatening to indict Drexel under the powerful Racketeer Influenced and Corrupt Organizations Act (RICO), under the legal theory that corporations are responsible for an employee's crimes, which had yet to be uncovered or even alleged. The threat of a RICO indictment, which would have required the firm to put up a performance bond of as much as $1 billion in lieu of having its assets frozen, unnerved many at Drexel, including top management, as simply being indicted would have put the firm out of business, regardless of whether Giuliani proved his case.

Drexel's CEO, Fred Joseph, observed at a meeting I attended that it had taken him some time to understand the difference between negotiating with a commercial counter party as compared to a government counter party. In the commercial case, the effort is to establish degree of damages done and agree on settlement, make reparations, and move on. The government counter party, on the other hand, did not want to agree on damages. What they wanted was to kill their counter party.

Soon his words would prove to be true. With little time to go before Giuliani planned to indict under RICO, Joseph reached an agreement with the U.S. Attorney in which it pleaded no contest to six felonies, including three counts of stock parking and three counts of stock manipulation. The firm also agreed to pay a fine of $650 million, at the time the largest fine ever levied under securities laws. It appeared then that both the SEC and Giuliani were having a hard time finding a smoking gun.

Milken Pleads, and NOT to Engaging in Insider Trading

Milken was indicted in 1989 and in a plea bargain pleaded guilty to securities and reporting violations but notably not to racketeering or insider trading. Milken was sentenced to ten years in prison, fined $600 million in a global settlement in which all recipients of the warrant strips mentioned above participated, and permanently barred from the securities industry by the SEC. His sentence was later reduced to two years.

Milken left the firm after his indictment in March 1989. In April 1989, Drexel settled with the SEC, agreeing to stricter safeguards on its oversight procedures, including appointment of three independent directors to its large board. No longer able to issue the controversial but effective highly confident letters, Drexel struggled to keep its franchise in high yield bonds alive without Milken. One result was that it did what it had never done before and offered bridge financing to a large client. Bridge financing is intended as a short-term vehicle to fund the transaction while the permanent financing is being put in place. This huge bridge loan placed added strain on Drexel's ability to finance its operations.

And Drexel Fails

When on February 13, 1990, Drexel could not refinance $300 million of its own short-term debt, as it came due, the firm was advised by the Secretary of the Treasury, the SEC, the NYSE, the Federal Reserve System, and other investment banking firms that no rescue package would be forthcoming. The holding company Drexel Burnham Lambert Group, Inc. and various subsidiaries filed for Chapter 11 bankruptcy protection. It was then the largest and likely the most notorious bankruptcy to date.

As a fairly obscure employee who nonetheless owned stock, I initiated a grassroots organization of the other shareholders, all but one of whom were employees and few of whom had been any part of the small group that attracted regulatory and criminal investigations. I was fortunate to find in attorney Claude Montgomery a very able advocate willing to serve as counsel to the Equity Committee, which we succeeded in getting the bankruptcy court to appoint as a fiduciary for all Drexel shareholders.

And Restructures Its Own Board of Directors

In exchange for our committee's support for certain company plans, we secured agreement from Drexel, now called the debtor in possession, to restructure the board to favor independent directors as a way to placate the enraged creditors and others who felt betrayed and humiliated and were extremely suspicious of incumbent management. Following protracted negotiations, two independent directors (Fred Zuckerman, former Treasurer of Chrysler, and Fletcher L. Byrom, retired CEO of Koppers, Inc.) whom I had recruited, and I took our seats, immediately thereafter, the SEC deem Drexel an inadvertent investment company required to be governed under the Investment Company Act of 1940.

Given that the shareholders were now dispersed to other jobs all over the Street, every sale transaction the debtor undertook involved a conflict resulting from the need to deal with what were defined as "affiliates" under the '40 Act rules. The independent directors, therefore, had to make most portfolio decisions, and many operating ones. Recoveries to all parties exceeded expectations. The irony of Drexel's influence in enfranchising disinterested directors by financing hostile takeovers and then needing disinterested directors to ride to the rescue during its chapter 11 proceeding is noteworthy.

Lasting Impact of Milken and Drexel Burnham

Drexel's financiers were pragmatic dealmakers. But in their search for profit they brought about what *The Economist* called in an October 2010 article a democratization of access to credit. In its view, firms that previously had to rely on conservative banks or expensive equity were given the ability to raise funds by offering fixed-interest instruments in which the investors that Mr. Milken had cultivated had invested. This was a boon to the American economy: limiting capital to investment-grade firms limits economic progress. If a firm can pay the rate for its risk, it should get the money it needs.

Unloved as it was, Drexel changed the face of corporate finance and of Wall Street. Drexel has left four enduring legacies: a junk-bond market that has grown at least sevenfold since the firm's demise; the firms and industries, from gambling to cable television, that owed their rapid expansion to Drexel's high yield bonds; the lasting influence of the "Drexel diaspora," the Drexel alumni, continuing leaders in the finance industry; and the acceleration of the rise of independent directors on America's public company boards.

With outstandings in excess of $1 trillion in 2010, approximately 40% of all outstanding corporate bonds in America were rated as "speculative", or below investment grade (BB+ or lower), according to Dealogic, a financial-data firm. Even better-class bonds are not as unassailable as they once were; many of the high-grade bonds issued since 1992 have since been rated BBB-, the lowest investment grade. Junk bonds, once despised, are now mainstream. And less noticeably but quite unmistakably, Milken's financing power changed the face of corporate governance.

Private Equity Goes Public

As private equity reemerged in the 1990s it began to earn respectability. Although in the 1980s, many of the acquisitions made were unsolicited and unwelcome, private equity firms in the 1990s focused on making buyouts more attractive propositions for management and shareholders.

Although there had previously been certain instances of publicly traded private equity vehicles, the convergence of private equity and the public equity markets attracted significantly greater attention when several of the largest private equity firms pursued various options through the public markets. Taking private equity firms and private equity funds public appeared an unusual move since private equity funds often buy public companies listed on exchange and then take them private.

In 2007, Blackstone Group, for example, offered shares in its management company, allowing shareholders to share in its management fees and carried interest earned. In 2006, Kohlberg Kravis Roberts completed an initial public offering for a new permanent investment vehicle (KKR Private Equity Investors or KPE) listing it on the Euronext exchange in Amsterdam (ENXTAM: KPE). They raised $5 billion, alleged to be more than 3 times what they had hoped for, perhaps an indication of the popularity of private equity as an asset class in that the form of the vehicle offered investors otherwise unable to invest in a traditional private equity limited partnership due to size or other restrictions to gain exposure to a portfolio of private equity investments.

Read More

The Predators' Ball: the Junk Bond Raiders and the Man Who Staked Them, Bruck, Connie, The American Lawyer and Simon & Schuster, 1988

The Rain on Macy's Parade, Trachtenberg, Jeffrey A., Crown Business, 1996

Barbarians at the Gate: The Fall of RJR Nabisco, Burrough, Bryan, Harper Business, 1990

Den of Thieves, Stewart, James B., Simon & Schuster, 1991

Highly Confident: The Crime and Punishment of Michael Milken, Kornbluth, Jesse, William Morrow & Company, 1990

Leveraged Buyouts: A Practical Guide to Investment Banking and Private Equity, Pignataro, Paul, Wiley Finance, 2013

Mastering Private Equity: Transformation via Venture Capital, Minority Investments and Buyouts, Zeisberger, Claudia & Prahl, Michael, Wiley, 2017

Chapter 13
The Rise of Hedge Funds and Emergence of Aggressive Activism

You may recall that in the securities regulations that became law in the 1930s, hedge funds were exempted from registration with the SEC. What is a hedge fund?

While the it now covers many different types of investing, the term hedge fund generally refers to a private investment vehicle available only to accredited investors that may be created on or offshore but is frequently offshore. The hedge part refers to what was once the common investment strategy of going long with certain securities and short with others, aiming to make the result market neutral, as in unaffected by market movement, while capturing the positive difference between the two securities as profit.

The main structural difference between a hedge fund and a private equity fund relates to the liquidity provided to investors. The hedge fund generally offers periodic opportunities, often quarterly or annually, to add new investment dollars and to redeem the shares of shareholders who desire to sell. While some achieve an initial two or three year lock up period in which an investor cannot redeem, most do not. Their investment strategies, therefore, would be expected generally to rely on liquid securities. In recent years, some appear to have forgotten that and have had to slow down payment of redemptions.

Private equity funds may accept funds at several different closing dates, but once the fund is closed, no further investors can join, and the fund will generally not redeem investor holdings until all investors are paid out. Private equity funds typically have a life of seven years, presumably long enough to find, acquire, improve, and sell their investments in companies. Such funds typically give the right to the sponsor, aka the general partner or the manager, to extend the life of the fund by one or more years to give them added flexibility as to when to harvest investments, which presumably benefits the investors who may realize greater value as a result. Hedge funds can use various legal forms, but generally are formed as offshore limited liability companies with a perpetual life.

Hedge Funds Remain Largely Opaque and Unregulated

Though under the 2010 legislation known as Dodd-Frank, hedge fund managers managing assets greater than a certain value or serving more than a certain number of clients must now register with the SEC. They must now as part of

DOI 10.1515/9781547400270-013

that process file annually a report of their activities including fee structures and assets under management with the SEC. The funds they control, however, remain unregistered and therefore opaque. One aspect of their activities that makes them tricky to deal with for corporations is their ability to invest without disclosure throughout the capital structure, and go long, short, or both. There were more than eight thousand hedge funds managing a cumulative $3.1 trillion in mid-2017 per the *Financial Times*, a threefold increase in assets over the decade since the 2008 debacle, according to Hedge Fund Research (HFR).

While hedge funds show up in many different guises in capital markets, for our purposes we will look briefly at their behavior as activists using their shares to effect change. Shareholder activism can take any of several forms: proxy battles, publicity campaigns, shareholder resolutions, litigation, and negotiations with management.

Hedge Funds Emerge as Activists

The goals of activist shareholders, who include both long term institutional investors and hedge funds, range from financial (increase of shareholder value through changes in corporate policy, financing structure, cost cutting, etc.) to non-financial (disinvestment from particular countries, adoption of environmentally friendly policies, etc.).

Within the hedge fund universe, those pursuing an activist investing style deserve particular attention. Activist funds, which include various investor types, have dramatically upped the pressure on corporate executives and boards. While activists can certainly not guarantee that their strategy or director slate will magically transform the prospects of an underperforming company, they are very good at getting attention from the media, from the proxy advisors, and from other investors.

One attraction of shareholder activism to a hedge fund lies in its comparatively low cost; a fairly small stake (less than 10% of outstanding shares) may be enough to launch a successful campaign. In comparison, a full takeover bid is a much more costly and difficult undertaking. Though there is no definitive source to my knowledge as to how much hedge fund money is allocated to activist strategies, and that number will change with perceived opportunity, Hedge Fund Research (HFR) pegs 2015 dollars at $200 billion.

While significant, there are a great many funds, and few are able to commit large percentages of their portfolio to one company's stock. But the addition of leverage to their equity amplifies their purchasing power, and the influence they can exert when they demand board seats, CEO replacements, or strategy shifts can be much larger than the dollars they have invested.

A 2012 study by London-based research firm Activist Insight showed that the mean annual net return of over forty activist-focused hedge funds had consistently outperformed the MSCI world index in the years following the global financial crisis in 2008. Activist investing was the top-performing strategy among hedge funds in 2013, with such firms returning, on average, 16.6% while other hedge funds returned 9.5%. Lucian Bebchuk, in his provocative paper "The Long-term Effects of Hedge Fund Activists" considered activist impact on corporate performance in universe of about 2,000 interventions during the period 1994-2007 Impact over the five-year interval following the intervention was analyzed. His findings showed no decline and seemed to show that operating performance improved during the five-year period following the intervention.

Hedge funds, unregulated as to their actions and able to invest across the capital structure as well as to short securities, pursue many tactics to achieve their desired results. Proxy fights are an obvious route. According to financial data company FactSet, 405 campaigns between 2001 and 2014 involved multiple parties, 220 of which included a dissident group seeking board seats. Of those, 107 won at least a single board seat.

Again, according to Millstein, some well-established activists were able to secure board seats without running a proxy contest in 2015. Shareholder activists are making their mark on M&A activity as well: 2015 survey of corporate development leaders found that 60% of respondents saw shareholder activism affecting transaction activity in their industry. One strategy hedge funds can employ is to operate as a wolf pack in which several funds acting not as a group but in parallel buy up shares in a target, using the securities law to their advantage by exploiting the ten-day window between the time the "lead wolf" starts buying shares and when he is required to disclose ownership in a 13D filing with the SEC. Mutual fund managers have been known to test the limits of securities law as well, arguing that they are not a single owner but instead have many beneficial owners and do not have to file 13D's.

Traditional Institutional Investors Join the Fray

The nature and style of activists may be changing from brash and demanding outsiders to influential insiders with a long-term stake. Much more politely given their general need to be long-term investors, but nonetheless forcefully, some large U.S. institutions are publicly stating their intentions regarding future activism in governance.

Vanguard, with $3 trillion in assets under management, is the largest mutual fund complex in the U.S. and a major shareholder in many of the biggest corporations. In a 2015 letter to several hundred public companies, CEO William McNabb wrote, *"In the past, some have mistakenly assumed that our predominantly passive management style suggests a passive attitude with respect to corporate governance. Nothing could be further from the truth."*

In an interview with *The Wall Street Journal*, McNabb noted, *"We are 5 percent of most major companies. We should be doing this. We felt like we should take it to another level."* McNabb's letter urged boards to appoint an independent chairperson, rather than a member of management, and to increase interaction with shareholders, possibly through a shareholder liaison committee. *"It's more about the behavior than the framework,"* he told the Journal. *"We're indifferent as to how a board chooses to engage. What's important is that it engages."*

Blackrock, perhaps the world's largest asset manager with $4.65 trillion in assets under management, has issued revised voting guidelines, signaling that it may now oppose U.S. directors' reelection over things like lengthy tenures, poor board meeting attendance, lack of diversity, and inadequate succession planning. Remarkably, too, Blackrock Chairman & CEO Larry Fink has written letters to a number of large corporate CEO's urging them to manage for the long term and offering support if they do. Here we have another paradox, as the daily pricing of mutual funds and the need for strong track records has played a large role in keeping management attention focused on the short term.

The Current Impact of Activism

According to law firm Gibson Dunn & Crutcher's informative annual report on proxy season developments, shareholders submitted approximately 827 proposals for 2017 shareholder meetings. This is significantly fewer than the 916 proposals submitted for 2016 and the 943 proposals submitted for 2015 meetings.

For 2017, the most frequently submitted proposals among the four categories (governance and shareholder rights; environmental and social issues; executive compensation; and corporate civic engagement), were environmental and social proposals, which garnered approximately 345 proposals. The number of social proposals submitted increased to 201 during the 2017 proxy season, up from 160 in 2016. Thirty-five social proposals submitted in 2017 focused on board diversity (up from 28 in 2016), 34 proposals, up from 16 in 2016, focused on discrimination or diversity-related issues, and 19 proposals focused on the gender pay gap, up from 13 in 2016.

Environmental proposals were also popular during the 2017 proxy season, with 144 proposals submitted (up from 139 in 2016). Furthermore, there was an unprecedented level of shareholder support for environmental proposals this proxy season, with three climate change proposals receiving majority support and climate change proposals averaging support of 32.6% of votes cast. This compares to one climate change proposal receiving majority support in 2016 and climate change proposals averaging support of 24.2% of votes cast.

Voting Results on Shareholder Proposals

Based on the 331 shareholder proposals for which ISS provided voting results in 2017, proposals received on average 29.0% of votes cast, slightly down from average support of 29.8% of votes cast in 2016. The proposal topics that received high shareholder support were:

- Board Declassification: Three proposals voted on averaged support of 70.2% of votes cast in 2017, compared to three proposals with average support of 64.5% in 2016
- Elimination of Supermajority Voting Requirements: Seven proposals voted on averaged support of 64.3% of votes cast, compared to thirteen proposals with average support of 59.6% in 2016
- Adopt Proxy Access: Eighteen adopt proxy access proposals voted on averaged support of 62.1% of votes cast. In 2016, average support for proxy access proposals where the company had not previously adopted some form of proxy access was 56.0%
- Majority Voting in Uncontested Director Elections: Seven proposals voted on averaged support of 62.3% of votes cast, compared to ten proposals with average support of 74.2% in 2016
- Written Consent: Twelve proposals voted on averaged support of 45.6% of votes cast, compared to thirteen proposals with average support of 43.4% in 2016
- Shareholder Ability to Call Special Meetings: Fifteen proposals voted on averaged support of 42.9% of votes cast, compared to sixteen proposals with average support of 39.6% in 2016
- Climate Change: Twenty-eight proposals voted on averaged support of 32.6% of votes cast, compared to thirty-seven proposals with average support of 24.2% in 2016

Overall, approximately 10.9% of shareholder proposals that were voted on at 2017 shareholder meetings received support from a majority of votes cast, compared to 14.5% of proposals in 2016.

Large investors have also begun publicly to post their positions on a number of issues on their websites. Blackrock, for example, posts "Our Engagement Priorities for 2017-2018" on www.Blackrock.com, and Vanguard lays out its Proxy Voting Guidelines, at www.Vanguard.com.

Blackrock notes explicitly that "when we do not see progress despite ongoing engagement, or companies are insufficiently responsive to our efforts to protect the long-term economic interests of our clients, we will not hesitate to exercise our right to vote against management recommendations. Climate-related risks and opportunities are issues we have become increasingly focused on at Black-Rock as our understanding of the related investment implications evolves".

Read More

The Emperor's Nightingale: Restoring the Integrity of the Corporation in the Age of Shareholder Activism, Monks, Robert, Basic Books, 1999

Shareholder Rights at 400: Commemorating Isaac Le Maire and the First Recorded Expression of Investor Advocacy, Frentrop, Paul; Jonker, Joost; (ed.), Remix Business Communications, 2009

"The Evolution of Shareholder Voting Rights: Separation of Ownership and Consumption" Hansmann, Henry; Pargendler, Mariana (Yale Law Journal, Vol. 123, 2014

Dear Chairman: Boardroom Battles and the Rise of Shareholder Activism, Gramm, Jeff, Harper Business, 2016

Barbarians in the Boardroom: Activist Investors and the Battle for Control of the World's Most Powerful Companies, Walker, Owen, FT Publishing, 2016

Fink Letter

Chapter 14
The Evolution of the New York Stock Exchange

As market composition has changed and many derivative instruments are actively traded, how has the NYSE adapted? "The Big Board" continued to be the world's largest stock exchange by market capitalization of its listed companies at U.S.$21.3 trillion as of June 2017. The average daily trading value was approximately U.S.$169 billion in 2013.

The NYSE continues to trade in a continuous auction format, where traders can execute stock transactions on behalf of investors. The auction process moved toward automation in 1995 through the use of wireless handheld computers (HHC), which enabled traders to receive and execute orders electronically via wireless transmission ending a 203-year process of paper transactions and ushering in an era of automated trading. By 2007, the process was fully automated.

NYSE's governing board voted to merge with rival Archipelago on December 6, 2005, and became a for-profit, public company. It began trading under the name NYSE Group on March 8, 2006. A little over one year later, on April 4, 2007, the NYSE Group completed its merger with Euronext, the European combined stock market, thus forming NYSE Euronext, the first transatlantic stock exchange.

Until the 2005 reorganization, the right to directly trade shares on the exchange was conferred upon owners of the 1366 "seats." The term comes from the fact that up until the 1870s NYSE members sat in chairs to trade. These seats were a sought-after commodity as they conferred the ability to directly trade stock on the NYSE, and seat holders were commonly referred to as members of the NYSE.

Seat prices varied widely over the years, generally falling during recessions and rising during economic expansions. The most expensive inflation-adjusted seat was sold in 1929 for $625,000, which, today, would be over six million dollars. In recent times, seats have sold for as high as $4 million in the late 1990s and as low as $1 million in 2001. In 2005, seat prices shot up to $3.25 million as the exchange entered into the agreement to merge with Archipelago.

Seat owners received $500,000 in cash per seat and 77,000 shares of the newly formed corporation. The NYSE now sells one-year licenses to trade directly on the exchange. Licenses for floor trading are available for $40,000 and a license for bond trading is available for as little as $1,000 as of 2010. Neither is resalable but may be transferable during a change of ownership of a corporation holding a trading license.

In 2008 NYSE Euronext acquired the American Stock Exchange (subsequently renamed NYSE Amex Equities). Four years later NYSE Euronext was acquired by

DOI 10.1515/9781547400270-014

Intercontinental Exchange, an electronic trader of energy commodities, which sold Euronext but retained ownership of the NYSE. In 2017 the NYSE acquired the National Stock Exchange, based in New Jersey.

What is driving these transactions? As technology has changed the face of securities trading and derivatives markets have grown so significant, stock trading is less profitable, and volume is declining. By combining various exchanges and platforms, not only can cost be significantly reduced, but the franchise in what have become highly competitive markets expanded.

The result today is a global exchange operator diversified across markets including agricultural and energy commodities, credit derivatives, equities and equity derivatives, foreign exchange and interest rate products. Global stock and derivatives franchises now include global clearing house businesses and commodity futures with trading ranging from coffee to coal and crude oil to currencies. And remarkably, this trading is done in a public company format, as the NYSE itself copes with the pressures of quarterly earnings reports.

Consider the change in the roughly 400 years since the Amsterdam Stock Exchange was founded with one issuer's stock listed, and in the two centuries since the Buttonwood Agreement. Also consider the potential impact on corporations who list their securities and the dealers who list them who find themselves having to recognize that they are no longer dominant players on the exchange.

During that period, and throughout the major systemic changes we have reviewed, the corporate form and its board of directors as an organizing structure has, however, endured. Its value is clear, yet the world in which it operates is not only radically changed but will only continue to change more rapidly. The corporation's ability to continue to develop that value depends increasingly on informed and effective boards of directors. The governance revolution at hand requires us to move from our historically somewhat passive position to actively manning the ramparts to protect the enterprises for which we are responsible.

Read More

The Big Board: A History of the New York Stock Market, Sobel, Robert, Free Press, 1965 and Beard Books, 2000

The New York Stock Exchange: Its History, Its Contribution to National Prosperity, and Its Relation to American Finance at the Outset of the Twentieth Century, Vol. 1, Stedman, Edmund Clarence, Classic Reprint, 2010

Wall Street: A History, Geisst, Charles R., Updated Edition, Oxford University Press, 2012

Part III: **The Role of The Board**

Perception of the board's role has changed quite a bit in last 75 years, and there are many legacies of former conventions clouding today's boardrooms. Despite improvements in orientation programs, now called onboarding, new directors can easily become *dis*oriented and it is easy for all directors to lose perspective. Functioning of the board can only be as strong as its weakest link, which is often weak due to lack of a clear and common understanding of board role and responsibilities. The debate over the board's proper role has never been as loud or litigious, though the principles have been in place for over 400 years.

As we marched through those 400 years of history, turmoil, ups and downs and ultimately huge growth, especially following World War II, there were precious few sightings of the board doing its job, and it seems safe to say that the understanding of what that job is has not been broadly understood. These glimpses occurred in response to various kinds of emergencies: getting a bad actor or weak CEO out of the way, serving as proxy for regulators in the '40 Act, providing defenses to unwanted changes of control, and finally, the spate of corporate disasters that piled up due to perceived governance failures in the early 2000s.

For many, the board's role tends to be ignored until it is too late for positive outcomes to occur. As a corporate turnaround executive, a great many of the ugly situations I have been called upon to diagnose and try to remedy over the last several decades have been either caused by or made significantly worse by ineffective board leadership.

Why is this? Confusion over role, perhaps the wrong people are seated and not able to stand up and be counted or challenge the CEO . . .head in sand, or up the river in Egypt, which is what is called denial. Sometimes the board lives in its own ivory tower and convinces itself that it is performing well even in the face of many contrary indicators, as boards are still somewhat cloistered, with relatively few inputs from sources other than the CEO, who can if allowed control the information provided.

Some of the worst corporate meltdowns over the past 60 years can be traced in whole or in part to passive directors. Thinking primarily about placating institutional investors, certain stockholders, proxy advisors, and corporate management, these inattentive and deferential board members seem to lack the basic understanding that their role is to care for the enterprise, to be sure their companies can sustain themselves for the long term.

We will take a look at the role of the board and its purpose, both hot topics, as is the very purpose of the corporation. We have seen that the board is a necessary element in the formation of a corporation in every jurisdiction in the world, and, looking at VOC, its use appears to have been inherited from earlier guild structures, rather than intentionally designed to fit corporations per se. We have also seen that corporations and importantly the limited liability they offer investors are devices used to attract and retain capital, and the board comes along as a corollary of the device.

This lack of clarity, based perhaps on the concept discussed above that the construct of the board is an inherited one, has likely been quite useful as it allows broad interpretation of the role. That broad interpretation also contributes to the continuing confusion surrounding the role of the board and its individual members as the blind men keep encountering different parts of the elephant.

In the years following enactment of SOX, getting governance right has become a significant concern not only in the United States but around the world. The question of what corporate governance is and how it should be done is a topic that is no longer obscure. Discussion of it is going on at a feverish pace around the world. From my point of view, I am thrilled as it has been a misunderstood backwater for far too long. When I walked into my first director role in 1990, I struggled to find a book on the subject. Now, governance codes and policies are proliferating exponentially. Too much may be as difficult to make useful, however, as too little. We will move through the various themes to try to distill the simplicity often found on the other side of complexity.

As we collectively confront continuing technological change, cybercrime and cyberterrorism, emerging cryptocurrencies and the possibilities of block chain technology, coordinated international response from corporate as well as government organizations is increasingly crucial. We no longer have the luxury of arguing over the role of the board. Directors and board must understand that the buck stops with the board, and the board is ultimately in charge. Management is an agent of the board.

Chapter 15
Clarifying the Rights and Roles of the Board and the Shareholders

As this book is being written a drama is unfolding at Wells Fargo & Company. Federal reserve regulators have prohibited further growth until a clean-up plan is submitted and governance issues are cleaned up. It is crystal clear from the Fed's actions that they consider the board to be in charge, and accountable. The publicity surrounding their actions should be a siren call to all directors, both independent and management, that the board must do its job as supervisor, or else consequences will follow. These actions signal that expectations for director and board performance are serious, and the seriousness of possible consequences for failure is rising.

On February 5, 2018, the *New York Times* offered an article about Wells Fargo and its penalties for poor oversight. Wells Fargo & Company got into trouble in 2016 for charging millions of customers for bank accounts they did not want and for auto insurance they did not need. The bank, repeatedly penalized by regulators since then, heard early in January 2018, that the central bank planned stiff new penalties. The Fed's central demand: no further growth until it proved that its governance was substantially improved. The bank would not be able to increase assets above its current level of about $2 trillion, and the bank would need to submit a clean-up plan.

Wells had replaced about half of its scandal-era directors and had seated a new chairman in January 2018. The Fed allegedly wanted more change, perhaps due to their notice of public anger about the government's past practice of taking action against corporations without also holding individuals responsible. The Fed appears to have agreed to the Wells plan to replace four more directors, leaving only three directors who had been around during the misconduct.

None of us wants to be one of the directors associated with Wells Fargo's massive failure of oversight and internal control, nor to be one of those former chairmen receiving a scathing and very public letter from the mighty Federal Reserve. All of us as directors want to help the companies we serve to flourish and provide good value to customers with an attractive return to our shareholders. We need to actively embrace the many and complex and often ambiguous demands of the work of the board of directors.

DOI 10.1515/9781547400270-015

The Board Serves the Corporation as Its Agent

The right to form a corporation, receive a charter, and offer limited liability to shareholders is as we have seen a privilege awarded by each jurisdiction. In the United States, it is each state that provides the power to incorporate, and their corporation statutes provide, with minor variations in language, that a corporation shall be managed by or under the direction of its board of directors. Thus, it is unambiguous that the board is legally responsible for the affairs and well-being of the corporation. This board-centered model of corporate governance is not only the universal norm in American corporate law, it is also the prevailing model of corporate governance around the world.

Corporations are considered legal persons by the laws of their particular jurisdiction. While these laws vary among countries, a corporation's legal person status is a fundamental tenet in all jurisdictions and is conferred by statute. This status allows, for example, the entity to hold property, in its own right, without reference to any particular person. Corporate persons may also sue and be sued and enter into contracts. It also results in the concept of perpetual existence that characterizes the modern corporation. This concept of perpetual life of the entity enlivens the specific role of its board, which is to safeguard that perpetual life as both shareholders and executive management often come and go.

The responsibility is similar to that of a parent. While the child, the corporation, is an infant, the parent, the board, carries a heavy burden of protecting the child and teaching it how to care for itself. As it grows, the parent is teaching it the tools of self-reliance, monitoring its health and safety and the development of its judgment carefully, prepared to step in at any moment should the child veer off course. While the parent may develop confidence in the ability of the growing child to care for itself, its vigilance never ends. And as with parents, the job requires active and careful discernment. There is no one size fits all handbook.

While legally persons, corporations have no ability to act on their own behalf and must rely on agents to act for them. In 1854, Lord Cranworth stated in his judgment in Aberdeen Ry v. Blaikie that: *"A corporate body can only act by agents, and it is, of course, the duty of those agents so to act as best to promote the interests of the corporation whose affairs they are conducting. Such agents have duties to discharge of a fiduciary nature towards their principal. And it is a rule of universal application that no one, having such duties to discharge, shall be allowed to enter into engagements in which he has, or can have, a personal interest conflicting, or which possibly may conflict, with the interests of those whom he is bound to protect... So strictly is this principle adhered to that no question is allowed to be raised as to the fairness or unfairness of the contract entered into..."*

Lord Cranworth references the agents' "principal," which refers to the corporation, or the child, in my analogy. From whom do these agents, protecting their principal, take instruction, and to whom are they accountable? With a single shareholder the answer is simple: the shareholder dictates. As the number of shareholders, and thus competing or conflicting objectives and directions also grow, the question becomes more difficult to answer.

The Powers of the Board

We know that the board is legally responsible for the well-being of the corporation, which, lacking the ability to act for itself, must rely on agents to carry out whatever actions may be required. And we know that in doing so, the agents must put the corporation's well-being above their own. What do we know about who can give instruction to the board?

Until the end of the 19th century, it seems to have been generally assumed that the supreme authority over company affairs rested directly with shareholders, whose wishes were expressed in periodic general meetings to which all shareholders were invited. The board of directors was deemed to act for the company subject to the control of the shareholders.

In 1906, however, the *Court of Appeal in England and Wales* in *Automatic Self-Cleansing Filter Syndicate Co Ltd v Cuninghame* made clear that the division of powers between the board and the shareholders depended on what powers were laid out in the organizing documents required legally to form the entity: the articles of association, known as the certificate of incorporation in the U.S. The decision further stated that where the powers of management were vested in the board, the shareholders could not interfere with their lawful exercise. The articles were held to constitute a contract by which the shareholders had agreed that "the directors and the directors alone shall manage."

In 1935, this doctrine was further expressed in *John Shaw & Sons (Salford) Ltd v Shaw* as follows: "A company is an entity distinct alike from its shareholders and its directors. Some of its powers may, according to its articles, be exercised by directors, certain other powers may be reserved for the shareholders in general meeting. If powers of management are vested in the directors, they and they alone can exercise these powers. The only way in which the general body of shareholders can control the exercise of powers by the articles in the directors is by altering the articles, or, if opportunity arises under the articles, by refusing to re-elect the directors of whose actions they disapprove. They cannot themselves usurp the powers which by the articles are vested in the directors any more than the directors can usurp the powers vested by the articles in the general body of shareholders."

Shareholders in the public company, therefore, are entrusting their money to the care of agents for the corporation with little direct control. In my view, that lack of control is, among other factors, what has prompted complaints and confusion through the centuries as to what on earth the board of directors is up to now, and why are they not doing their job. Shareholders are impotent, and some do not like being in that position.

Public Company Ownership

We move next to the question of who owns the public company. The answer seems clear: its shareholders. Companies, therefore, should be managed in their interest. Yet this widely held assumption is a subject of some intense debate. Let us look further, as better understanding the arguments regarding the nature of ownership of public companies and their related governance rights has important implications for how boards and directors comport themselves.

In 1948, the Court of Appeal of England and Wales ruled that "shareholders are not, in the eyes of the law, part owners of the company." The House of Lords strongly reaffirmed that ruling in 2003, recently echoed in the EU's 2015 Shareholder Directive. Ownership of capital is therefore legally not the same as ownership of the company. Companies are not "owned" by their shareholders but are incorporated bodies which bring together a range of stakeholders — owners and suppliers of capital, labor, suppliers and customers.

In this version of reality, no one "owns" a public company. Public companies should instead be seen as institutions designed to facilitate a dense web of contractual relationships between management, shareholders, employees, and creditors, among others, each providing a mix of tangible and intangible assets. The EU Directive stated that "The position of shareholders is similar to that of bondholders, creditors and employees, all of whom have contractual relationships with companies, but do not own them."

This is a controversial position. Following this approach, shareholders are critically important given their role in contributing their capital to the enterprise, but as an investment for which they expect to receive a return. As such, corporations are the mechanism by which various investments and forms of labor come together to produce goods and services for profit which can be provided to shareholders as beneficiaries. Shareholders are important in this process, but they are not owners of the enterprise.

Adolf Berle and Gardiner Means eloquently phrase the issue in their enduring 1932 book *The Modern Corporation and Private Property:*

> The direction of industry by persons other than those who have ventured their wealth has raised the question of the motive force back of such direction and the effective distribution of the returns from business enterprise.
>
> . . . Such an organization of economic activity rests upon two developments, each of which has made possible an extension of the area under unified control. The factory system, the basis of the industrial revolution, brought an increasingly large number of workers directly under a single management. Then, the modern corporation, equally revolutionary in its effect, placed the wealth of innumerable individuals under the same central control.
>
> By each of these changes the power of those in control was immensely enlarged and the status of those involved, worker or property owner, was radically changed. The independent worker who entered the factory became a wage laborer surrendering the direction of his labor to his industrial master. The property owner who invests in a modern corporation so far surrenders his wealth to those in control of the corporation that he has exchanged the position of independent owner for one in which he may become merely recipient of the wages of capital.
>
> Though the American law makes no distinction between the private corporation and the quasi-public, the economics of the two are essentially different. The separation of ownership from control produces a condition where the interests of owner and of ultimate manager may, and often do, diverge, and where many of the checks which formerly operated to limit the use of power disappear. Size alone tends to give these giant corporations a social significance not attached to the smaller units of private enterprise.
>
> By the use of the open market for securities, each of these corporations assumes obligations towards the investing public which transform it from a legal method clothing the rule of a few individuals into an institution at least nominally serving investors who have embarked their funds in its enterprise. New responsibilities towards the owners, the workers, the consumers, and the State thus rest upon the shoulders of those in control.
>
> In creating these new relationships, the quasi-public corporation may fairly be said to work a revolution. It has destroyed the unity that we commonly call property—has divided ownership into nominal ownership and the power formerly joined to it. Thereby the corporation has changed the nature of profit-seeking enterprise. This revolution forms the subject of the present study.

Functional Principles of the Board

Whether shareholders are owners or not, they certainly have a significant stake in the health and wealth of the corporation in which they are invested, and thus depend on its board of directors to help them realize a return on their investment. As we have seen there are various theories as to the board's intended function, inherited as it was from the pre-corporate era. These are by no means mutually exclusive; each of them has merit and all are useful. Their relative emphasis has shifted over time, from the advisory role expected during the post-war period to the supervisory role we see prevalent today. A brief discussion of the range of roles is summarized below.

Political Legitimacy. This theory suggests that the existence of the board as a group functioning between management and shareholders helped reduce fears of legislatures when asked to enact general incorporation statutes that provided for unelected, unaccountable managers to control the corporation's prospective economic power.

The unifying theme behind medieval parliaments, town councils, guild councils, councils of the Church, and the boards of the trading companies is that they provided the means to comply with the long standing common law principle first seen in Roman law and later repeatedly cited in the Magna Carta and elsewhere that "what touches all shall be consented to by all." This concept has been critical in circumstances when consent by assembly of the entire group was impractical. This reflects the notion that legitimate authority requires consent, regardless of the impact of consent on the quality of decisions and governance.

Central Management. As the number of shareholders grows, the need for centralized decision making regarding allocation of corporate resources as well as acceptance if risk becomes increasingly necessary, especially when shareholder interests are trading, and investment horizons vary. Similarly, management may benefit from the checks and balances of an independent body responsible for long-term health, so it is not buffeted by possibly conflicting and inconsistent demands of disparate shareholders.

Group Decision Making. Stephen Bainbridge in his book *Why a Board?* moves beyond the need for central management in asking why corporate law calls for a board, rather than just a chief executive officer, to be at the apex of the corporation's management. He points to behavioral psychology studies which suggest that groups, such as corporate boards, often produce better decisions than do single individuals when it comes to matters of judgment.

Mediating Claims to Distributions. A different explanation for the use of corporate boards focuses on the need to mediate competing claims of those who have an interest in distributions from the corporation.

Continuity. Another rationale is that the inclusion of multiple parties on the board may have been viewed as a simple mechanism to ensure the ongoing life of the corporation in the event that the chief executive vacates the office, is removed, or dies.

Monitoring of Management. A further argument for the board-centered model of corporate governance holds that boards elected by shareholders exist as a necessary tool to monitor corporate management. Typically, this view starts with the assumption that corporate hierarchy exists to gain the advantage of team production, while minimizing the corporation's agency costs (i.e., shirking and disloyalty) by having higher-level agents monitor lower-level agents. The problem becomes, however, who monitors the highest-level monitors, and on whose behalf.

The traditional economics answer is that the shareholders, as the residual claimants, have the best incentives to monitor the highest-level agents of the corporation. The monitoring rationale supports the rationale that the shareholders should elect the board and the board should appoint the senior executives. It also may contribute to the confusion of the those who believe that the board is intended to be the agent of the shareholders.

Accountability of the Board

The role of the board becomes more complex when we consider it in terms of its goal. What are the markers of its success? You may feel quite comfortable saying that its purpose is to maximize shareholder value, which may seem correct given that shareholders elect directors and have, as we have established, very little further say on what goes on thereafter. Though this shorthand is familiar and maybe even generally accepted, as far as I can see there is little basis for it in the law, though a good many court decisions seem to support it.

Defining Board Success

Two general theories as to the goal of the board have been debated for decades, as corporations have become such enormous factors in industrialized economies. These are often presented as mutually exclusive: the board's purpose is to maximize shareholder value, which is often linked to focus on current share price, versus its purpose is to build a healthy enterprise sustainable over the long term. To my mind as a director, maximizing shareholder value sounds clean and clear until you consider the path to achieving it. Maximize in what time frame, for which shareholders, compared to what standard to enable us to believe we have maximized? A trader's idea of value is different and even opposed to that of a shareholder who plans to hold their shares indefinitely. Its use in conversation can be a showstopper.

Taken to its extreme, maximizing shareholder value can be considered to be at odds with the director's fiduciary duty, which is owed not to the shareholders but to the enterprise. To my mind, working to make the enterprise healthy, profitable and sustainable is the best path to ensuring that the enterprise is delivering value to shareholders, which *can* be considered to be maximizing return to shareholders. In short, in my view boards of directors are charged with developing and sustaining corporate enterprise value.

Years ago, while serving as chairman of a recently reorganized company, the company received a windfall tax refund. A great majority of the shareholders wanted that money distributed to them, as they, former creditors, saw that money as owed to them. The company's position was that the funds were needed to rebuild the enterprise weakened by the reorganization process and a cyclical downturn.

As chairman, I offered to call a special shareholder meeting or to discuss with them the situation if they would sign confidentiality agreements. Accepting neither offer, they instead sued for breach of fiduciary duty and lost. Sometime later, they apologized to me, saying they had simply not understood the legal realities. My view was that my duty to them was owed through building a profitable enterprise; they thought that as the majority of shareholders they could direct me to distribute the money.

This debate may seem academic, but following the financial meltdown of 2008, the earlier major corporate collapses and enactment of Sarbanes Oxley and later Dodd-Frank, focus on corporate governance mechanisms and effectiveness has been broad and intense. Various initiatives that attempt to clarify expectations have brought forth both discussion of the corporate purpose and various agreed principles. There is also continuing disagreement.

We need as a society and as directors and investors to address these concerns as anti-business rumblings are deep and wide. To quote a January 2011, *Harvard Business Review* article called "Shared Value" by Harvard Professor Michael E. Porter and Mark R. Kramer: "The capitalist system is under siege. In recent years business increasingly has been viewed as a major cause of social, environmental, and economic problems. Companies are widely perceived to be prospering at the expense of their communities. Trust in business has fallen to new lows, leading government to set policies that undermine competitiveness and sap economic growth. Business is trapped in a vicious cycle. A big part of the problem lies with companies themselves, which remain trapped in an outdated approach to value creation. Focused on optimizing short term financial performance, they overlook the greatest unmet needs in the market as well as broader influences on their long-term success."

The Purpose of the Corporation Project

There is sufficient concern across various jurisdictions and professional roles that The Purpose of the Corporation Project has gained significant attention. Led by law firm Frank Bold from the Czech Republic, The Purpose of the Corporation Project, provides a strategic, open-source platform for those interested in promoting the long-term health and sustainability of publicly listed companies. The Project has held a series of roundtable discussions around the world and published the results in *Corporate Governance for a Changing World: Report of a Global Roundtable Series*.

* * *

Their rallying cry, as laid out in the Frank Bold Concept Note describing the project, is compelling, and has led to a series of governance roundtables around the world.

We are at a moment in history when we need our corporate businesses more than ever to help us cope with the unprecedented challenges ahead. Many corporations have a greater turnover than the GDP of most countries. 500 corporations control about seventy percent of world trade and each year approximately 3 million new limited liability companies are registered. Therefore, the way these corporations are managed can affect the potential for either positive or negative change.

The maximizing shareholder value theory that came to dominate our thinking and policy-making over the preceding decades has contributed to the recent financial crises. It has been blamed for some of the worst excesses in corporate behavior, externalization of costs, and growing inequality. Academics are now broadly questioning the basic tenets upon which it was built. Policy makers are alive to one of its manifestations, short-termism, and are seeking ways to mitigate that type of thinking. A problem in that regard is that they often simply seek to fix the problem by deploying solutions which serve to further entrench shareholder primacy and in turn facilitate capital markets' pressure on companies. They never think to ask the fundamental question: "Does this paradigm actually work?"

There is now ample evidence that the maximizing shareholder value paradigm is flawed economically, legally and socially. What is lacking is a platform for the development of a coherent vision for a new paradigm of corporate governance which will be more beneficial for society than the present one, but which will still allow corporations to remain profitable and provide jobs and innovative solutions to society's growing needs. In order for such a beneficial paradigm shift to occur there must be a collaboration between academics across a number of disciplines, business leaders, policy makers and civil society.

These words are both ominous and inspiring; ominous in that they suggest that pressure may see further change coming from government, and inspiring in that there may be an opportunity for business and directors to heed these words and refocus their efforts on more than shareholder value as reflected in immediate stock price alone.

As we saw in Part I, for the first 200 years of the existence of the corporate form, corporate charters were approved by government for the purpose of activity that was deemed to be in the public interest, as well as private. Once the use of the corporate form was established and available without government approval specific to the circumstances, you may recall that such charters were limited in life and other restrictions applied.

Short Termism Really Is a Problem

While it can seem heretical to argue with proponents of the maximizing shareholder value mantra that it is counterproductive and often not in shareholders' best interest to run the company that way, the impact of short term focus is clearly damaging. The damage, however, is difficult to measure.

Some commentators link pervasive short termism to the acceptance of maximizing shareholder value as the board and management's focus, a concept that as we have seen took root in the 1970s. As stated above it is difficult analytically to define what maximizing shareholder value means, so we default to the simplest measures: the current stock price, and quarterly earnings trends. The 2008 financial crisis, like the Great Depression and World War II before it, defines important before and after timeframes. Scrutiny of its causes has been significant, and many look to the short termism as the culprit.

In his October 2015, *Harvard Business Review* article "Yes, Short-Termism Really Is a Problem" Roger Martin describes the difficulty of measuring the effect of short termism. He points out that it is not easy to isolate specific causes of results; in his words it is "much more likely that a whole lot of x's combine to cause y and a bunch of other stuff."

He traces the inputs to output back to examine the behaviors of actors in the system to infer their likeliest impact. Results produced by businesses will be a function of the decisions made by executives, and if those decisions do not focus on the long term, it seems reasonable to expect long-term performance of business will suffer.

Several studies help us to see this effect. In one study, John Graham, Campbell Harvey, and Shiva Rajgopal interviewed 400 CFOs of large U.S. public companies. Almost 80% of them said that they would sacrifice economic value in order to meet that quarter's earnings expectations. Though in reality it may be that all respondents would do it, it was remarkable that 80% would actually admit it. Executives might reasonably be expected to avoid any answer that would identify them with that unsavory activity called earnings manipulation.

The second and third studies are linked. Research into the extraordinary rise of corporate buybacks by Bill Lazonick demonstrates that a disproportionate share of corporate earnings are being dedicated to repurchasing company stock rather than investing in future growth. Maybe not an unreasonable action in certain market conditions. A University of Illinois study, however, shows that a large share of buybacks occur when a corporation would miss its earnings per share (EPS) target if not for the effect of the buyback. And the research in general demonstrates that buybacks do boost share price in the short term. So, buybacks, plain and simple, are a tool for boosting short-term performance, regardless of their impact over the long haul.

We believe that executives want to ensure that their companies do as well as possible in the long run. They believe, however, that the capital markets place unproductive constraints on them. According to Martin, they are constantly assessing how much they can invest in the long term before Wall Street makes their lives so miserable that their ability to manage productively at all is at risk. For stronger companies, they can invest nearly all that we would wish them to. But CEOs already under pressure, especially from activists, can invest almost nothing at all.

The current focus of research analysts on organic growth continues the relentless demand for profit growth this quarter and every quarter. Companies respond by underinvesting in long-term growth and buying back stock. For many, buybacks are an explicit, ongoing part of their EPS growth formula, which may include, for example, 5% from organic growth, plus 3% from acquisitions, plus 2% from stock buybacks to arrive at the desired double-digit EPS growth. Then the markets hammer their companies for low top-line growth, telling executives that they won't be able to maintain profit growth without revenue growth. This is hardly a surprise as we reap what we sow — except for hedge funds, which will just swarm unhampered by fiduciary care as they descend like locusts onto the next company they destroy.

Martin offers a compelling analogy. As Malcolm Gladwell pointed out in his piece about concussions and chronic traumatic encephalopathy (CTE) in football, when clever interested parties employ lack of definitive scientific evidence as their defense, they can keep the gravy train going for a long, long time. Coal-mining companies did this to stave off concerns about black lung for half a century. Tobacco companies did it to ignore concerns about lung cancer for decades.

Despite unclear scientific data, if you were a coal miner's wife or the husband of a two-pack-a-day smoker, you would not need definitive scientific evidence. You could see the damage with your own eyes. Yes, we see it with our own eyes. Short-termism is chronic, pervasive, damaging, and a problem.

Read More

"Shared Value", Porter, Michael E. and Kramer, Mark R., Harvard Business Review, January 2011

"Yes, Short-Termism Really Is a Problem" Martin, Roger, Harvard Business Review, October 2015

Corporate Governance for a Changing World: Report of a Global Roundtable Series, Veldman, Jeroen; Gregor, Filip; Morrow, Paih, Purpose of the Corporation Project, 2015

Chapter 16
Assessing the Proliferating Policies and Principles

To continue the thread regarding increased global focus on corporate governance, we turn next to the Organization for Economic Co-operation and Development Principles. The OECD, formed in 1961 by twenty member countries including the United States and later expanded, promotes policies designed to achieve the highest sustainable economic growth and employment and a rising standard of living in member countries, while maintaining financial stability, and thus to contribute to the development of the world economy.

The *G20/OECD Principles of Corporate Governance*, first published as the *Organization for Economic Co-Operation and Development Principles* in 1999, revised in 2004 and revised again and endorsed by the G20 in 2015, are among the most influential guidelines on corporate governance, often referenced by countries developing local codes or guidelines.

This internationally agreed framework consists of more than fifty distinct disclosure items across five broad categories:
- Auditing
- Board and management structure and process
- Corporate responsibility and compliance in organization
- Financial transparency and information disclosure
- Ownership structure and exercise of control rights

The OECD Principles describe the responsibilities of the board; summarized below:
- Board members should be informed and act ethically and in good faith, with due diligence and care, in the best interest of the company and the shareholders.
- Review and guide corporate strategy, objective setting, major plans of action, risk policy, capital plans, and annual budgets.
- Oversee major acquisitions and divestitures.
- Select, compensate, monitor and replace key executives and oversee succession planning.
- Align key executive and board remuneration (pay) with the longer-term interests of the company and its shareholders.
- Ensure a formal and transparent board member nomination and election process.

DOI 10.1515/9781547400270-016

- Ensure the integrity of the corporations accounting and financial reporting systems, including their independent audit.
- Ensure appropriate systems of internal control are established.
- Oversee the process of disclosure and communications.
- Where committees of the board are established, their mandate, composition and working procedures should be well-defined and disclosed.

OECD Encourages Adoption of National Codes of Governance

OECD is careful to point out that there is no single model of good corporate governance. However, work carried out in both OECD and non-OECD countries and within OECD itself has identified some common underlying elements. The Principles build on these common elements and embrace the different models that exist. Following the promulgation of these Principles by OECD and its member countries. OECD has undertaken a review of the governance policies and practices of its members. This has resulted in many countries adopting corporate governance codes of their own.

Other Voices Join in

Building on the work of the OECD, other international organizations, private sector associations and more than twenty national corporate governance codes formed the United Nations Intergovernmental Working Group of Experts on International Standards of Accounting and Reporting (ISAR) to produce their Guidance on Good Practices in Corporate Governance Disclosure.

Other active organizations include investor-led International Corporate Governance Network (ICGN) set up by individuals centered around the ten largest pension funds in the world in 1995 to promote global corporate governance standards. The network is led by investors that manage $18 trillion and are located in fifty different countries. In 2009, the International Finance Corporation and the UN Global Compact released a report, *Corporate Governance: The Foundation for Corporate Citizenship and Sustainable Business,* linking the environmental, social and governance responsibilities of a company to its financial performance and long-term sustainability.

In short, confusion is to an extent increased by those trying to reduce it, in that every organization that touches governance has felt required to climb on the bandwagon and issue its own guidelines. This attention, however, is a marker of the increased importance that all such organizations are placing on getting governance righter. While the proliferation of such codes may be a harbinger of greater regulation to come, they may also indicate that we are at a moment in time in which that attention can be corralled and possible solutions addressed. As major economic power today is concentrated in the hands of a small number of huge corporations on the one side and huge investors on the other, we may be able to find and act on common ground.

Read More

G20/OECD Principles of Corporate Governance, Organization for Economic Co-Operation and Development Principles, 1999, revised 2004 and revised and endorsed by the G20 in 2015

Guidance on Good Practices in Corporate Governance Disclosure, United Nations Intergovernmental Working Group of Experts on International Standards of Accounting and Reporting (ISAR), 2014

Corporate Governance: The Foundation for Corporate Citizenship and Sustainable Business, International Finance Corporation and the UN Global Compact, 2009

Chapter 17
Considering the Proposed New Paradigm

Perhaps the most intriguing proposal as it purports to offer a practical plan to engage investors in the effort to move both investors and corporations to focus on the long-term, the International Business Council of the World Economic Forum released *The New Paradigm, A Roadmap for an Implicit Corporate Governance Partnership Between Corporations and Investors to Achieve Sustainable Long-Term Investment and Growth.* In September 2016. Attorney Martin Lipton, Senior Partner of Wachtell, Rosen, Lipton, & Katz, played a leading role in crafting the ideas below. Whether you agree with it in its entirety or not, it is thought provoking.

Summary Roadmap for the New Paradigm

The following is a snapshot of key expectations for boards of directors and CEOs under the New Paradigm. While its authors argue that it applies to all corporations, they recognize that it particularly applies to larger listed corporations and investors. It offers valuable content for all.

In summary form, under the New Paradigm the corporation's board and senior leadership should jointly:
- *Long-term Strategy and Performance.* Guide, debate and oversee a thoughtful long-term strategy for the corporation and the communication of that strategy to investors using clear, non-boilerplate language. Define the corporation's business model and its vision, taking into account key drivers of strategy, risks and business outcomes. Play a front-and-center role in ensuring that the corporation pursues sustainable long-term value creation.
- *Engagement.* Develop an understanding of shareholder perspectives on the corporation and foster long-term relationships with investors by using appropriate methods of engagement. Establish communication channels with investors and be open to dialogue between independent directors and investors on a "clear day," not just in the midst of a crisis or activist challenge. Respond to investor requests for meetings to discuss governance, the business portfolio and operating strategy, and for greater transparency into the board's practices and priorities. Consider cultivating relationships with government, community and other stakeholders.

DOI 10.1515/9781547400270-017

- *Social Responsibility and ESG/CSR.* Set high standards for the corporation, including with respect to human rights, and the integration of relevant sustainability and environmental, social and governance ("ESG") and corporate social responsibility ("CSR") matters into strategic and operational planning for the achievement of long-term value.
- *Risk Management.* Determine the corporation's reasonable risk appetite, oversee the implementation of state-of-the-art standards for managing risks and seek to ensure that necessary steps are taken to foster a culture of risk-aware and risk-adjusted decision-making. Oversee the implementation by management of standards for compliance with legal and regulatory requirements, monitor compliance and respond appropriately to "red flags."
- *Monitoring and Partnering with Management.* Maintain a close relationship with the CEO and work with management to encourage entrepreneurship, appropriate risk-taking and investment to promote the long-term success of the corporation and to navigate changes in domestic and world-wide economic, social and political conditions. Monitor management's execution of the corporation's long-term strategy and provide advice to management as a strategic partner. Maintain a CEO succession plan in case the CEO becomes unavailable or fails to meet expectations.
- *Tone at the Top.* Establish the appropriate "tone at the top" to actively cultivate a corporate culture that gives high priority to ethical standards, principles of fair dealing, professionalism, integrity, full compliance with legal requirements, ethically sound strategic goals and long-term sustainable value creation.

Investors. Importantly, the New Paradigm also lays out expectations for institutional investors. To summarize, an investor should:
- *Consistent Support for Long-Term Strategies.* Provide steadfast support for the corporation in pursuing reasonable strategies for long-term growth. Speak out publicly against short-term demands in order to minimize the disruptive impact of activists.
- *Integrated Long-Term Investment Approach.* Establish a firm-wide culture of long-term thinking and patient capital that discourages over-reliance on short-term performance metrics. Promote stewardship principles by encouraging portfolio managers to act consistently with the long-term time horizons of its clients and asset owners. Design employee compensation to discourage sacrificing long-term value to capture short-term swings in stock prices. Consider value-relevant sustainability, citizenship and ESG/CSR factors when developing its own investment strategies.

- *Engagement.* Actively listen to corporations and review their communications about strategy, long-term objectives and governance. Communicate preferences and expectations with respect to engagement with the corporation. Provide candid, direct feedback on the corporation's strategy, performance, management, board, governance and engagement.
- *Collaboration and Feedback.* If the investor is concerned about a corporation's strategy or performance, give prompt notice to the corporation of its concerns and invite the corporation to privately engage with the investor. If the investor publicly discloses a negative opinion about the strategy, performance, compensation or management of a corporation, as part of that disclosure, state whether the investor provided an opportunity to the corporation to engage.
- *Voting Decisions.* Actively vote, or refrain from voting, shares on an informed basis in a manner consistent with the best interests of its clients that have long-term investment goals, without abdicating decision-making to proxy advisory firms.
- *Disclosures.* Proactively disclose the investor's policies and preferences, including with respect to its adoption of the New Paradigm, preferred procedures and contacts for engagement, long-term investment policies and evaluation metrics, positions on ESG and CSR matters, policies on outside consultants, governance procedures it considers significant, views on quarterly reports and earnings guidance, guidelines for its relations with short-term financial activists and voting policies.

The New Paradigm Attempts a Synthesis of Good Corporate Governance Concepts

The New Paradigm is a synthesis of corporate governance codes and various efforts underway to articulate a new corporate governance framework, including Common Sense Principles of Corporate Governance issued by a group of CEOs of major corporations and investors on July 21, 2016 and the Business Roundtable's Principles of Corporate Governance issued on August 4, 2016. At its core, the New Paradigm is a simple quid pro quo that recalibrates the relationship between public corporations and their major institutional investors.

Following this approach, corporations are to embrace core principles of good governance and, in seeking to cultivate relationships with investors, demonstrate that they have engaged, thoughtful boards overseeing reasonable, long-term business strategies. Institutional investors are seeking not simply accountability, but also active involvement and credibility, from CEOs and boards of directors. In exchange for corporations' commitment, institutional investors are consistently to provide the support and patience needed to permit the realization of long-term value and engage in constructive dialogue as the primary means for addressing subpar strategies or operations.

Institutional investors are to embrace stewardship principles and develop an understanding of a corporation's long-term business strategy. This requires going beyond compliance-oriented governance mandates and, instead, working to develop relationships with corporations and thoughtful analyses of the needs and goals of each corporation. Financial metrics such as total shareholder return and earnings targets will be balanced against a more holistic understanding of firm value.

Where institutional investors have concerns, they are exhorted to directly engage with the corporation, quietly. Investors are also clearly to communicate their expectations and policies for engagement and long-term investment by a corporation, as well as their methods of evaluating a corporation's success in meeting expectations. Finally, they are to describe steps they have taken in structuring their own business and compensation policies to support a long-term perspective.

Its proponents argue that without a private-sector consensus around something like the New Paradigm, the unprecedented power of a relatively small number of institutional investors over virtually all major corporations combined with the demonstrated success of activists in exploiting short-term opportunities will provoke further regulatory and legislative reforms.

These purportedly include imposing robust fiduciary duties on asset managers to take into account the long-term objectives of their ultimate beneficiaries when engaging with issuers or voting; using tax laws to encourage long-term investment or to significantly discourage short-term trading; prohibiting quarterly reports and quarterly guidance; regulating executive compensation to discourage managing and risk taking in pursuit of short-term incentives; imposing enhanced disclosure obligations on both corporations and institutional investors; reversing shareholder governance rights in order to restore a more director-centric governance model; imposing higher standards with respect to institutional investors' independence and others.

Over the course of history, the concentration of power in the hands of a few has stimulated governmental action in adopting sweeping reforms, which can be both beneficial and overreaching, or even detrimental. As we have seen, the corporate form is a creation of the state, conceived originally as a privilege linked to securing the public good and welfare. Though often forgotten in our daily life, government retains its prerogative to alter the rules governing corporations, notwithstanding claims by shareholders to spurious "intrinsic" rights.

To my mind, the extraordinary aspect of the so-called New Paradigm is not the prescriptions for improved corporate governance, which offers a nicely articulated statement of the work directors and boards have long been charged with doing. Instead, it is that it purports to get and keep the commitment of institutional investors in significant enough volume that the pressures brought by "quarterly capitalism" might be reduced. Yes, we have a small number of investors who are so large they have little choice but to invest in the shares of large companies for the long haul.

What percentage, however, do these shareholders represent of the capitalization of the companies involved? And how does this tally with the short holding period and the high turnover rates of shares we have discussed? Many of these investors, if not most, are in turn fiduciaries for their investors, who may in fact be long-term investors. That does not, however, make them long-term investors in the particular manager's strategy. Mutual funds and ETFs are priced daily and offer daily liquidity. Their investors, therefore, long accustomed to measuring comparative performance based on near term results, can become impatient and vote with their feet, as they routinely do.

Pension funds, generally long-term investors, are overseen by boards who serve as fiduciaries for plan beneficiaries. Most engage investment management firms to manage the plan's funds. Such managers are not only chosen on the basis of relative performance compared to a universe and often unmanaged indices of market results as well but are periodically measured against such benchmarks. The measurement periods include monthly, quarterly, and annual periods. Pension plan fiduciaries are working to ensure that they can meet their plan liabilities to beneficiaries and may not be able to overlook performance that is not competitive for more than a short period.

That said, the broad dialogue about these possibilities between and among large corporations and large investors must be seen as a positive step, and one that might assist in offsetting the pressure that activist hedge fund shareholders bring to bear. If we have an extraordinary opportunity at hand based on major corporate boards and their largest investors agreeing to adopt and act on these common principles, we do not want to have failed to consider it.

Larry Fink, in his capacity as chief executive officer and chairman of the board of Blackrock, has developed the habit of sending an annual letter to large corporate chief executive offers, and making it public. In his letter, Mr. Fink implores CEOs to lay out long-term plans each year and indicates that Blackrock will expect to see these plans, reviewed and approved by their boards, as part of its investment process. In its own words on its website, Blackrock is the leading global asset manager, serving many of the world's largest companies, pension funds, foundations, and public institutions as well as millions of people from all walks of life.

Without taking a position regarding the content of Mr. Fink's letter, it is clear that his comments reflect a trend. In March 2016, The Investment Association, a British organization that represents leading institutional investors, issued a report with the encouragement and participation of the British government that describes its stewardship principles:

> While the primary responsibility for promoting the success of a company rests with the Board and its oversight of management, investors play a crucial role in holding the Board to account for the fulfillment of its responsibilities. Shareholder stewardship should aim to promote the long-term success of companies in such a way that the ultimate providers of capital will also prosper. In this sense, there should be a natural alignment of interests: effective stewardship should benefit companies, investors and the economy as a whole.
>
> Supporting long-term investment and productivity requires effective dialogue between investors and companies. By exercising stewardship responsibilities effectively, investors are well placed to ensure companies adopt a long-term approach. For example, through purposeful dialogue, shareholders can demonstrate support for expenditures that will boost productivity and challenge companies compromising it as a result of poor capital management.

So, too, the 2016 International Corporate Governance Network Stewardship Principles:

> Engage and Communicate with Corporations. Investors should be active listeners and, where appropriate, they should be proactive in engaging in dialogue with a corporation as part of a long-term relationship. Engagement can be an especially effective means of bringing about change when the relationship between a corporation and an investor is based on trust, respect and a collaborative mentality, all of which require time and energy to develop. In order to dedicate sufficient time and attention to effective engagement, investors should increase their in-house staffing and capabilities, should not hire a consultant that will not engage with a corporation on the same basis on which the investor will engage and should take the time to understand a corporation's business plan and long-term strategy and get to know its management.

Proposed Investor Behavior

The proposed New Paradigm calls for investors to consider going on the public record to speak out against the short-term demands of activist investors, to help reduce the disruption their demands can have when unchallenged by other shareholders whose interests are inconsistent with their purportedly short-term investment horizon. It also calls for institutional investors to be mindful of the message their support will send to other corporations that may be considering whether to tailor their business strategies to meet short-term objectives and avoid attack by an activist.

New Paradigm Proposes Integrated Long-Term Investment Approach

The March 2015 "*Long-Term Portfolio Guide*" by Focusing Capital on the Long Term, an organization founded by the Canada Pension Plan Investment Board and McKinsey & Company, provides a number of suggestions for actions an investor should consider to promote a long-term perspective throughout its own organization. These suggestions include establishment of a firm-wide culture of long-term thinking and patient capital that persists through cycles of short-term turbulence, emphasizes disciplined research of corporations' fundamentals that have the ability to generate real long-term value, discourages over-reliance on stock price and short-term quantitative metrics as performance indicators, and allows portfolio managers to remain focused on long-term outcomes and to act consistently with the time horizons of its clients and asset owners.

The New Paradigm stresses that investment professionals should be compensated by the institutional investors for whom they work in a way that encourages them to invest for the long term and discourages them from sacrificing long-term value in order to capture short-term swings in stock prices. Some institutions, for example, have implemented clawback arrangements or required employees to invest in "parallel portfolios." Evaluations and compensation based on qualitative assessments, such as consistent adherence to agreed-upon strategies, are described as useful.

Proposed Integration of Citizenship Matters into Investment Strategy

The New Paradigm asserts that institutional investors may wish to consider the following, some of which are already underway by leading institutional investors: (i) creation of portfolio ESG risk profiles to stimulate discussion among portfolio managers on ESG factors; (ii) incorporation of ESG metrics into firm-wide risk management and investment platforms; (iii) training of portfolio managers on identifying material ESG factors for corporations; (iv) research of individual ESG factors and their materiality to corporations in specific sectors to help inform investment analysis and risk measurement; and (v) engagement in robust dialogue with corporations with respect to the thinking of management and boards on the importance of ESG factors.

Proposed Disclosure of Investor Policies and Preference

As part of their engagement efforts, the New Paradigm asks that investors clearly communicate their policies and consider disclosing:
–   Whether it has adopted the New Paradigm as a framework for its relationship with a corporation
–   Its preferred procedures for engagement and its primary contacts for engagement with corporations
–   Its investment policies, the metrics it will use to evaluate a corporation's success and any other expectations that the investor has for corporations
–   Its position on ESG and CSR matters, including with respect to integration of relevant metrics into strategy, effects on long-term firm value and a corporation's disclosure of such matters
–   Whether it uses consultants to evaluate strategy, performance and transactions and how a corporation can engage with those consultants
–   The governance procedures it considers significant and how the investor considers those procedures in evaluating strategy, performance and transactions
–   Its views as to the manner in which a corporation should make its mandatory quarterly reports and its views as to the desirability of a corporation giving guidance as to quarterly earnings
–   Whether it invests in short-term financial activists and its policy with respect to discussing its questions or concerns about a corporation's performance with short-term financial activists
–   Its procedures and policies with respect to voting, or refraining from voting, on issues submitted by a corporation for shareholder approval, including the identity and qualifications of the investor's employees who are making those decisions.

Many if not most of these recommendations for institutional investor behavior would be valuable to corporations as well as to the underlying investors in their investment strategies.

There are significant challenges, however, regarding achieving adoption beyond the largest investors. Institutional investors operate in a highly competitive marketplace. Many may not have the ability to fund some of the above concepts without penalizing performance. Those that do have the funding are comprised of many portfolio managers charged with executing various strategies, measured by their underlying investors on a short-term basis, and bringing them all together to adopt a single set of policies may not be feasible. The effort, however, will be interesting to watch.

And Now Comes CIRCA, Council for Investor Rights and Corporate Accountability

At the other end of the spectrum, we find Pershing Square, Carl Icahn, Elliott Management, Third Point and JANA Partners forming the Council for Investor Rights and Corporate Accountability (CIRCA) to advocate for legislation to protect the agendas of short-term financial activists. From its website: "CIRCA's mission is to get out the facts about activist investing and the role activist investors play in our economy. Activist investors directly benefit all public shareholders, including the investment vehicles for all of the country's stock-based savings vehicles, such as mutual funds and public and private pension funds. We seek to promote a dialogue that respects the value created by activist investors and fosters their involvement in improving the governance and business policies of all of our public companies, which are so vital to our economy and the health of our public and private pension systems."

And more from their blog: "Are activist investors mainly out to make a fast buck or are they a long-term plus for the companies they target? A paper that can lay claim to being the largest and broadest investigation of this hotly debated issue finds the latter to be generally the case.

A study published in 2017 *Are Activist Investors Good or Bad for Business? Evidence from Capital Market Prices, Informed Traders, and Firm Fundamentals* by Edward Swanson and Glen Young of Texas A&M University essayed the largest sample of activist events yet examined – some 5,000 initiatives over 21 years. They report that the interventions not only occasioned a short-term boost in stock price but, on average, superior stock performance and strengthened company fundamentals over the long term. In all, the study embraces 4,870 activist campaigns involving 2,652 unique firms, with the researchers monitoring indicators from two years before interventions to two years after.

Turning now to looking directly at what activists often do and the impact they can have on corporate management and boards, we look at the 2014 effort by Pershing Square Capital Management's Bill Ackman to complete a takeover of Allergan by Valeant. This description and the analysis that follows are drawn from the work of Harvard Business School Professors Joseph Bower and Lynne

Paine presented in the *Harvard Business Review* article "The Error at the Heart of Leadership," which appeared in the May–June 2017 issue.

Activist Playbook

As a first step, the activist acquires shares in the targeted company—typically somewhere between 5% and 10%, but sometimes less than 1%. He then asserts himself by issuing directives, often publicly released. To add to his leverage, he will often alert other hedge funds to his actions, and separately they may also invest, firming what has come to be called a "wolf pack." The directives make liberal use of the language of ownership.

In 2014, for example, to advance a takeover of Allergan by Valeant Pharmaceuticals, Ackman attacked Allergan's board for failing to do what the directors were paid to do "on behalf of the Company's owners." In one letter to the Allergan board, Ackman challenged the board's professionalism: "Your actions have wasted corporate resources, delayed enormous potential value creation for shareholders, and are professionally and personally embarrassing for you."

Whether true or not, there is nothing to stop him from making and publicizing whatever assertions he likes and depending on the size of his position and the length of time he has held it, he may not need to disclose his holdings. To add further to the damage such behavior can cause, his firm is free to invest throughout the capital structure and even to short the target's stock, which reminds us of Isaac de la Maire.

As Ian Gow and Suraj Srinivasan (with others) have documented in their study of nearly 800 campaigns at U.S. companies from 2004 to 2012, activists tend to focus on capital structure, strategy, and governance. They typically call for some combination of cutting costs, adding debt, buying back shares, issuing special dividends, spinning off businesses, reconstituting the board, replacing the CEO, changing the strategy, and selling the company or its main asset. Tax reduction is another element of many activist programs.

Unheeded, an activist may initiate a proxy fight in an attempt to replace incumbent board members with directors more willing to do the activist's bidding. In a few instances, activists have even offered their chosen nominees special bonuses to stand for election or additional incentives for increasing shareholder value in their role as directors, which certainly betrays their lack of respect for the role.

More companies may be being targeted—473 worldwide in the first half of 2016 (including 306 in the United States), up from 136 worldwide in all of 2010—and activists' demands seem to be being met in a number of cases. In the United States in 2015, 69% of demands were at least partially satisfied, the highest proportion since 2010. Activists are also gaining clout in the boardroom, where they won 397 seats at U.S. companies in 2014 and 2015. Although activist hedge funds saw outflows of some $7.4 billion in the first three quarters of 2016, assets under management were estimated at more than $116 billion in late 2016, up from $2.7 billion in 2000.

Proxy Fights and Shareholder Candidates

While we look at activist strategies, let us also look at the shareholder's right to present director nominees at annual meetings. The most important barrier facing the presentation of such candidates continues to be the expense of compliance with the SEC's proxy rules as well as cost of the printing, mailing and publicity involved in engaging in an election contest in a diffusely-owned firm. The rules that emerged in the 1950s strongly favored the incumbents, finding that the dissidents must fund their campaign from their own pockets.

As a practical matter, the dissidents are reimbursed only if they successfully gain control of the board. Proposals for proportional reimbursement based on the dissident's fraction of the vote have not gained traction. In January 2007, however, the SEC adopted a rule that would allow an insurgent to provide internet availability of proxy materials rather than to have to print and mail the materials, though it must provide a paper copy to any requesting shareholder. Given increasingly concentrated shareholdings, it may be that shareholder candidates will emerge.

The Bower and Paine Analysis of Maximizing Shareholder Value as Corporate Goal

In the fall of 2014, Allergan shareholder Pershing Square Capital Management leader Bill Ackman became increasingly frustrated with Allergan's board of directors. The reason: their apparent failure: refusing to negotiate with Valeant Pharmaceuticals about its unsolicited bid to take over Allergan—a bid that Ackman himself had helped engineer in a novel alliance between a hedge fund and a would-be acquirer.

Ackman cited Valeant's plan to cut Allergan's research budget by 90% as "really the opportunity." Valeant CEO Mike Pearson assured analysts that "all we care about is shareholder value." These comments encapsulate a way of thinking about the governance and management of companies that seems to have become pervasive in the financial community and much of the business world, perhaps because all parties in the financial system are evaluated and compensated based on short term results, as in "what have you done for me lately?"

It again showcases the idea that management's objective should be maximizing value for shareholders, but it addresses a wide range of topics—from performance measurement and executive compensation to shareholder rights, the role of directors, and corporate responsibility. This thought system has been embraced not only by hedge fund activists like Ackman but also by institutional investors more generally, along with many boards, managers, lawyers, academics, and even some regulators and lawmakers. If this book achieves nothing else, I hope it will help thoughtful people consider these concepts and the dangerous folly they represent.

In the contest between Allergan and Valeant, the playing field was famously not level. A member of Allergan's board who held shares in Valeant would have been expected to refrain from voting on the deal or promoting Valeant's bid. But Allergan shareholders with a stake in both companies were free to buy, sell, and vote as they saw fit, with no obligation to act in the best interests of either company. Institutional investors holding shares in thousands of companies regularly act on deals in which they have significant interests on both sides, while preaching publicly about the need for companies to manage for the long term.

Consider this: should managers and boards follow the edicts of letters like Mr. Fink's and focus on long-term value to the detriment of short term results, organizations such as Blackrock might take advantage of lower values to increase their positions and possibly engineer corporate combinations to improve their own results. Taken to an extreme degree, Mr. Fink's letters, written as they are, by the head of an organization that is assessed on its own short- term results, could be seen as a way of jawboning market behavior in his own firm's interest.

My point is that in a well-ordered economy, rights and responsibilities go together. Giving shareholders the rights of ownership while exempting them from responsibility creates a malicious hazard by fomenting opportunism and misuse of corporate assets. When shareholders use their positions, visible and invisible, to influence specific corporate decisions, they present a serious risk.

The issue is at its most stark when temporary holders of large blocks of shares determine that they should and will reconstitute a company's board, change its management, or restructure its finances. Their goal is to win and unfettered by securities regulation or the rules of discretion and decorum that inhibit corporate response, they will stop at nothing in their effort to drive up its share price. Victorious, they can then sell and move on to another target without ever having to answer for their intervention's impact on the company or other parties.

Reliance on what can be said to be a spurious doctrine of alignment between company and shareholder gain spreads moral hazard throughout a company and narrows management's field of vision. Among other issues, this agency theory depends on an impossibility: that all shareholders want the company to be run in a way that maximizes their own economic return in the same investment horizon.

Shareholders have varying investment objectives, tolerance for risk, and time horizons. Pension funds may seek current income and preservation of capital. Endowments may seek long-term growth. Proxy voting records indicate that shareholders are divided on many of the resolutions put before them. They may also view strategic opportunities differently.

In the months after Valeant announced its bid, Allergan officials met with a broad swath of institutional investors. As cited by Bower and Paine's article, according to Allergan's lead independent director, Michael Gallagher, "The diversity of opinion was as wide as could possibly be."

The notion that all shareholders have the same interests and that those interests are the same as the corporation's masks provides intellectual cover for powerful shareholders who seek to divert the corporation to their own purposes while claiming to act on behalf of all shareholders. To combat this, we need to govern in a way that takes the corporation seriously as an institution in society and centers on the sustained performance of the enterprise.

The Dangers of Agency Theory

Since Meckling and Jensen laid it out in their 1976 paper mentioned above, agency theory has attracted a wide following and provided the intellectual rationale for changes in practice that have enhanced the power of shareholders and shifted governance toward a shareholder centered model. This is a dangerous trend that needs correction, as taken to its logical extreme, it may ultimately drive value out of public markets.

In 1997 the Business Roundtable issued a statement declaring that "the paramount duty of management and of boards of directors is to the corporation's stockholders" and that "the principal objective of a business enterprise is to generate economic returns to its owners." A response to pressure from institutional investors, it revised the Roundtable's earlier position that "the shareholder must receive a good return, but the legitimate concerns of other constituencies also must have the appropriate attention." According to surveys by the Aspen Institute, many business school graduates regard maximizing shareholder value as their top responsibility.

The sources of alleged value creation by activists need to be analyzed carefully. Though research on this question is limited, one study suggests that the positive abnormal returns associated with the announcement of a hedge fund intervention can be, for example, a transfer of wealth from workers to shareholders. The study found that workers' hours decreased, and their wages stagnated for the three years after an intervention.

Other studies have found that some of the gains for shareholders come at the expense of bondholders. Still other academic work links aggressive pay-for-stock- performance arrangements to various misdeeds involving harm to consumers, damage to the environment, and irregularities in accounting and financial reporting. Shareholders' gains are sometimes simply transfers from the public purse, such as when management improves earnings by shifting a company's tax domicile to a lower- tax jurisdiction—a move often favored by activists, Similarly, budget cuts that eliminate exploratory research aimed at addressing some of society's most vexing challenges may enhance current earnings but at a cost to society as well as to the company's prospects for the future.

It may be that measures to enhance shareholders' accountability can be useful. Suggestions include the notion that activist shareholders seeking significant influence or control could, for example, be treated as fiduciaries for the corporation or restricted by securities laws in their ability to sell or hedge the value of their shares. Regulators might be inclined to call for greater transparency regarding their beneficial ownership of shares and their own governance. Regulators might close the ten-day window currently afforded between the time a hedge fund acquires a disclosable stake and the time the holding must actually be disclosed.

The time has come to challenge the agency-based model of corporate governance. Its mantra of maximizing shareholder value is distracting companies and their leaders from the innovation, strategic renewal, and investment in the future that require their attention. History has shown that with enlightened management and sensible regulation, companies can play a useful role in helping society adapt to constant change.

Read More

The New Paradigm, A Roadmap for an Implicit Corporate Governance Partnership Between Corporations and Investors to Achieve Sustainable Long-Term Investment and Growth; Lipton, Martin, Rosenblum, Steven A., Niles, Sabastian V., et al and Drexler, Michael, World Economic Forum, September, 2016.

"Long-Term Value Summit Discussion Report", Focusing Capital on the Long Term, 2015

"Global Stewardship Principles", International Corporate Governance Network, 2016

"Focusing Capital on the Long Term", Barton, Dominic and Wiseman, Mark, Harvard Business Review, January-February 2014 Issue

"The Kay Review of UK Equity Markets and Long-Term Decision Making", European Corporate Governance Institute, 2012

"Commonsense Principles of Corporate Governance", Popper, Margaret and Verbinnen, Sard, 2016

"Hedge Fund Activism and their Long Term Consequences: Unanswered Questions to Bebchuk, Brav and Jiang" Allaire, Yvan and Dauphin, Francois, Institute for Governance of Private and Public Organizations, August 2011

"Is Short-Term Behavior Jeopardizing the Future Prosperity of Business?" The Conference Board, 2015 Report

"Overcoming Short-termism: A Call for a More Responsible Approach to Investment and Business Management", The Aspen Institute Business & Society Program, 2009

"Securing Our Nation's Economic Future: A Sensible, Nonpartisan Agenda to Increase Long-Term Investment and Job Creation in the United States", Keynote Address by Leo E. Strine, Jr., First Annual American College of Governance Counsel Dinner, 2015

"Principles of Corporate Governance", The Business Roundtable, 2016

"The UK Stewardship Code", Financial Reporting Council, September 2012

Long-Term Portfolio Guide: Reorienting Portfolio Strategies and Investment Management, Focus Capital on the Long Term, 2015

"The Error at the Heart of Corporate Leadership", Bower, Joseph L. and Paine, Lynne S., Harvard Business Review, May-June 2017

"Consequences to Directors of Shareholder Activism" Gow, Ian D., Shin, Sean Sa-Pyung & Srinivasan, Suraj; Working Knowledge Review, Harvard Business School, 2014

Part IV: **Doing the Job**

Only directors themselves can improve governance, and then only if they know the rules of the game and play, as Einstein said, better than the rest. Learn the rules, play as a team with clear goals, and work together to win, which means winning and keeping the confidence of investors and stakeholders by delivering sustainable results in an ethical manner and leading them all toward well-developed corporate goals. It is time and past time for directors and boards to move from defense to offense in fulfilling their responsibilities.

Boards Must Protect Corporation Regardless of Conflicting Agendas

Whatever conclusions we form from the above discussion of the role of shareholders, the pressures of short termism, the behavior and motives of shareholder activists, the purpose of the corporation, and the potential of the New Paradigm in Corporate Governance, it is absolutely clear that the board has an ever more critical role to play in discerning the corporation's path forward and helping management achieve it. Attorney Ira Milstein calls for a new breed of "Activist Director" to seize the initiative and partner with management to reject short-term outlooks, plan a future based on growth and innovation, and take responsibility for corporate organization, strategy, and efficiency.

To do that, and to transform boards as a whole into effective active parties, there needs to be both education and agreement as to the functioning of the board. Much of this is in place. We have good templates for board structure, as spelled out by exchange listing requirements and the SEC. There are, however, various ways of carrying them out, which I will oversimplify and call active vs. passive engagement, or playing offense versus defense.

We have established that by law the board of directors is the corporation's ultimate authority. Turning this into reality in terms of behavior is, however, not simple. Of course, in emergencies, boards, like parents, are expected to somehow fix the problem. But how to include the board in corporate activities in such a way as to reduce emergencies? How to create agreement on the part of both management and directors as to how they can best perform their respective duties every day?

As we have seen, the voices aligned against the traditional view, the view of the board that adheres to corporate law and the clear role of the board as fiduciary for and agent of the corporation, are loud in their insistence that the board exists to serve shareholders as owners. Discussion of the New Paradigm inevitably focuses on the bookends involved: the largest corporations and investors.

These super-sized organizations may be able to find common cause as to how to encourage long-term thinking on both the invested and the investor's parts. Interestingly, if they can, the result will bring us full circle. The concentration of investor ownership and the scale of the largest companies may make possible an alliance that is remarkably comparable to what was possible when companies and capital were private. And these companies and investors provide an important bellwether for everybody else.

Even the discussion of the whys and wherefores of doing so will bring thought provoking and we hope helpful dialogue into the boardroom and between boards and shareholders. Regardless of this discussion, however, boards continue to have primary responsibility for protecting the enterprise and its prospects. Lessons for all directors can be gleaned regarding the best standards expected in the doing of the job.

In this section we will review the organization of the board and its work and attempt to offer some context to its execution. We will draw from, among others, the New York Stock Exchange, various surveys, and the New Paradigm's cogent description of the longstanding mechanisms of fulfilling board responsibilities. Its repetition, with some newer bells and whistles, and apparent endorsement by multiple investors and investor groups provides valuable reinforcement to directors and boards doing battle with proponents of the meretricious but difficult to refute arguments associated with Jensen and Meckling and proponents of agency theory.

Chapter 18
Review Issues for Boards to Address Highlighted by NYSE

To begin our journey through understanding the specific responsibilities of the board now, we turn to the *New York Stock Exchange Governance Guide*. I lay out the whole list here, and in the chapters that follow further explore the areas most critical in my experience. The 2014 edition identifies the following list of expectations (boldfaced emphasis added):

- *Establish the appropriate "tone at the top"* to actively cultivate a corporate culture that gives high priority to ethical standards, principles of fair dealing, professionalism, integrity, full compliance with legal requirements, and ethically sound strategic goals.
- *Choose the CEO,* monitor his or her performance, and have a succession plan in case the CEO becomes unavailable or fails to meet performance expectations.
- *Maintain a close relationship with the CEO* and work with management to encourage entrepreneurship, appropriate risk-taking, and investment to promote the long-term success of the company (despite the constant pressures for short-term performance) and to navigate the dramatic changes in domestic and worldwide economic, social, and political conditions.
- *Organize the business, and maintain the collegiality, of the board* and its committees so that each of the increasingly time-consuming matters that the board and board committees are expected to oversee receives the appropriate attention of the directors.
- *Approve the company's annual operating plan* and long- term strategy, monitor performance, and provide advice to management as a strategic partner.
- *Develop an understanding of shareholder perspectives* on the company and foster long-term relationships with shareholders, as well as deal with the requests of shareholders for meetings to discuss governance and the business portfolio and operating strategy.
- *Evaluate the escalating demands* of corporate governance activists designed to increase shareholder power.
- *Work with management and advisors to review the company's business and strategy,* with a view toward minimizing vulnerability to attacks by activist hedge funds.
- *Evaluate the board's performance,* and the performance of the board committees and each director.

DOI 10.1515/9781547400270-018

- *Determine the company's reasonable risk appetite* (financial, safety, cyber, political, reputation, etc.), see to the implementation by management of state-of-the-art standards for managing risk, monitor the management of those risks within the parameters of the company's risk appetite, and oversee that necessary steps are taken to foster a culture of risk- aware and risk-adjusted decision making throughout the organization.
- *Plan for and deal with crises, especially crises where the tenure of the CEO is in question,* where there has been a major disaster or a risk management crisis, or where hard-earned reputation is threatened by a product failure or a socio-political issue. Many crises are handled less than optimally because management and the board have not been proactive in planning to deal with crises, and because the board cedes control to outside counsel and consultants.
- *Determine executive compensation to achieve the delicate balance* of enabling the company to recruit, retain, and incentivize the most talented executives, while also avoiding media and populist criticism of "excessive" compensation and taking into account the implications of the "say-on-pay" vote.
- *Face the challenge of recruiting and retaining highly qualified directors* who are willing to shoulder the escalating workload and time commitment required for board service, while at the same time facing pressure from shareholders and governance advocates to embrace "board refreshment", including issues of age, length of service, independence, expertise, gender and diversity, and provide compensation for directors that fairly reflects the significantly increased time and energy that they must now spend in serving as board and board committee members.
- *See to the implementation by management of state-of-the-art standards for compliance* with legal and regulatory requirements, monitor compliance, and respond appropriately to "red flags."
- *Take center stage whenever there is a proposed transaction that creates a seeming conflict between the best interests of stockholders and those of management,* including takeovers and attacks by activist hedge funds. Recognize that shareholder litigation against the company and its directors is part of modern corporate life and should not deter the board from approving a significant acquisition or other material transaction or rejecting a merger proposal or a hostile takeover bid, all of which is within the business judgment of the board.
- *Set high standards of social responsibility for the company,* including human rights, and monitor performance and compliance with those standards.
- *Oversee relations with government, community, and other constituents.* Review corporate governance guidelines and committee charters and tailor them to promote effective board functioning.

Interestingly, the NYSE recognized that to follow these general principles, it is not always necessary to follow the common governance gospel, such as the arbitrary edict that says, "independence is good, insiders are bad." The guide continues:

To meet these expectations, it will be necessary for major public companies
- To have a sufficient number of directors to staff the requisite standing and special committees and to meet expectations for diversity;
- To have directors who have knowledge of, and experience with, the company's businesses, even though meeting this requirement may result in boards with a greater percentage of directors who are not "independent";
- To have directors who are able to devote sufficient time to preparing for and attending board and committee meetings;
- To provide the directors with regular tutorials by internal and external experts as part of expanded director education; and
- To maintain a truly collegial relationship among and between the company's senior executives and the members of the board.

In addition to overseeing compensation and risk and finding the right company leaders, board members must keep profitability and increasing shareholder value in their crosshairs. Without meeting these goals, all the others hold little value. Therefore, the board's role in shepherding strategic planning for future growth is imperative, particularly in an environment where competitive change happens quickly.

Executing the Work of the Board

There are now many sources of information on how the work of the board is typically organized. Directors and other students of governance will want to review a few of them and will also want to consult their own legal counsel for current interpretations. In addition, many law firms provide excellent handbooks covering the legal requirements and fiduciary standards relevant to the board's work. Another important source to consult is the NYSE's listing requirements.

In the following chapter, I take some headlines from the NYSE's guide and elaborate on why and how to implement these directives. I also add my own thoughts on other mission critical areas of focus.

Chapter 19
Establish the Appropriate "Tone at the Top"

No matter how many policies and guidelines a corporation issues regarding standards of behavior, the lessons that matter are not expressed in writing. Tone at the top is all about trust. Absent trust, leaders cannot lead. Trust and clarity as to values go hand in hand. Employees, senior and middle management, vendors, professional advisors who work with the company are people. People watch what leaders do, and how they do it. And they talk about it, at the water cooler, on social media, in the bathroom. If leaders do not act in a trustworthy and ethical manner following consistent shared values, it will be noticed, its effect amplified throughout the organization and beyond, and morale and productivity will plummet.

Remember that the corporation is a community of people; people working and often playing together, with common interests and a shared goal of building a successful organization. People everywhere are eager to feel a sense of belonging and want to work for an organization that values them and offers a sense of purpose beyond simply making a profit. They want to work for a company whose values they can see and respect. They want to take pride in what they produce. They want to admire the people with whom they work.

- Make values and expected standards of behavior clear. Work with the CEO and management to design and publish operating principles that reflect the company's values and provide specific expectations for acting in an ethical manner at all times.
- Strive for consistency between stated principles and action. When dealing with possible unethical behavior, assume that both the ethical breach and company response to it will be widely known and rapidly spread. Consider congruence with, or departure from the company's stated values, and how that will reinforce or tear down the fabric of trust.
- Lead with your ears. Monitor the corporate buzz and see and hear what employees, customers, vendors, shareholders and other stakeholders are saying about the company's culture in person and on social media.
- Reward principled performance: develop a framework for recognizing and rewarding ethical performance, especially in ambiguous or difficult circumstances. Find examples from high to low in the company and spotlight them.
- Manage upward path carefully. Do not promote anyone who has blemishes on their ethics or compliance track record. Examine the matter carefully to avoid later surprises in such difficult areas as sexual impropriety or harassment or use of racially charged language, for example.

DOI 10.1515/9781547400270-019

- Engage with people as a person. Tone at the top demands that the CEO and the board connect with people inside and outside the organization. Leaders must openly communicate their values on an ongoing and transparent basis, using different platforms and distribution systems. People are suspicious of leaders who are closed about their values or standards. Stakeholders assume if you value nothing, you'll value anything.
- Communicate, and communicate again, in words and action. While the behavior of all members of the community has an impact, remember that it is the CEO's behavior that tells employees what counts, and what's rewarded and punished. The CEO is the face of the company, the one to whom employees ultimately look for vision, guidance, and leadership. The board has a direct responsibility to see and understand how the CEO's character and behavior are perceived.

Getting the tone right has enormous impact. It permeates the corporation's relationships with investors, employees, customers, suppliers, regulators, local communities, and other constituents. Trust is difficult to establish and very easy to lose. Many corporate failures, notorious and unknown, can be linked to CEOs and boards who have neglected to develop a culture based on integrity.

Sometimes, all it takes is a rumor or hint of impropriety or malfeasance, or a social media post "gone viral," to negatively impact the stock price. Corporate reputations can be destroyed in an instant. There are conversations going on between and among all stakeholders at any given moment. Due to increased transparency and the ever-present smartphone with video, gaps between a leader's words and actions can "go viral" in a nanosecond, thus undermining efforts to build a consistent message and tone. Where there are actions that cannot be spoken about, or words that cannot be put into action, the moral fiber of the enterprise will be undermined by cynicism.

Translating tone at the top and building the sense of trust in leadership can be enhanced by certain operational practices, including for example:

- *Recruiting process.* Explicitly include screening for people's character as well as competence. Everyone in the hiring process should understand that character comes first.
- *Orientation and training.* Create constant reinforcement regarding the importance of trustworthy, ethical behavior consistent with the values and purpose of the company. Ensure that further training and mentoring continue to offer and reinforce consistent messages about what's valued.
- *Evaluation Metrics.* Performance evaluation should measure not only what is done, but how it is done, in accordance not only with ethical standards but in a consistent style that reinforces corporate values and personal trust.

- *Reporting Mechanism.* Whatever the method employed, employees must know where to go if they see something that troubles them. It is not always prudent to report concerns to one's supervisor, so it may be valuable to create a hotline or a designated person. Such communications must be kept confidential unless the employee is willing to be named.
- *Employee Departures.* People leaving the company must be treated with the same respect accorded to those remaining. It may be valuable to conduct an exit interview to collect insights perhaps not otherwise available.

While the above are not directly the purview of the board, board members will want to know that the tone set at the top is permeating the organization. It may be helpful to ask for periodic reports on activities intended to reinforce trust and ethical behavior. We are not referring to a checklist compilation or a pile of signed codes of conduct, though those may not hurt the effort. We are looking for recognition of key decision areas and opportunities to actively inculcate and demonstrate the ethical values if the company. The insights gained may be valuable in themselves and requesting such report signals that such matters are taken seriously by the board.

Certain areas may require additional attention from the board and senior leaders. These include:

- *Mergers, Acquisitions, and Divestitures.* Additional measures beyond completing transactional details must be addressed in any transaction. CEO, board and leaders throughout the company need to pay particular attention to the people involved. There will be fear, excitement, and uncertainty. Be sure that the plan to bring new people and processes into the organization or to say an appreciative farewell are developed with care and executed seamlessly top to bottom.
- *Providing Time and Space for People to be People.* This will go a long way toward building a successful combined operation. Leaders must focus on the fact that the new employees have choices and do their best to be sure they do not feel plundered or exploited. Appreciate them, which will help to reduce the pain of inevitable road bumps and mitigate potentially unforeseen risks. Be sure they know where to go with concerns.
- *Decentralized Operations.* Companies are increasingly likely not only to have far flung operations but to have a remote or flex time workforce. The board should ensure that the methods of communicating values and encouraging ethical behavior are effective across all employee cultures. This may take extra time and effort, as understanding the context in which employees operate is not simple when they work autonomously or are drawn from a different culture,

for example. Command and control approaches may work, but approaches based on listening, respecting, and adapting will pay dividends.

- *Malcontents.* Be sure that such people are not left alone to fester and allow their germs to spread. Identify them, try to understand and if possible address their concerns, and if not possible, remove them, respectfully. Nothing will undercut the desired tone faster than not addressing and dealing with individuals whose actions are contrary to the organization's beliefs.
- *Be Mindful of Institutionalization.* We have all seen the value statements stuck on the wall, sometimes covered with impromptu employee remarks. Beware of value statements that become stuck and meaningless, which will only underline that they longer apply. Encourage leaders throughout the corporation to keep the expected behavior fresh and vivid by living it. Stories about values in action are often helpful.

Relentless Focus on Ethical Behavior and Discerning the Right Thing to Do

Implicit in setting the tone at the top is the need to oversee the effectiveness of compliance and ethics programs. In order to exercise such oversight, boards need to receive expanded information regarding a company's ethics and compliance activities in order to adhere to the requirements of SOX requirements, SEC and Department of Justice (DOJ) guidance, and applicable law.

SOX gave the SEC a Congressional directive to ensure that procedures were in place sufficient to "deter and punish organizational criminal misconduct." A broad range of experts were drafted onto an Advisory Group and spent 18 months examining the effectiveness of various compliance criteria. They recommended that the SEC promulgate a stand-alone guideline to highlight effective ethics and compliance program dictators and to "specify the responsibilities of an organization's governing authority . . . for compliance."

An effective ethics and compliance program is defined therefore as one through which an organization exercises "due diligence to prevent and detect criminal conduct" and otherwise promotes "an organizational culture that encourages ethical conduct and a commitment to compliance with the law." A among the descriptors of an effective program is whether the "governing authority" is knowledgeable about the content and operation of the ethics and compliance program and exercises reasonable oversight of its functioning.

Training as to What Ethical Behavior Means is Important in Our Changing World

The board may delegate such oversight responsibility to a committee, such as the audit committee, though if it does, it must ensure that it is still receiving sufficient information to fulfill its oversight obligations. Importantly, the requirement for board training on their company codes of conduct, high-level risk areas, or other ethics and compliance program components was clearly addressed, and the training requirement applies to directors and high-level personnel, in addition to all other employees. Regardless, some companies still fail to train their board members.

Directors may feel, for example, that they receive sufficient training by virtue of sitting on more than one board, and thus not make it a priority to undergo such specific training. Mandatory training on each company's code of conduct, as well as on industry-specific risk topics of significance, is mission critical to complete. It both allows directors to be and demonstrates that they are sufficiently familiar with the policies, procedures, and training initiatives to exercise reasonable oversight of those programs. Not only does such training protect the organization in the event of corporate malfeasance, it also protects the individual directors from civil and/or criminal liability.

Ensure Reports on Compliance are Made Directly to the Board Periodically

An additional component of an effective ethics and compliance program is the requirement that a compliance officer report to the board or its designated committee at least annually about the implementation and effectiveness of the program. Since the results of the Advisory Group's work were compiled into "Organizational Guidelines" issued by the SEC in 2004, many companies now include such reports at each board meeting.

In 2010, the Organizational Guidelines were further clarified to address the desired relationship between the board and the compliance officer. Under the Organizational Guidelines, an organization is deemed to have an effective ethics and compliance program, even if high-level personnel are involved in a criminal offense, so long as the individual with operational responsibility for the program has "direct reporting obligations" to the board of directors or its designated committee.

This change reflects the importance of providing timely information to the board regarding misconduct, potential misconduct, and the operation of the organization's ethics and compliance program in general. While not requiring changes to existing reporting relationships between the board and the executive level of the organization, the amendment suggests that a formal procedure for the individual with day- to-day operational responsibility for the program to communicate with the board be adopted. In a further step, boards should consider whether they are receiving regular reporting on the operation of the ethics and compliance program from individuals who have the "expressed authority" to communicate with the board should they need to.

In short, compliance practices have developed significantly in a relatively short period of time. Best practices continue to evolve. The level of scrutiny of a board's oversight, or failure to oversee, a corporation's ethics and compliance activities has increased dramatically. The challenge for boards, executive officers, and ethics and compliance officers is to view the increased scrutiny not as an added burden but as an additional opportunity to enhance their corporate governance practices and continue to reinforce the desired "tone at the top."

Read More

"Organizational Sentencing Guidelines: Past, Present and Future", Grilli, Kathleen Cooper, General Counsel, U.S. Sentencing Commission; 2016 Compliance and Ethics Institute, 2016

"A Business Ethics Perspective on Sarbanes-Oxley and the Organizational Sentencing Guidelines" Hess, David; Law Review, University of Michigan, 2007

"Navigating Global Compliance: Establishing Rules for Taking the High Road in the Borderless Corporation", Bellerjeau, James T., General Counsel & Secretary, Mettler-Toledo International Inc.; Dillon, Michael A., General Counsel, Sun Microsystems, Inc.; Gnazzo, Patrick, Business Practices & Chief Compliance Officer, CA, Inc.; Rise, Martha, Vice President, Compliance & Business Conduct, Boeing Corporation; Association of Corporate Counsel Annual Meeting, 2006

"Power and Politics in Organizational Life", Zaleznik, Abraham, Harvard Business Review, May 1970

Chapter 20
Choose the CEO Wisely and Actively Plan for Succession

Choose the CEO, monitor his or her performance, and have a succession plan in case the CEO becomes unavailable or fails to meet performance expectations.

It follows from the above that the integrity and dedication of the CEO is vital to enabling the board to meet all of its responsibilities. The board and the CEO embody a symbiotic relationship, in which each depends on the actions of the other. If and when concerns about the CEO's actions, ability, or integrity arise, the board cannot allow the issues to fester. Raise worries in executive session or privately with the chair or lead director. Together you may decide whether any further knowledge or action is required, and when. The chair or lead director may raise concerns with the CEO or consult counsel should that be required.

A strong, capable and committed CEO and management team, subject to both robust oversight by the board and collaborative teamwork with the board, is essential to long-term value creation. To add some perspective, consider that the number of CEO changes at U.S. companies in 2017 totaled 1,160, according to a report from outplacement consultancy and executive coaching firm Challenger, Gray & Christmas, Inc.

Ensuring that such a CEO is in place and functioning well with the tools he or she needs is a major preoccupation of the board. Embrace it head on. And when the company has the right CEO, there remain at least two scenarios to continue to plan for: the unexpected loss of the current CEO, whatever the reason, and the longer-term process of selecting the successor CEO in the normal course.

Keep the Emergency Succession Plan Current

To plan for an emergency situation requiring a sudden change in leadership, the board and the CEO should together establish a strategy in advance and agree on the steps to take if an emergency vacancy occurs. Identify potential candidates, which may include a board member willing to take on management responsibility in an emergency on an interim basis. Have a general compensation plan at the ready. Boards also should discuss accelerated succession possibilities that could be implemented if the board begins to have concerns about the performance of the CEO.

DOI 10.1515/9781547400270-020

Build a Future View of Company Needs into Longer Term Succession Planning

Regarding longer term succession planning, both the future needs of the company and the resulting profile of the next CEO deserve attention. What will the company look like, and what skills and personality attributes will be particularly important to that future? Wise boards address these strategic issues first. Once the outline is established, go as far as possible in developing a specific profile of the leader the company will need and considering the impact the future CEO needs to have on the organization.

Building consensus on a future-looking strategy to develop the criteria for the next CEO is a critical step that helps the process go smoothly. It also helps boards avoid the trap of choosing an executive whose strengths resemble those of the incumbent. Without these steps completed it is hard to evaluate the possible future candidates and their fit, or to develop needed leadership qualities among the internal candidates. Some executives are skilled at growing a company; some are experienced in turnarounds; some maintain the company's current course. Some are operations oriented, or transaction oriented, or sales oriented. Get specific about the company's needs.

Cultural fit is another factor to consider strategically when seeking the next CEO. If culture is viewed as a valuable asset, that might lead to favoring a compatible profile. Sometimes, however, company culture can inhibit success. A culture too invested in its own ways may require transformational change, in which case, for example, the board may weigh more heavily the capabilities needed to transform the culture. Culture, therefore, needs to be evaluated as part of this process.

Setting Criteria and Developing Possible Candidates

A board's ability to choose a CEO successor requires a frank view of internal and external candidates' readiness, including an understanding of their development needs based on the future direction of the company and the likelihood of their being able to close any gaps in a reasonable amount of time. Executives' analytical capabilities, social intelligence, and self-awareness are all skills that speak to their ability to succeed in more complex and demanding contexts. CEOs must operate amid greater ambiguity and complexity than in their previous roles, so understanding whether executives have the skills to navigate these challenges is critical. This is no small consideration when the one thing boards know is that the challenges facing the new CEO will change.

As an anecdote, one CEO created formal mentor relationships between each board member and a member of senior management and changed them every two years. This allowed strong relationships to form without fear of being perceived to undercut the CEO and gave board members over time a lively ability to evaluate prospective candidates for elevation to various roles.

An additional component of candidate assessment is benchmarking internal executives against proven executives outside the organization, critical to giving the board a good sense of the relative strength of the internal candidates. According to research from The Conference Board, in 2016, nearly 86% of newly appointed S&P 500 CEOs were "internal." Just five years ago, in 2013, the percentage of insiders elevated was 76%. Boards are making a substantial commitment to grooming internal talent.

Succession planning can be one of the most time intensive board responsibilities, requiring significant work between meetings. While the entire board should be involved at critical points, a smaller succession planning or nominating committee that includes directors who are the most qualified for the work and have the necessary time can steer the process for the board and handle the heavier workload associated with assessment and benchmarking. The succession planning group often includes the current CEO ex officio.

As this committee takes ownership of the details, it should keep the rest of the board up to date and ensure its continued buy-in to ensure that the board understands the process; agrees with the identified key selection criteria; has the opportunity to participate in the assessment of internal candidates; and reviews any benchmarking information on external executives. In the end the selection must reflect the choice of the entire board and must not be seen by directors not involved in the subcommittee as a fait accompli.

Work with the Incumbent

In most cases, the incumbent CEO plays a significant role in succession planning, by driving management succession at senior levels and developing succession-ready executives, and a forward-looking approach to executive talent development. As the transition nears and the process turns toward the board's selection of finalist candidates and a possible outside search, the incumbent CEO's participation clearly diminishes.

Know Your Senior Management Team

While the board needs to be deeply involved in succession planning for the CEO role, less agreement exists among experienced directors about how involved the board should be in talent decisions further down. Regardless, the board should ensure that the CEO has a strong team and an effective succession planning process in place for other key executive roles. Many boards monitor talent development and succession planning for the top ten or twelve positions, and the process and philosophy employed throughout.

Directors can get to know senior leadership through presentations in the boardroom and regular engagement outside of it. An annual talent review which includes having the CEO and top HR executives lead a discussion about forward-looking leadership requirements can be very useful and gives all an agreed framework against which the talent pool can be evaluated. By being involved on an ongoing basis, the board can observe patterns of performance and develop a nuanced point of view on executives' strengths and weaknesses.

Among companies that do it best, succession planning focuses on selecting the next CEO and also stimulates an ongoing top-down and bottom-up process for developing talent throughout the company. These companies seem to have several common characteristics:

- Their boards are deeply involved in the succession planning process with the CEO on a continuing basis, linking it to the strategic planning process to ensure a fit between where the business is going and the skills of likely successors.
- They frequently expose their senior management team to the board and encourage "next-generation" CEOs to gain exposure to the media, the investment community, and fitting outside board service opportunities. Likely internal candidates for CEO are periodically compared to possible outside leaders.
- They develop a "succession culture" in which all levels of the organization plan for the inevitability of change by ensuring that top executives and high-potential leaders throughout the organization are given the proper tools, exposure, and training to develop into contenders for advancement.

Maintain a close relationship with the CEO and work with management to encourage entrepreneurship, appropriate risk-taking, and investment to promote the long-term success of the company (despite the constant pressures for short-term performance) and to navigate the dramatic changes in domestic and worldwide economic, social, and political conditions.

The interests of the corporation are best served when directors and management work together as business partners to improve sustainability of results and operations and develop and execute strategy. So long as independent directors are able and willing to assert their independent judgment, directors and management are well served by developing relationships of mutual respect, trust and a degree of friendship. This gives directors greater insight into key business decisions and gives management the ready ability to draw on the judgment, experience and knowledge of directors. Building and nurturing respect and trust enables each to benefit from the considerable value of the other.

It may be useful to see the work of the board as involving multiple roles, in which the choice among them is dependent on the nature of the material being considered and the circumstances of the company. Some decisions require board action, some situations require board advice, some require simply that the board be informed. Clarifying who make what kinds of decisions at each level helps. Some companies not only list but list publicly those types of decisions that are reserved for the board. Whether released to the public or not, the creation and periodic review by the board and the CEO of such a list could be a very helpful guide.

Maintaining the balance is, however, easier said than done, but remains an important aspiration. Friendship needs to be treated very carefully. As a corporate turnaround executive, I have been approached for help by two independent chairmen of NYSE listed companies, each with a similar issue. Their friendships with their CEO's had rendered them unable to look at them objectively and take the steps each knew were needed to remove the CEO. Beware.

Read More

"A Practical Guide to CEO Succession Planning: Ensuring a Successful Leadership Transition", Russell Reynolds & Associates, 2016

"CEO Succession Starts with Developing Your Leaders", Björnberg, Asa, and Feser, Claudio; McKinsey & Co., 2016

"7 Tenets of a Good CEO Succession Process", Luby, Victoria and Stevenson, Jane Edison; Harvard Business Review, December 2016

Chapter 21
Develop a Strong Organizational Framework

Organize the business, and maintain the collegiality, of the board and its committees so that each of the increasingly time-consuming matters that the board and board committees are expected to oversee receives the appropriate attention of the directors.

The business of the board and its committees should be organized in a way that ensures matters requiring board or committee attention receive such attention, are prioritized appropriately, and adequate time for consideration and review is provided.

Before we sally forth into the mechanisms for organizing the business of the board, let us spend a few minutes on a subject that is receiving much current attention: corporate culture. Culture begins with the board. If the board is a passive rubber stamp and fails to probe deeply into corporate behavior, the rest of the company will undoubtedly follow suit.

As you observe the board at work, note the interactions, behaviors, language, and data visible. Often the agenda is jammed full of technical content, or too many topics to allow thoughtful consideration. Many board meetings continue to be designed to prevent engagement in conversation.

Creating an environment in which candid discussion of sensitive topics can take place is the first order of business when ordering board function, and can not be accomplished in a single meeting. Few boards possess explicit expertise in assessing and changing culture to support candor and trust. Boards often assume that having some experience with corporate culture is sufficient to effect and supervise issues of culture. That assumption can be a dangerous illusion.

Board members feel pressure to be seen as knowledgeable, and the assumption that everyone is on the board because of previous achievements and expertise often creates an environment that is hostile to true learning. Creating the ability for the board to learn together how to address new material is not easy. Acknowledging limited understanding is the first step required for boards to begin to develop their knowledge of corporate culture and how they can influence it.

In the 2017 Board Leadership of Corporate Culture in Europe Report, prepared by the Mazars firm in association with Board Agenda and INSEAD, 450 chief executive officers, chief finance officers, board chairs, executive and non-executive directors, company secretaries, risk officers, and investment managers were polled. Sixty-three percent of respondents said they either work on boards

DOI 10.1515/9781547400270-021

that exclude culture from formal risk considerations, or fail to routinely assess the risks associated with their own corporate cultures.

While believing that the culture of business can be influenced from the top, particularly through the role of the CEO, only one in five board directors believe they are spending the right amount of time addressing cultural issues. Overall, the findings indicate that although the importance of corporate culture to business success is recognized, boards have yet to find a way to discuss corporate culture in a meaningful way.

The survey suggests that three sources seem to predominate when assessing actual culture: first is feedback from employees, from surveys and dialogue, for example, followed by customer complaints and satisfaction surveys, and finally from risk events such as rule breaches, HR issues, and compliance-monitoring. Interestingly, far less attention seems to be paid to information from external sources, such as social media and newspaper commentary or investor engagement.

It points out that approximately 85% of the value of leading businesses takes the form of intangible assets, most of which are linked to people, reputation, and brand—and all of which are critically influenced by organizational culture. While to me this number is difficult to assess, the point it is making is an excellent one. Intangibles strongly influenced by culture are very important to business success. Therefore, investing attention and effort in the mindful development of culture has an important payoff.

In her 2009 book *SuperCorp: How Vanguard Companies Create Innovation, Profits, Growth, and Social Good*, Harvard Business School professor and prolific author Rosabeth Moss Kanter draws on stories of such businesses as Procter & Gamble, Digitas, and Cemex, to describe how they have exploited their strong cultures to adapt and innovate, often harnessing the momentum of change to capture market share or squash competition. Those companies that will thrive in the future, maintains Kanter, have stamina, energy, long lists of contacts, an appetite for communication, comfort with ambiguity, and a belief that the company's values and principles mean that they are part of something bigger than just a job.

Read More

SuperCorp: How Vanguard Companies Create Innovation, Profits, Growth, and Social Good, Kanter, Rosabeth Moss, Crown Business, 2009

"Board Leadership of Corporate Culture, European Report 2017," Mazars and Board Agenda with INSEAD, 2017

"The Board's Most Important Function," Wommack, William W.; *Harvard Business Review*, September 1979

"Why Corporate Culture Is Becoming Even More Important," Alton, Larry, *Forbes Magazine*, 2017

Chapter 22
Tailor Board Work to the Company

Now to look at how to organize the work of the board. There are so many statements of principles, recommended best practices, and other prescriptions proliferating that rule number one in organizing board work has got to be questioning what makes sense in the context of the board and corporate circumstance. Thinking about the related benefits will help filter out the noise and allow the board to develop its own practices. It is not necessary or desirable to adopt a policy only because it is labeled a best practice. Such fashions come and go.

This sentiment was expressed by Myron Steel, former chief justice of the Delaware Supreme Court, in his 2010 comments in NACD Directorship Magazine's Verbatim Column "Common Law Should Shape Governance":

> Until I personally see empirical data that supports in a particular business sector, or for a particular corporation, that separating the chairman and CEO, majority voting, elimination of staggered boards, proxy access with limits, holding periods, and percentage of shares— until something demonstrates that one or more of these will effectively alter the quality of corporate governance in a given situation, then it's difficult to say that all, much less each, of these proposed changes are truly reform. Reform implies to me something better than you have now. Prove it, establish it, and then it may well be accepted by all of us.

Board Leadership

Chairman & CEO. Nowhere is the need to evaluate company specific benefits better illustrated than in the debate over combining or separating the roles of chairman and CEO. Many assert that the job of the CEO and management is to run the business of the company and the role of the board is to oversee management, thus leadership of the board should be separated from leadership of management. While this is an elegant construct and one I generally agree with, the best choice may depend on circumstance and directors need to decide this for themselves.

Looking at other systems, in the United Kingdom, for example, the CEO generally does not also serve as chairman of the board, whereas in the United States one person filling the dual role has been common. According to the 2015 Spencer Stuart Board Index, the CEOs of 50% of corporations surveyed also chair the board. This percentage continues to decline, however, given concerns expressed

DOI 10.1515/9781547400270-022

by shareholders in various ways such as the recent challenge of the combined CEO and chairman role at JP Morgan.

To my mind, there is a substantial amount of work involved in building the board as an effective team able to debate candidly, apply a skeptical turn of mind, make space for diverse points of view, and be sure that they are heard. For practical reasons, therefore, there needs to be a board leader able to focus on such issues, and to develop the board's agenda, with the CEO. Such a role can be played by a designated director such as a lead director, or by the chairman.

An independent chairman can be beneficial, for example, when a company appoints a new CEO, or when company performance has declined and significant changes to strategy, operations, or culture are needed that require management's complete attention while the board considers whether a change in leadership or sale of the company is necessary. Some argue that separating the roles can inhibit decision-making when specialized information does not easily transfer from the CEO to the chairman, creating an information gap. The desirable structure will, therefore, depend on context. This is true not only for the issue of whether to require an independent chairman but also for the majority of corporate governance policies. Beware.

Regardless of the leadership structure, one simple device that can go a long way toward making the issue less troublesome is to have the board and the CEO agree on and periodically review the specific decisions that are reserved to be made by the board. Other issues may be added as board or management desires, but building a clear list can save a great deal of time and maneuvering.

Committee Structure

Public company boards hold annual meetings with shareholders each year, at which directors are formally elected and other issues decided, based on what has been presented to shareholders via formal proxy statements. Following the annual meeting, the board has traditionally held the organizational meeting of the board formally to elect its officers as needed and to handle updated committee assignments. The work of the board is handled in various ways, including board meetings, which typically are held four to ten times each year.

Public companies are required by the NYSE and NASDAQ listing requirements as approved by the SEC to appoint three standing committees comprised of independent directors: audit, compensation, and nominating/corporate governance. The board may appoint other committees appropriate to the corporation's industry as it sees fit, consistent with its bylaws, such as a risk management committee, a science committee, a compliance committee, or a committee on social responsibility, and so on. Given the time required from the board and the board members available, it behooves the board to form additional committees only if they are really needed. Each committee reports on its activities including significant actions it recommends during the board meeting.

Committee Appointments. In determining committee appointments, the nominating and corporate governance committee generally develops a set of goals for each committee. Its chair should also consult with the CEO to determine what will be needed from the committees to accomplish success. The CEO may consult other leaders who will rely on the committees. For example, the CFO might want an audit committee member with recent capital markets experience to review the desired capital structure if a financing is planned. Or the internal audit executive might want an audit committee member who is familiar with the Sarbanes-Oxley Section 404 internal controls provisions, as well as with how other companies in the same industry handle those provisions. Questionnaires may be useful to determine and document both qualifications and requisite independence.

Next, board leadership, including the chair or presiding director, the nom/gov committee chair, and the chair of the applicable committee, should think about what the board needs from each committee. If a charter exists, be sure it is reviewed and updated as needed prior to or at the annual organizational meeting. The combination of the charter and the more immediate needs the board has should give rise to an outline of the specific strengths needed on each committee.

Committee Function. The advance work includes creating a 12–18-month calendar and rolling agenda for each committee. A useful step is to ask the corporate secretary to annotate each committee charter to show meeting dates where each charter requirement is to be covered with a brief description. This makes it easy for all to ensure that all requirements are met. If practical, include the result in the advance materials for every committee meeting and post it on the board portal, so that everyone can easily access it from time to time.

The advance work also includes developing, where appropriate, the use of consent agendas and other techniques to be sure the committees are not bogged down in the many public company requirements they must meet and thus less able to focus on the thoughtful work required. It is important that the committee understands the requirements and oversees the needed work. Many committees, however, report that in hindsight they spent too much time on technical details and not enough on critical substance. The advance work allows much of the technical detail to be covered there rather than during meetings. The committee must feel comfortable that the requirements will be adequately addressed but still leave time to oversee business matters that contribute to creating long-term value.

Though committees generally have authority to retain consultants and advisors, use them sparingly and cultivate the committee members' own independent judgment. It is worth noting that in the past, committees have sometimes relied on advisers or counsel who are also advising management, reflecting lack of awareness of potential conflicts, or perceived inability to engage an independent advisor. While in most cases, their interests are one and the same, in some cases, such as compensation consultants and in certain circumstances legal counsel, will reduce the value of the independent judgment the committee is tasked with applying. Thus, it is important for each committee to know that it has the right to retain help, and does not need to seek permission other than as a courtesy. This can be especially important when considering a significant transaction.

Our review of methods to execute the work of the board would not be complete without at least some discussion of the three required standing committees for public companies as well as others that are often used circumstances. As there is much discussion about committee charters available, however, along with the charters themselves of the committees of public companies, we will content ourselves here with being brief.

Audit Committee

The audit committee is a standing committee of the board charged with oversight of financial reporting and disclosure. This has grown to include oversight of the financial reporting process, selection of the independent auditor, and receipt of audit results both internal and external. The committee assists the board of directors to fulfill its corporate governance and oversight responsibilities in relation to its financial reporting, internal control system, risk management system and internal and external audit functions. Committee members are drawn from members of the company's board of directors, with a chair selected from among the committee members. Audit committees have become increasingly important since the passage of the SOX, and continue to evolve. Many audit committees also have oversight of regulatory compliance and risk management activities.

Increasingly, audit committees are looking at the quality of what they report, not just its compliance with required accounting standards. One aspect of this is recent focus on integrated reporting, which follows a framework adopted in 2013 by the International Integrated Reporting Council (IIRC), a coalition of regulators, investors, reporting companies, accounting firms, and other parties interested in providing clearer financial reports with a focus on value creation and sustainability.

External auditors are also required to report to the committee on a variety of matters, such as their views on management›s selection of accounting principles, accounting adjustments arising from their audits, any disagreement or difficulties encountered in working with management, and any identified fraud or illegal acts.

Internal control includes the policies and practices used to control the operations, accounting, and regulatory compliance of the entity. Management and both the internal auditing function and external auditors provide reporting to the audit committee regarding the effectiveness and efficiency of internal control.

Audit committees discuss litigation or regulatory compliance risks with management, generally via briefings or reports of the General Counsel and/or the Chief Compliance Officer or Ethics Officer that report incidents or risks related to the entity's code of conduct. Should significant problems be identified or alleged, a special investigation may be directed by the audit committee, outside consulting resources as deemed necessary.

Finally, SOX introduced the notion of the audit committee financial expert. Though it pains me to use its acronym ACFE, it has passed into common usage. What is an ACFE? Under SEC rules, an ACFE is defined as an individual possessing the following attributes:

- An understanding of GAAP and financial statements
- The ability to assess the general application of GAAP to accounting for estimates, accruals, and reserves
- Experience preparing, auditing, analyzing, or evaluating financial statements of a breadth and level of accounting complexity generally comparable to that expected to be present in the company's financial statements (or experience actively supervising others engaged in such activities)
- An understanding of internal control over financial reporting
- An understanding of audit committee functions

To qualify, an individual must have gained these attributes through any of the following means:

- Education and experience (1) in a position as a principal financial or accounting officer, controller, public accountant, or auditor; or (2) in a position involving similar functions
- Experience actively supervising a principal financial or accounting officer, controller, public accountant, or auditor (or an individual performing similar functions)
- Experience overseeing or assessing companies or public accountants in the preparation, auditing, or evaluation of financial statements
- Other relevant experience

The listing standards of neither the New York Stock Exchange (NYSE) nor NASDAQ require an ACFE. The NYSE does, however, require at least one member of the audit committee to have "accounting or related financial management expertise," as evaluated by the board of directors, and NASDAQ requires one member to be "financially sophisticated."

Compensation Committee

The compensation committee, another standing committee required to consist entirely of independent directors, generally serves in an advisory role to the board on most executive compensation matters, and recommends components of the CEO pay package, the amounts of each component, and the value of the total compensation package. It is also typically responsible for establishing performance measures and specific targets.

Its function is both strategic and administrative in that the committee must consider how the achievement of overall corporate goals and objectives can best be supported by using specific compensation programs. In my view, if you believe that you get what you pay for and financial incentives drive behavior, it is possible to see the compensation committee as the true strategic planning committee. At the least, the compensation committee must be inextricably involved in strategic planning processes.

From an administrative standpoint, the committee must undertake the necessary studies of comparable organizations and executives, evaluate alternative structures, and oversee the development, implementation, and effectiveness of the company's compensation philosophy. It must also complete the loop and see to it that all compensation and benefit programs help to achieve intended results.

As the pressures and scrutiny on the compensation committee continue to mount, it is important that the committee's responsibilities be clearly defined so that there is no question as to what it must do, and that the limits of its authority are also clear. Be careful of placing undue weight on benchmarking as such are not always comparable. The goal is to ensure that compensation is competitive, commensurate with the level of performance attained, consistent with the organization's business strategy and compensation philosophy, and that it complies with all ethical, legal, tax, and accounting requirements.

As discussed above, compensation practices can be a minefield, rife with unintended consequences. The committee and the board itself need to stand back from the many charts and tables and ask themselves whether the resulting proposed compensation makes sense within the context and culture of the corporation as well as at the human level. Is the compensation package understandable, and is it structured to reward the right kind of achievement? Many will disagree with this, but to my mind it is treacherous for a CEO to have too much of his or her net worth tied up in company stock, as perspective can be seriously distorted, for example. While consultants can offer reassurance as to general norms, they can not answer those fundamental questions for the committee and the board. It may help to role play a conversation about the proposed compensation with an imaginary large shareholder to be sure that it has been looked at from multiple points of view.

Nominating and Corporate Governance Committee

The nomination and corporate governance committee is another standing committee of the board required to be comprised of independent directors. Its mandate is broad in that it typically oversees the composition and functioning of the board and its committees. It is charged with attracting and nominating candidates for consideration by the full board. It also provides leadership to the board in the development and organization of its corporate governance principles and practices.

Specific responsibilities may include the following:
- Develop and recommend corporate governance guidelines to full board
- Establish director qualification standards and recommend term limits and tenure length
- Annually verify independence of directors for inclusion in the annual proxy statement
- Review director candidates from various sources and recommend director nominations
- Engage with board leadership to recommend committee appointments and leaders
- Develop recommended board and committee assessment method; ensure its completion, and follow up on recommended improvements
- Oversee process of succession planning for CEO and executive talent development for discussion with full board (some companies include this in the work of the compensation committee)
- Oversee CEO evaluation and work with compensation committee to determine CEO compensation for review with full board
- Develop new director orientation and continuing director education programs
- Recommend director compensation to full board
- Retain as needed independent advisors including executive recruiters

Other Committees

The board may appoint additional standing or special committees as it sees fit, in accordance with its bylaws and circumstances. Risk oversight committees are common, as are industry specific committees such as Investment Committees, Science Evaluation Committees, and so on. Formation of standing committees needs to be done with considerable thought as each committee needs to be populated with seated directors, supported by staff, and time for meetings and committee work needs to be found. Too many committees can dilute the effectiveness of both the committees and the board.

Special Committees

Boards may form special committees to deal with specific matters on an ad hoc basis. Unlike a standing committee, such committees do not usually operate under a formal written charter since their assigned tasks are usually concerned with a single issue that is not on-going in nature. The special committee's responsibilities and authority are established pursuant to board resolutions that identify its members and the committee's resources, duties, and powers.

Special committees must be composed of directors who are disinterested parties with respect to the matter at issue. Absent that, the work of the committee will be vulnerable to attack regarding its impartiality. There have been numerous cases in which a special committee's process was rejected by the courts because the committee members were, from the start, not truly independent. Accordingly, a board must be careful care in selecting the members of a special committee.

Special Negotiation Committee

The need for a special negotiation committee is triggered by the need to consider a transaction among interested parties within the company. Definitions of these include (1) a majority of the board of directors has a conflict of interest with respect to such transaction, (2) a minority of the board of directors (who has a conflict of interest with respect to such transaction) controls or dominates a majority of the board, or (3) such transaction involves a merger of the company with a controlling shareholder.

The purpose behind using a special negotiation committee can demonstrate fair dealing with the interested party at arm's length. In addition, Delaware courts have determined that the use of a special negotiation committee will shift the burden of proving the entire fairness of the interested transaction from the company to the plaintiff should litigation ensue. To obtain the benefit of these Delaware decisions, the special negotiation committee must run a "legitimate process." It must be clear in the resolutions forming the committee that the special negotiation committee has the proper and unbridled authority to negotiate the transaction, that the special negotiation committee has full authority to select its own advisors, and what compensation will be paid to those directors serving on the committee. The special negotiation committee must be comprised entirely of "independent" directors.

Special Litigation Committee

When a shareholder makes a demand on a corporation with respect to a derivative claim against directors, often some or even all the directors are made defendants and thus, they may be deemed to have a conflict of interest in considering whether the pursuit of the claims would be in the best interests of the company. In such event, it is common practice for a board to appoint a special litigation committee consisting of disinterested directors charged with the authority to investigate the claims and to determine if their pursuit would be in the best interests of the corporation. Following an affirmative determination to pursue litigation, the special litigation committee would continue to be responsible for pursuing the claims made against the defendants.

Special Investigation Committee

Due to the increased number of whistle-blower complaints by employees, the growing activity of government regulators in investigating corporate wrongdoing, the expanded responsibilities of independent directors (especially the audit committee) in monitoring corporate conduct, and the heightened sensitivity to accounting irregularities, boards of directors are more frequently encountering internal issues that raise the need for independent internal investigations.

Whenever corporate wrongdoing is suspected, the board must immediately decide (1) whether an investigation should be conducted, and (2) whether it should be handled by management or by a special investigation committee. Some internal investigations may be readily handled by a company's general counsel staff. But when there are credible allegations of serious corporate wrongdoing (e.g., issuance of fraudulent financial statements or wrongdoing by corporate executives), it is usually prudent to appoint a special investigation committee of the board to conduct an independent investigation with the assistance of independent legal counsel, forensic accountants and other independent third-party advisors as needed. Most importantly, where wrongdoing is found, the committee must determine the appropriate action for the company to take.

The credibility of the findings and conclusions of a special internal investigation will depend on how thorough, impartial and fair the investigation was perceived in be in its conduct, and how impartial and fair the special investigation committee and its advisors were to all parties. It is imperative to start with a clear board mandate as to the responsibilities, authority and resources of the special investigation committee as well as the scope of its investigation. Additionally, it is important to determine with counsel what record of the activities of the special investigation committee and its advisors is required and who should collect and preserve the pertinent evidence developed.

Board Information

The board and CEO generally together determine the information the board should receive and periodically reassess its information needs, with support from counsel in many cases. The goal is to provide useful and timely information without overloading the board. In addition to current financial and operating information, significant security analysts' reports, media reports, information on key competitors, market trends, and, increasingly, investor behavior might be deemed useful to include.

Some boards work with management to distill key performance indicators as well as major customer, supplier, industry, investor, or regulatory developments into a brief flash report that can be distributed to all board members frequently to keep them current between meetings. There are many simple ways to convey information today, so consider as needed periodic video conferences, brief e-mails on critical subject matter, or other simple methods of including board members. The information required to be conveyed and digested can be overwhelming to both those who prepare it and those who receive. Make active management of the content a priority, and find ways to share it that are both easy and secure.

Information Security

Safeguarding the information shared is an increasingly important issue. Many boards have moved to digital portals for transmitting information as securely as possible and just as importantly controlling its dissemination. These platforms make it easy for management to keep information current and add up to the minute updates. They help directors by avoiding heavy board books that are too easily left behind in the hotel room. The board or the corporate secretary or general counsel needs to develop thorough procedures for maintaining information security for the board, and be sure all directors understand them and know how to comply. This includes the question of individual director note taking. Whatever the policy, be sure it is understood and followed.

Collegiality

The stated need in governance literature to maintain collegiality covers a multitude of issues. Fundamentally, the goal is to promote an environment in which directors can speak candidly with each other and the CEO, avoid the toxicity of dysfunctional politeness, be comfortable enough to disagree with each other, while in so doing avoiding damaging the fabric of trust, stay the course to find agreement, and walk out of the cloistered pressure cooker with a smile and whole-hearted commitment to the chosen path. Easier said than done, and the term collegiality can be interpreted to mean as many undesirable behaviors as "team player," referenced above. Not the point.

It takes a great deal of often unsung work to achieve collegiality in the best sense. While actively working on it is the responsibility of everyone in the boardroom, directors and management, the largest laboring oar belongs to the lead director or the chairman, not the CEO. Instilling in all a common sense of corporate and board purpose and values offers a good place to start. Beyond that, be mindful of the strength of the board's own culture, and build understanding of its formal and informal methods of communicating into the consideration of director candidates and orientation of new directors. Be sure that every voice is heard, not just the loudest. Encourage one on one conversations with the lead director if individual concerns develop. Bullying takes many forms and is to be stamped out but quick.

Manage Communication Mindfully

Trust is founded on communication and the credibility of communication is, accordingly, a fundamental element in the successful creation of trust. Understanding different communication styles and building space for them into board activities gets even more challenging as the boardroom includes a broader range of diverse people and backgrounds.

It will not surprise anyone that women in general communicate differently from men. Different age cohorts may also operate based on differing assumptions about the world around them. Add cultural and ethnic differences, and potential for misunderstanding grows exponentially. The chair or lead and each committee chair needs to learn how to draw out every director, and be sure to take the time to understand the meaning of what they say.

As an example, I often ask questions in board meetings, finding that a more comfortable way to lead than to assert my conclusions. In so doing, I am working to build consensus by being sure all directors are hearing the same interpretations. In one situation where I was a fairly new director, my colleagues interpreted my propensity to ask questions as an indication that I was unprepared, when in fact I was hyper-prepared. This sounds minor, but often boards as a group have developed highly ritualized ways of navigating meetings, and are not expecting perceived disruption.

Regardless of board size, the group in the room is small, and protected by layers of cushioning. The need to keep discussion not only collegial but fresh and lively instead of formulaic is critical to effective, active ownership of results. In another example, the board met in its own building with portraits of former leaders on the walls. The trappings were lovely. The meetings were highly choreographed, and the dreaded PowerPoint presentation filled every minute. I began asking questions, which made everyone squirm, until slowly, the chairman and then each director joined me. The use of power points diminished, dialogue increased, posture changed from stiff to engaged, and every single one of those very polite gentlemen thanked me. Fish can not see water.

Generally, board members today do not have the preexisting social ties common in days gone by, and efforts to counterbalance the valued but very strong influence of the CEO by reducing his or her role in director selection compounds this issue. When a new director arrives, therefore, it is important to the collegial fabric of the board, to its tensile strength, that the new director feel a strong sense of sponsorship. This can take many forms but must include time with the CEO. The CEO needs to understand and trust his board. When connection to the CEO does not occur, and this can happen when boards are being very careful to observe what they think are best practices, tissue rejection often ensues.

The board dinner the night before the board meeting is of great importance in building the comfort and confidence of board members in each other. While the dinner can often be effectively used to showcase a particular business unit or team, it is important to protect social, unstructured time for the members of the board including the CEO to simply be together, able informally to explore thoughts and ideas and concerns that may be emerging, and simply to get to know each other. A casual breakfast before the meeting might also be useful.

Regardless of the mechanisms used, investing in building the fabric of the board is essential to its ability to fulfill its role. Some board leaders call each director before each board meeting to see what may be on his or her mind. Others carefully debrief each director following each meeting, to see what issues may have needed more time, what may have been missed altogether, and so on. I am no expert on team building, and there are many out there to learn from. Consider thinking of the board as a team, needing to learn the various plays and positions required, the strengths and weaknesses represented, and the ability to move smoothly from offense to defense as the game changes. And importantly, the team's goal is not just to work through a process, though process is very important. The team's goal is to help the company win.

Executive Session

Companies listed on the New York Stock Exchange must provide for such sessions as part of their governance guidelines, as mentioned earlier when discussing the nominating and governance committee. The use of the executive session without management present following each meeting can be a very helpful tool to building the fabric of the board, and is another area to be evaluated in terms of its benefits. Some boards work to be sure that whatever anyone wants to say can be said with management present. More typically, though, the executive session provides a valuable safety net for all. One caution: either use them routinely or not at all. It is not helpful at the end of the board meeting for the lead to ask if anyone wants an executive session. This puts board members in an awkward position.

Veteran director Betsy Atkins suggested in a recent televised interview that in the executive session, the lead go around the room and ask each board member what is on his or her mind, what issues have surfaced during the meeting that need attention, and what he or she wants to explore on future agendas. If this approach is used, she suggests that the lead assemble all the comments following the session, anonymize them, and share them with the CEO as soon as practicable. The worst thing that can happen is failure to report back to the CEO, as that lack of fundamental courtesy will likely have a corrosive effect.

Meeting with Management

In my experience, a great deal of the value of board meetings comes from the work done to prepare for them, by both management and the board. Management likely finds it painful to assemble the materials, but in so doing is forced to look at trends and consider the last year or quarter as a whole, which may not happen in daily work. In supporting the committees, the senior management team learns different points of view to use in completing their work. The effort required to summarize can lead to unexpected insight. For board members, investment in preparation allows each to use the comparatively small amount of actual meeting time in a focused manner. Where possible, and subject of course to advice of counsel, using consent agendas can increase the meeting time available for substantive discussion.

Setting the Agenda

The first matter to consider is ownership of the agenda. The agenda will include recurring items such as financial review and committee reports as well as any required approvals of proposed actions. Ideally, all board members will feel as if they have influence over the agenda and it is not beyond their control. Where possible, technical information may best be presented in advance, with assistance in interpreting it as well. Questions and discussion can then take place while all are present, but this can help avoid the meeting stalling due to technical overload. In my experience it is all too easy for the smallest details to take up the largest amount of time. Guard against this by finding ways to preserve time for in depth discussion of mission critical substance, and build the rest of the agenda around that. Where possible push detailed work to committees.

Facilitate Candid Communication and Trusting Relationships

There are many ways to encourage connections to develop between board members and senior executives in a way that does not undermine the CEO nor take excessive amounts of time. The idea is to formally recognize the need for all parties to be comfortable that they are not behaving improperly. Familiarity and the ability for directors to pick up the phone and ask a question is another way to keep valuable meeting time free for substance.

The corporation may find it useful to have an annual board retreat with the senior executives and, where appropriate, outside advisors, at which there is a full review of the corporation's strategy and long-range plans, budget, objectives and mission, ethical and compliance programs, financial statements and disclosure policies, risk profile, succession planning, and current developments in corporate governance.

In Crisis the Buck Stops with the Board

Plan for and deal with crises, especially crises where the tenure of the CEO is in question, where there has been a major disaster or a risk management crisis, or where hard-earned reputation is threatened by a product failure or a socio-political issue. Many crises are handled less than optimally because management and the board have not been proactive in planning to deal with crises, and because the board cedes control to outside counsel and consultants.

No matter how good a risk management program is, crises will emerge and test the board. Potential situations can range from unexpected departures of the CEO and other senior executives, sharp deterioration of business conditions, impending liquidity shortfalls, compliance violations, risk management failures or major disasters, public uproar over executive compensation and beyond. These are best regarded as opportunities for the board to grow and learn, as lamenting them does no one any good. The board must rise to the occasion.

Understanding the vulnerabilities of the corporation with a view toward anticipating and preparing for potential crises requires significant attention. Consider how many boards in recent years appear to have been utterly blindsided by the unexpected, and suffered both humiliation and serious damage to their companies as a result.

Each crisis is different, but when a crisis arises, and it will, directors are in most instances best advised to manage through it as a collegial body working in unison with the CEO and management team. The only way out is to go straight through it. Once a crisis starts to unfold, the board needs firmly, with the CEO in most cases, to take charge. This requires having defined communication processes, as in who notifies whom and how, who speaks in public and who does not. Agreeing upon the battlefield leader, whether chairman, CEO, or lead director also helps board members to act in close order formation, with no loose lips or panicky moves.

Should the board engage outside advisors, the board, which may create a crisis subcommittee for this purpose, needs to select and engage them, and be sure they understand they report to the board, not to management, as it is uniquely the role of the board to ensure the perpetual life of the enterprise. Be mindful not to overreact, including by reflexively displacing management or ceding control to outside lawyers, accountants and other consultants. Allegations of legal or regulatory impropriety require prompt and careful investigation, to be undertaken calmly with professional advice.

No Time to Resign

A word to the wise: some directors react to crisis with dismay, and consider resigning. That impulse should if possible be resisted. Beyond being sure there is a well-functioning CEO, leading the company successfully through a crisis is a crucible that only the board, the guardian of its perpetual life, is positioned to do. Well done, the trial of going through it may offer new opportunities, as the Chinese proverb suggests. Regardless, it is an important way to create strong bonds of teamwork among board members. Leaving the board at that time might leave a director open to later blame, and does not help the company, which every director has promised to do. Resilience is the goal, and the board needs to assert command during the emergency.

Read More

"Common Law Should Shape Governance," Steel, Myron, former chief justice of the Delaware Supreme Court, Verbatim Column, NACD Directorship Magazine, 2010

"Chairman and CEO: The Controversy over Board Leadership," Larcker, David F., and Talan, Brian, Graduate School of Business, Stanford University, 2016

"The Structure of Board Committees," Chen, Kevin D., Department of Economics, University of Pennsylvania, and Wu, Andy, Strategy Unit, Harvard Business School. Working paper, Harvard Business School, 2016

Chapter 23
Focus Intently on Compensation

Determine executive compensation to achieve the delicate balance of enabling the company to recruit, retain, and incentivize the most talented executives, while also avoiding media and populist criticism of "excessive" compensation and taking into account the implications of the "say-on-pay" vote.

We have amply discussed the complexities of compensation, its design, and the incidence of unintended consequences when choosing the form of compensation consideration above. We have also reviewed the sensitivity of investors to this issue, and the importance, when seeking outside assistance, of finding professionals whose only client in the organization is the board. Thus, here we will content ourselves with a summary.

Executive Compensation

Design reasonable executive compensation to allow the corporation to recruit, retain and incentivize the most talented executives to generate long-term value, while avoiding incentive compensation that might cause executives to pursue short-term results at the expense of long-term results and considering the views of investors as expressed through "say-on-pay" votes or otherwise.

Fairly Compensate Directors

Director compensation, too, needs attention. Directors now devote significantly increased time and energy to the enterprise, accept major responsibility, and tolerate exposure to public scrutiny and potential liability involved with board and committee service. The compensation committee or the nominating and governance committee should determine or recommend to the board the form and amount of director compensation with appropriate benchmarking against peer companies. In addition to determining compensation, the board should determine appropriate stock holding requirements.

It is legal and appropriate for additional amounts to be added to basic directors' fees for chairs of committees and members of committees that meet more frequently or for longer periods of time, including special committees

DOI 10.1515/9781547400270-023

formed to review major transactions or litigation. While there has been a trend to establish stock-based compensation programs for directors, the form of such programs should be carefully considered to ensure that they do not create the wrong types of incentives for directors.

Following World War II, director compensation was low and sometimes non-existent. The tradition, going back to the 19th century, was not to pay outsiders, on the view that the opportunity to monitor management was reward enough for a substantial stockholder. As bringing independent directors on to boards became desirable, compensation for their time became necessary. Such compensation, of course, can undercut director independence so must be carefully developed.

One 1990s-era governance innovation was to compensate directors as well as management in stock (or stock options) to strengthen the alignment of director and shareholder interests. Stock-based compensation may create a set of perverse incentives for the directors, as demonstrated by the wave of financial disclosure problems in the late 1990s and early 2000s. The director receiving stock-based compensation, like the similarly-compensated CEO, may be tempted to accept aggressive accounting rather than stock-price-puncturing disclosure. Many companies provide a mix of cash retainers and longer-term equity linked compensation, often roughly equal in current value.

In one circumstance, it was clear to me that the compensation from the board we served together was too important to a fellow director. An academic, he was not well paid in his primary profession compared to corporate compensation. He was able because of the board work to acquire a luxury car and other items otherwise beyond his means. As much as we want diverse views and backgrounds on the board, it is difficult to preserve independence of thought and behavior if a standard of living is substantially changed because of the board compensation. This is a very sticky wicket, but must be considered.

Read More

"CEO Compensation," Larcker, David F. and Tayan, Brian; Corporate Governance Research Initiative, Stanford Graduate School of Business, 2017

"Executive Compensation Is Out of Control. What Now?" Karabell, Shellie, *Forbes Magazine,* February 2018

"How Companies Actually Decide What to Pay CEOs," Clifford, Steven; *The Atlantic Magazine,* June 2017

"Board of Directors Compensation: Past, Present and Future," Lerner, Diane; Pay Governance, LLC, 2017

Chapter 24
Seek Wisdom, Courage and Breadth of Experience in Director Recruitment

Face the challenge of recruiting and retaining highly qualified directors who are willing to shoulder the escalating workload and time commitment required for board service, while at the same time facing pressure from shareholders and governance advocates to embrace "board refreshment," including issues of age, length of service, independence, expertise, gender and diversity, and provide compensation for directors that fairly reflects the significantly increased time and energy that they must now spend in serving as board and board committee members.

When I joined my first board in 1990, boards were obscure and few wanted to take on what were thought to be the serious risks of a directorship. Now a wealth of talent is eager to serve and actively campaigning for the opportunity. Numerous organizations have sprung up to prepare aspiring directors and help them network their way into a board seat. Their clamor notwithstanding, identifying and recruiting a good mix of directors is far from a simple process. It is a challenge to identify and attract those who possess skills and experiences that are in high demand, and finally to determine which possess the traits of courage, character, and collegial frame of mind that will click with the group and be effective for the company.

Many candidates may be discouraged from serving on boards due to the reputational risks of negative publicity campaigns, proxy contests and various public and personal attacks on directors, lurid headlines over executive compensation, shareholder litigation and the potential for high-profile risk management lapses. Some are attracted precisely because of the difficulty of the role, and the strength of their conviction that they can make a difference to the company, its people and leadership, and its community.

Cast the net widely, understand what you are looking for not in terms of a skills matrix but in terms of the human qualities the board needs. I am generally drawn to people who have experience in multiple fields, as their skills and insights are cross functional and tend to give them broad vision. Your board may need something else. Think hard, and look beyond the inevitable spreadsheets and checklists to assess character and courage.

Think specifically about your board's approach to dissent, which is discouraged in the name of maintaining collegiality by many boards that are trying to follow good governance principles. Consider former Home Depot chairman

DOI 10.1515/9781547400270-024

Bernie Marcus remark that he would never serve on a board where dissent was discouraged. In his view, when he serves on a board, both his reputation and his fortune are on the line. He can not restore a damaged reputation, and D&O insurance is not likely to protect a fortune. Marcus has remarked, "I don't think you want me on your board. Because I am contentious. I ask a lot of questions and if I don't get the answers, I won't sit down."

Some would find these characteristics highly desirable on a board, whilst some would run as he suggests. Regardless, be mindful of treacherous filters such as "team player," which can mean too many different things, from adaptable to biddable to compliant to docile. Such a person could be valuable, or a waste of a perfectly good board seat. According to data compiled by Kathleen Eisenhardt and L.J. Bourgeois, the highest-performing companies have extremely contentious boards that regard dissent as an obligation and that treat no subject as undiscussable.

Directors at these companies scoff at some of the devices more timid companies use to encourage dissent such as outside directors asking management to leave while they discuss company performance. What's the point of criticizing management, they ask, if management isn't there to answer the criticism? It should be noted that skepticism and dissent don't constitute disagreement for its own sake but rather are the by-products of a constantly evolving view of the business and of the world. The result of such candor is not that the board wins, and management loses, but rather that, after passionate disagreements had been voiced, together they arrive at new conclusions.

Get the Right Mix of Directors in the Boardroom

Board effectiveness depends on the quality of the individuals involved. Balancing board composition, more an art than a science, generally includes consideration of the following factors:

Independence. As we have seen, there has been continuing movement toward boards consisting of a preponderance of independent directors, and the definition of independence has become increasingly narrow. It behooves the board, however, and investors and regulators as well to remember that being independent under various legal definitions is only part of the desirability of independence. What the corporation needs are directors who possess sufficient character, confidence, and integrity to allow them to make judgments that are unbiased by personal considerations, and communicate them persuasively.

Diversity. Directors with diverse backgrounds and experiences may strengthen board performance. While boards are under pressure to attract and seat candidates defined as diverse such as women and candidates of color, the board also needs to keep in mind that the goal is to build a rich mix of points of view to render its decision-making more robust. Checking the box may be a worthy start, but the board then needs to find ways to capitalize on the resulting diversity by being sure that all directors are comfortable speaking their minds. All too often, newcomers fit in by mimicking those already in the room. Often, candidates who are different in gender, age, experience, or ethnicity are misunderstood by sitting directors, and odd choices can result.

Age and Tenure. While age and tenure may be relevant factors in ensuring a balanced board, bright-line rules can force the arbitrary loss of valuable directors and are a poor proxy for what really matters. In some cases, lengthy service can enhance independent behavior. A director, for example, who has served since long before the current CEO or is a generation older than the CEO may likely have greater ability successfully to challenge management should the need arise than will more recent additions. In addition, long-serving motivated directors with a deep understanding of the corporation and personal knowledge of its evolution can be irreplaceable.

Competence and Integrity. Intelligent, dedicated and well-qualified individuals with appropriate skills, experience, expertise, education, background and perspectives are not enough to make a board effective. The board, with its necessary mix of qualities must learn to function as an effective team. The quality of team dynamics may have a significantly greater impact on performance than the sum of individual director contributions. This is an important issue to consider, and thinking of the board as a sports team with several different players and positions and tactics may be very useful. Board roles must be fluid.

While qualities such as mutual respect, sense of common purpose, energy, business sense, and openness may be difficult to quantify or describe with precision, they are very much at the heart of effective board functioning. In thinking about board composition, directors should take a long-term strategic view focused not merely on filling immediate vacancies on an ad hoc basis, but on constructing a well-rounded board that works well together in handling the multidimensional responsibilities inherent in its role. Trust and respect are earned and must be treasured.

Commitment to Director Responsibilities. Individual candidates need to understand and embrace the substantial work load and time commitment required for board service. To ensure that the increasingly complex and time-consuming matters that the board and committees need to oversee receive the appropriate attention of directors, the board may want to limit the number of other boards on which a director sits. While not easily reduced to a formula, it is undeniable that serving on multiple boards, especially with committee involvement, may place significant and conflicting demands on time. Some boards ask members to report in real time on any significant changes in their work or even charitable activity. Some watch this aspect less formally through conversation.

Beware Overuse of the Skills Matrix. Some boards employ a skills matrix to be sure they have the mix of skills and experience they need on the board. While keeping an inventory of skills represented and needed is valuable, the skills matrix can often take on too much importance. One issue to consider is whether the desirable skills highlighted should be sought in board members, or instead be contracted for as a service or possibly brought in to the mix of skills in the employee population. For example, with respect to cybersecurity, what can a board member, whose skills almost by definition will be out of date in this rapidly changing world, do with his or her direct expertise to address cyber risk? It may be riskier for the company to create the illusion of board level expertise than it is to recognize that it needs state of the art up to the minute knowledge and engage a firm who focuses on nothing but cybersecurity.

Value Tempered Judgment over Technical Expertise

What all boards can benefit from is not so much specific expertise, but enough familiarity with company businesses to be able to offer the benefits of seasoned judgment. The wisdom that comes from surmounting difficulty and working in multiple formats, capacities, and industries is valuable to the company's ability to recognize problems early and to resolve them well. It takes x-ray vision to be able to see into the organization and identify emerging issues while not engaged with it every day. To get the real benefit of independence, seeking that kind of skill may trump the skills listed in the matrix as needed. In the wrong hands, the matrix can be used to divide and conquer.

Director Training. In addition to the periodic mandatory requirement for all directors to refresh themselves on the corporate governance code, code of conduct and business ethics, new directors need orientation. Onboarding not only addresses company and industry business and competitive matters, but also addresses the intangibles such as corporate and board culture and history. The goal is to provide insight into the corporation's business, strategy and risk profile, and method of making decisions in such a way that the new director can take his or her seat with confidence and not slow down proceedings with the need to explain basics.

Make explicit commitments to ongoing director education so it does not end up taking place in the board meeting. It can be comprised of specialized tutorials and/or site visits. It can be helpful to promote lines of communication that will foster open and frank discussions with senior management. Some boards hold their board meetings at a rotating list of company locations that can be used to highlight production, sales, and other mission critical activities. This gives the directors direct exposure to company operations, and, as important, makes them visible and human to managers and employees, and vice versa. It builds important awareness and connective tissue.

Another approach that can be effective is to bring key executives from various operations and divisions to the board, and include them in board dinners to facilitate informal exchange of information and the building of relationships. The executives may be asked to provide a presentation on their area of responsibility before the formal board meeting starts. Yet another technique to foster interaction is to have directors arrive a day early, with the expressed purpose of meeting with whichever executives they need to see, for committee work or general information. Executives keep themselves available that day.

One company developed a standing two-day meeting agenda, in which one day was dedicated to the general business of the board and the other was reserved for a day long exploration of key issues in a business area.

Read More

"What Makes Great Boards Great," Sonnenfeld, Jeffrey A., *Harvard Business Review,* September 2002

"Different Is Better: Why Diversity Matters in the Boardroom," Russell Reynolds Associates, 2017

"What Makes a Great Board Member? (You Really Need to Get This Right)," Stolle, Bryan; *Forbes Magazine,* June 2014

Chapter 25
Actively Evaluate Board Performance
to Constantly Improve

Evaluate the board's performance, and the performance of the board committees and each director.

Candid assessments of director, board, and committee performance are a necessary tool in determining areas for improvement. Typically, the nominating and corporate governance committee recommends to the full board the mechanisms to use to do this, and shepherds the process through to completion and beyond. There are a variety of approaches to formulating an effective evaluation process, and each board may choose to develop its own path. The challenge is to do it without creating distractions and taking time away from the work of the board while also developing meaningful results that can be used in the constant improvement effort of the company. Make the choice an active one, to ensure that the results are valued by all.

One of the greatest benefits of the effort to evaluate the board is that it forces an opportunity to consider what the goals are against which the board believes its collective and individual performance should be measured. This discussion, with and with management, can be very enlightening and useful. Do not squander it.

Developing the Process

Many consulting firms have published recommended procedures for conducting evaluations and have established advisory services in which they meet with a board and committee members to lead them through the evaluation process. While these services may be helpful, it is not required that the board receive outside assistance or that multiple-choice questionnaires and/or essays be the means of evaluation. Suggested aspects to consider when developing the process follow.

Given the way the board likes to work, determine whether a process managed from within the board would yield the most valuable insights, or whether a process managed from outside the board would be more useful. When undergoing a major transformation, an outsider with experience in the transformation process, such as an IPO, might be a good fit. When under attack, counsel may

DOI 10.1515/9781547400270-025

advise that outside counsel lead the evaluation. These possibilities are provided to stimulate thinking on the subject and are not intended as a prescription.

Design decisions include:
- Will directors provide oral input? Individually, or in a group?
- Will directors also or instead provide electronic or written input?
- Is it to be anonymized, or for attribution?
- Will members of management who interact with the board provide input?
- What topics will be covered, and in how much detail?
- Will there be questions about the performance of individual directors in addition to questions about the collective performance of the committees and the board?
- Who will have access to the raw data obtained or participate in analyzing the data?
- Are all comments anonymous?
- Will results be reported in summary or will directors see the granular data for each question? Will there be a written report?
- Who will participate when the board reviews the report and considers any actions based on the results?
- Will the same process be used for each committee as for the board? Unique questions for the committee can provide useful feedback for the committee chair and management in agenda planning.
- Would a change of process be helpful, or would the continuity derived from using the same process as in prior years be useful?
- What records will be retained when the process is completed? It is important to include company counsel in the retention plan. All who may create records should be aware in advance whether the records might be subject to discovery or litigation holds and receive advice from counsel regarding retention.

When gathering responses:
- Be sure that directors understand the process as well as its goals in advance
- Be considerate of time required of all parties
- Be sure that directors' responses are clearly understood

Results are of course reviewed considering the context of circumstances and the company's goals. Both numerical and qualitative results must be digested carefully to best advise the board as to how it might increase its effectiveness. A concise report on strengths and weaknesses, followed by deliberations by the board to choose areas of focus, is one method of helping the board work on continuous improvement without being overwhelmed.

Regardless of the process chosen, follow-up is an essential part of gaining value from the exercise, and can easily be overlooked. Choose a responsible party which can, for example, be the nominating committee chair. Or assign follow-up responsibility based upon the content. Setting a target completion schedule is also helpful.

Some boards use self-assessments or peer to peer techniques to help directors understand themselves, each other, and the group. In such self-assessments, board members can review the use of their time, the appropriate use of their skills, their knowledge of the company and its industry, their awareness of key personnel, and their general level of preparation. The peer review can consider the constructive and less constructive roles individual directors play in discussions, the value and use of various board members' skill sets, interpersonal styles, individuals' preparedness and availability, and directors' initiative and links to critical stakeholders.

Read More

"How Boards Should Evaluate Their Own Performance," Larcker, David; Griffin, Taylor; Tayan, Brian; *Harvard Business Review,* March 2017
"Performance Evaluation of Boards and Directors," Deloitte, 2014

Chapter 26
Manage Risk Effectively

Determine the company's reasonable risk appetite (financial, safety, cyber, political, reputation, etc.), see to the implementation by management of state-of-the-art standards for managing risk, monitor the management of those risks within the parameters of the company's risk appetite, and oversee that necessary steps are taken to foster a culture of risk-aware and risk-adjusted decision-making throughout the organization.

Identify Risks that Can Kill the Company. Thinking about risk is fascinating and can be an endless exercise unless framed in a useful format. Boards will want to choose carefully their own definition of significant risk and their risk appetite. To my mind, focus needs to be first on defining the types of risk that can take the company out or do such damage that recovery is not feasible. While of course we can not list risks we do not know about, we can list those we are aware of, and consider probabilities and thence protective actions.

One risk that we do know about and can understand better is liquidity risk, which we will devote some attention to shortly. Though there are many causes or corporate failure we can identify, the immediate proximate cause is almost always driven by cash, or lack of same. The company in its woes just plain ran out of money and sources of funds. In my time as a corporate turnaround CEO or advisor, I have yet to see a company that has a good grasp on where its cash is, how much it has, what claims are against it, and what sources of more funds are available. It is not especially difficult to track the information, but someone must decide that it is worth doing, and set up and maintain the process of monitoring it.

Often companies are blindsided by the unforeseen, when sometimes the reason it was unforeseen is that the relevant eyes were closed. One way to incorporate vigilance into board processes is a simple one. Ask each director and each business unit head as enumerated by the CEO to write down his or her own top ten risks; the worries that keep them awake at night. Do this before every board meeting; aggregate and review them quickly at the next meeting. This exercise keeps various risks top of mind, and not necessarily the risks one would expect. Resulting discussion can be very enlightening for all.

One of the most challenging tasks facing the board is risk management, which has evolved from being viewed primarily as a business and operational responsibility of management to being characterized also as a key governance issue that is squarely within the purview of the board. In fulfilling this function, the board's role is one of informed oversight. The directors should determine the corporation's reasonable risk appetite and satisfy themselves that the risk

DOI 10.1515/9781547400270-026

management processes designed and implemented by management suit the corporation's strategy, are functioning as expected, and that necessary steps have been taken to foster a culture of risk-adjusted decision-making throughout the corporation.

Through its approach to the oversight role, the board can send a message to management and employees that comprehensive risk management is neither an impediment to the conduct of business nor just a supplement to the corporation's overall compliance program, but is instead an integral component of corporate strategy, culture and the value-generation process.

A great deal has been written about this area. Much of it seems circular to me, or unduly full of jargon to the point where a common understanding of meaning is defeated. This creates its own risk, that of eyes and ears glazing over just when the alert focus of all is needed. Discussion surrounding overall risk appetite is often perfunctory, and sometimes non-existent. At the same time, any strategy and projected return is intrinsically linked with a given set of risks. It can help to break the risk discussion into chunks. Moody's Investor Services specifies four elements they want to see present in a company promoting a risk focus: (1) risk governance, (2) risk management, (3) risk analysis and quantification, (4) risk infrastructure and intelligence.

It is important that the board understand and accept not only a certain return target and strategy, but also the level of risk that achieving that return target entails, and beyond that must understand and approve the company's risk appetite, and the method used to assess and measure the level of risk inherent in any strategy. Best practice calls for the risk appetite to be clearly and explicitly identified in terms of both types of risks and the magnitude of total exposure it is comfortable with, expressed in a quantified form, such as a percent of earnings or equity.

Drivers of Risk. Explore the relationships between various risks and revenue drivers. Request regular presentations of alternative scenarios for future financial results. In financial institutions this handy process is called stress testing. Shell Oil famously calls it *scenario-based planning*.

Whatever it is called, the idea is not to depend on a single set of projections in an uncertain world, but instead to learn more about the relationships among various forces by examining alternative situations. At a minimum there should be three scenarios (worst case, expected case, and best case), but some companies have implemented more nuanced simulations following the model of financial institutions. These simulations can be based on historical events or hypothetical developments. In all cases, directors should be aware of the assumptions embedded in the scenarios.

Directors need to understand both the nature of the risks to which their company is exposed, and their potential materiality, to engage forcefully with executive management on strategic and tactical matters. Key components to focus on include:

Identification of Risks. Pay attention to the total bundle of risks, such as market, credit, operational, business, liquidity, reputational, litigation. Seek update regularly on the key risks faced by the organization and, more broadly, on the firm's risk profile, including a quantification of the risk, even if it is a rough approximation, which of course it will be.

Question risk professionals to be sure they are always working on an integrated and coherent picture of the risks facing the business and the quality of the firm's control environment when set alongside reports from other control functions, such as audit, compliance, and legal.

Study the Risk Management Environment. As risk and risk management increase in complexity, directors need to learn on an ongoing basis about trends in risk management and in new risks facing the business or embedded in new products. Training is particularly important in enabling boards to use the risk information shared with the board by management, some of which can be obscure in its detail.

Broad risk matters, such as setting the firm's risk appetite and ensuring its fit with strategy are matters for the full board. However, in most cases, the detail of risk oversight is undertaken in a committee setting, where other major agenda items are not vying for attention. A committee setting also provides a more relaxed setting for interactions among board members and risk professionals.

Promote a Risk Aware Environment. The support of the board is key to creating an overall culture that promotes decision-making at all levels of the firm that is sensitized to risk matters and risk-adjusted performance. This culture feeds from well-established business and ethical principles emphasizing openness in communication and the right to fail. Otherwise risk managers tend to care more about their career and reputational risks than about doing the right thing.

Build a Vital Risk Management Policy. The board should sponsor and approve a risk management policy that outlines the objectives of risk management, its own key responsibilities in the risk process, as well as the mechanisms to delegate responsibilities and to elevate issues and conflicts. The policy should highlight clearly how the board or risk-focused committee(s) monitors action plans to remedy deficiencies in the key risk framework, controls and risk systems, where required.

Integration of Risk Insights into Planning Processes. Beware the siloing of risk thinking. The board or it committees should ensure that other control functions actively use the intelligence on key risks in their planning processes. For example, internal audit should use these insights as a major input into their risk-based audit plan.

All of that having been said, I must say that I have no patience with directors who, for example, claimed that they did not understand the complex products on their financial institution's balance sheets in or before 2008. While no one can be expected to understand everything, directors are expected to ask why when balance sheet composition changes significantly or an area is growing disproportionately. Failure to understand is understandable. Failure to ask to understand, and to do so until the issue is clear, is unforgivable. Such behavior represents a serious risk to the company.

Further Comments on the Board and Cybersecurity

Online security breaches, theft of proprietary or commercially sensitive information and damage to information technology infrastructure are a constant threat. Increasing reported cyberattacks make clear the urgency of the task, and the need for thorough defenses to this ballooning set of issues. The board needs to help ensure that the corporation understands it vulnerabilities and designs, implements, and monitors effective cybersecurity measures. This is an unfamiliar landscape to most directors, but that should not Inhibit the review process nor the formulation of questions to ask the Chief Information Security Officer (CISO) and staff to guide the adoption of the right policies, processes, organizational culture, technologies, and, most important, the cyber team.

This is a delicate and complex arena, in which the target is constantly moving. To me, there are several actions to take to help protect the company. Acknowledge that cyberattacks, whether driven by greed or terrorist motives, happen constantly and rare is the company or person, large or small user of technology, who has not been confronted by a breach of some kind.

While preventing breaches is desirable, the more pervasive arena on which to focus resources is on detection and neutralization: the ability rapidly to identify the source of the breach, to reduce the time from breach to detection, and then the time from detection to neutralization. Get regular reports on these trends from the CISO. Identify the most critical data and take additional steps to secure that, including redundancy.

Never Underestimate the Impact of Human Error

Recognize that a great many breaches do not occur because of technical weakness but instead succeed because of avoidable human error. Thus, build awareness of cyber hygiene practices among the entire corporate community. Simple steps such as not opening emails from unfamiliar addresses, not clicking unexpected attachments, paying attention to possible phishing, turning off Wi-Fi on mobile devices when not in use, changing passwords regularly, using company sanctioned data storage procedures, keeping all personal communication away from company devices, and so on can have real impact mitigating the degree of damage, and heightened awareness can not hurt.

Put data protection and cybersecurity front and center on the board agenda. It is all too easy for director eyes to glaze over as technical matters are discussed, but do not succumb to the temptation to declare cybersecurity someone else's problem. Instead, consider elevating the CISO position in a similar way to the approach taken to internal audit, and request that reports be provided in plain English. Otherwise your board may end up like the Equifax board, in the dark during a crucial point in time.

Equifax, a company whose entire business is about collecting consumer data, often without consumer knowledge or consent, exposed sensitive personal information of 143 million American consumers, over half of our citizens, between mid-May and late July 2017. Hackers accessed people's names, Social Security numbers, birth dates, addresses and, in some instances, driver's license numbers and credit card data. The Equifax CEO and chairman did not inform the rest of the board of this development for three weeks, and consumers were not informed of this massive disaster for several months. Whatever else your company does, be sure that from bottom to top, every person knows that bad news must be reported up the line of command instantly.

Importance of Plans

Finally, ensure that incident response plans are in place which include reporting of breaches to National Institute of Standards and Technology (NIST), a unit of the Department of Commerce charged with tracking breaches and coordinating responses as a matter of national security. Incident response is one of the fourteen requirements outlined in the NIST's Special Publication (SP) 800-171—Protecting Controlled Unclassified Information in Nonfederal Information Systems and Organizations, and enforced by the U.S. Department of Defense. If your organization contracts for the government, you must implement all of these security requirements. Regardless of whether the company is contracting with government, the NIST approach provides an excellent method to use to review the company's posture regarding cyber risk. The NIST Framework contemplates five functions that comprise the risk management system and its lifecycle of dealing with threats: identify, protect, detect, respond, and recover.

Read More

Risk Management: Concepts and Guidance, Fifth Edition, Pritchard, Carl L., Auerbach Publications, 2014

"Five Steps to Developing a Comprehensive Risk Appetite Framework," Dixon, Don; *Wall Street Journal,* January 5, 2017

Risk Assessment for Mid-Sized Organizations: COSO Tools for a Tailored Approach Mackay, Scott; Wiley & Sons, 2017

"Special Publication (SP) 800-171—Protecting Controlled Unclassified Information in Nonfederal Information Systems and Organizations," *National Institute of Standards and Technology,* 2015

"The Evolving Role of the Board in Cybersecurity Risk Oversight," EY Center for Board Matters, July 2017

Chapter 27
Independently Evaluate the Impact and Execution of Transactions

Take center stage whenever there is a proposed transaction that creates a seeming conflict between the best interests of stockholders and those of management, including takeovers and attacks by activist hedge funds. Recognize that shareholder litigation against the company and its directors is part of modern corporate life and should not deter the board from approving a significant acquisition or other material transaction, or rejecting a merger proposal or a hostile takeover bid, all of which is within the business judgment of the board.

The board is the only authority within the corporation that can approve or reject a major corporate transaction, such as a merger or takeover proposal, a significant acquisition, spin-off, investment or financing. It would seem to follow therefore, that the board will receive the information it needs to evaluate the proposition, and be provided with the time and analytical support required fully to understand the situation. It is remarkable how often boards do not receive such tools, do not demand them, and allow themselves to become an afterthought, relegated to a simple voice vote once management has done the heavy lifting.

Management should build a strong foundation to support any major transaction, and provide the results of its due diligence investigation to the board. Depending on scale, materiality, and complexity, the board may choose to retain independent advisors to assist them, particularly where there are complicated financial, legal, integration, culture, or other issues. Before making the choices involved, the board meets to consider whether it needs to retain advisors who are not also advising management, as it can be presumed that management's advisors may be further down the learning curve and thus see their role as selling the board on the deal.

Look at the possible outcomes for management with and without consummation of the transaction in question. There may be areas in which the board is well advised to engage its own experts, especially in the arena of legal advice to the board as well as independent valuation professionals. Even when they do not do so, it should be as a result of examining the issues and determining that the concerns of management and the board in the instance are one and the same.

Importantly, as we learned by reviewing the evolution of the board's role, we have seen that the courts generally respect the business judgment of the board so long as it is clear that the disinterested directors, have exercised their business

DOI 10.1515/9781547400270-027

judgment and acted on an informed basis, pursuant to a thorough process, and in good faith.

Volumes can and have been written on the board's role in transactions. In the best functioning situations, the board is involved early on in considering strategic issues and acquisition or divestiture candidates, and then an iterative, back and forth process ensues with management as the transaction takes shape. Though it is easy to think of transactions only in terms of mergers, acquisitions, and divestitures, be sure that the decision-making framework in place also requires board review and approval of any major capital transaction and its terms.

Read More

"Role of the Board in M&A," Lajoux, Alexandra R., National Association of Corporate Directors, September, 2015

"Modernizing the Board's Role in M&A," Bhagat, Chinta and Huyett, Bill; *McKinsey Quarterly,* February 2013

"How Boards Should Deal with M&A," Atkins, Betsy; *Forbes Magazine,* January 2010

The Art of M&A: A Merger Acquisition Buyout Guide 4th Edition, Reed, Stanley Foster; Lajoux, Alexandra R., Nesvold, Peter H., McGraw Hill Education, 2007

The Art of M&A Due Diligence: Navigating Critical Steps and Uncovering Crucial Data, Second Edition, Lajoux, Alexandra R., and Elson, Charles M., McGraw Hill Education, 20

Art of M&A Valuation and Modeling: A Guide to Corporate Valuation, LaJoux, Alexandra R., Nesvold, Peter H., Nesvold, Elizabeth Bloomer, McGraw Hill Education, 2015

"Making Capital Structure Support Strategy," Goedhart, Marc H., Koller, Timothy; Rehm, Werner, *McKinsey & Company Series on Corporate Finance & Strategy,* 2006

Chapter 28
Communicate Clearly, Consistently and Constantly

Moving beyond the hot buttons highlighted by the NYSE, we focus now on communication, a word all too frequently used in this book. Doing it well at all levels can make the difference between success and failure.

First, we must all remember to protect confidentiality of boardroom discussions. Confidentiality is essential for an effective board process and for the protection of the corporation. Moreover, directors generally owe a broad legal duty of confidentiality to the corporation with respect to information they learn about the corporation in the course of their duties.

Maintaining confidentiality is also essential for the protection of individual directors, given that directors can be held responsible for any misleading statements attributable to them. Even when a director believes the subject matter of his or her statements is within the public domain, it is good practice for an individual director to avoid commenting on matters concerning the corporation. A director who receives an inquiry may or may not have all of the relevant information, and his or her response could involve the corporation, as well as the director, in a disclosure violation. Directing public communications through a single spokesperson, such as the CEO, allows the corporation to speak with a unified voice.

Communicate the Right Things. Maintaining credibility and building mutual trust between board members and each other, between the board and management, employees, and between the corporation and its customers, vendors, investors, and lenders are absolute imperatives for the board to foster. All parties want to know that there is an engaged, thoughtful board overseeing a reasonable, long-term business strategy that is on track to achieve long-term value creation. Such communications should address the following:

- Describe the strategy and confirm board involvement in the strategy.
- Make the case for long-term investments. Explain where appropriate capital projects and investments. Particularly when short-term pressures are at their peak, adhering to a strategy that prioritizes long-term investments can demonstrate the board's conviction regarding its strategy.
- Describe capital allocation priorities.
- Address sustainability, citizenship, and ESG/CSR. The corporation should communicate how management and directors view relevant sustainability matters in relation to firm value and strategy.
- Articulate the link between compensation design and corporate strategy. The corporation should describe how compensation practices encourage

DOI 10.1515/9781547400270-028

and reward long-term growth, promote implementation of the strategy, and achieve business goals.
- Explain why the right mix of directors is in the boardroom. The corporation should present the diverse skills, expertise, and attributes of the board and of individual members and link them to the corporation's needs and risks.
- Discuss how board practices and board culture support independent oversight. Articulate the actual practices and responsibilities of the lead director or nonexecutive chair, independent directors, committee chairs, and the board as a whole in providing effective oversight, understanding stakeholder perspectives, evaluating CEO performance, and organizing the board to ensure priorities are met.

Consider adopting the Integrated Reporting Framework developed by the International Integrated Reporting Council (IIRC) and/or the Global Reporting Initiative (GRI) both of which are designed to supplement financial reports to better align capital allocation and corporate behavior to wider goals of financial stability, sustainable development, long-term value creation and improved investor dialog.

Use the Right Methods of Engagement. Direct engagement through disclosure—including earnings calls, periodic reports, proxy statements and other SEC filings, the corporation's website and the corporation's social media presence is often the most practical means of engagement. In other cases, in-person meetings, one-on-one calls or interactive communications (such as at conferences or investor days) may be more effective or efficient. Whatever approach is taken, the key is quality rather than quantity. Establishing channels of communication in advance of a crisis or activist challenge is extremely important.

Determine Appropriate Director Involvement in Engagement Activities. Major institutional investors expect that a corporation will provide access to its independent directors, and these investors have stated that it will color their attitude toward a corporation if the corporation first begins to provide such access only after it has been attacked by an activist. Participating directors should be thoroughly briefed on discussion topics as well as the constraints of disclosure rules.

Read More

"Communicate Effectively to Create Better Board Relationships," Smith, Hardy, BoardSource Blog, December, 2016

"Best Practices in Board Communications," ResultsMap, 2013

"Communication and Decision-Making in Corporate Boards," Malenko, Nadya, *Review of Financial Studies*, Vol. 27, No. 5, Carroll School of Management, Boston College, May 2014

"Choosing the Right Strategy When Communicating with Investors," Hull, Patrick, *Forbes Magazine*, October 16, 2013

"Communicating with the Right Investors," Palter, Robert N., Rehm, Werner, and Shih, Jonathan, *McKinsey Quarterly*, April 2008

"Engagement—Succeeding in the New Paradigm for Corporate Governance," Lipton, Martin; Harvard Law School Forum on Corporate Governance and Financial Regulation, January 23, 2018

Part V: **Hazards and Their Navigation**

Here is the fundamental question that everyone involved in the corporation—employees, top management, shareholders, lenders, even vendors—want to answer. To whom do we entrust the responsibility of corporate governance? And why is it so difficult to build and sustain a highly effective board?

In hindsight, we often look at major corporate disasters and ask ourselves "What were they thinking?" It boggles the mind to think that disasters such as WorldCom, Enron, and the rest can happen without serious negligence on the part of board members. Yet it is difficult to find a pattern of incompetence or corruption. Members showed up for meetings; they invested in the company; audit committees, compensation committees, and codes of ethics were in place; the boards were not too small, too big, too old, or too young. Board composition was generally similar between companies that failed and companies that succeeded.

Bottom line: to what can we ascribe the repeated failures attributed to governance? It appears that many boards simply go through the motions, which may be exactly what management wants them to do so that management can avoid be distracted by an active board. Most of these failures are not due to sins of commission, but instead of omission, of failing to see that a step in a process was missing, that the right hand was not aware of what the left hand was doing, and so on. Boards are often blind, which may explain why it seems they are often blindsided by events.

There are many minefields of which to be wary, and no one can list them all. Some significant ones are discussed here, as food for thought, and not as a definitive list. Most of these hazards are hazards because we are people; people with foibles and idiosyncrasies. And for the most part, realizing value in the companies we serve depends on working well with people at all levels, and trying to discern what is driving them. We aim here to consider the bigger rocks that can take the company down, and some of the smaller pebbles that when ignored can cause real injury.

Chapter 29
Address Individual Hazards and Personal Fear

We have beaten to a pulp the notion that directors are fiduciaries for the corporation. Black's Law Dictionary defines "fiduciary relationship" as "a relationship in which one person is under a duty to act for the benefit of another on matters within the scope of the relationship. Fiduciary relationships . . . require an unusually high degree of care." In exercising their powers to act on behalf of the corporation, directors are bound by two important duties:

- *The duty of care.* "Directors are not merely bound to be honest; they must also be diligent and careful in performing the duties they have undertaken."
- *The duty of loyalty.* "An undivided and unselfish loyalty to the corporation demands that there be no conflict between duty and self-interest . . . the duty of loyalty mandates that the best interest of the corporation and its shareholders takes precedence over any interest possessed by a director, officer or controlling shareholder and not shared by the stockholders generally."

Liability Concerns

Both state law and the federal securities laws require director care and loyalty when attending to the affairs of the corporation, which can be seen as a precondition to the exercise of independent judgment and the related protections of the business judgment rule. Many in and out of the boardroom see the possibility of monetary liability for being found to have breached these duties to be an overarching preoccupation. This concern can seriously undermine the ability of directors individually and the board to acquit themselves of their jobs. Often, we find directors cowering, determining their course of action not by discernment of the most attractive path for the company, but by estimating which action or nonaction will minimize their risk of being sued.

But how real is such exposure? Liability for breach of the duty of care uncomplicated by self-dealing has been famously described as the search for a very small number of needles in a very large haystack and the risk of securities fraud liability as nonexistent. Professors Black, Cheffins, and Klausner tell us that liability in duty of care cases is still quite rare, and that outside director liability exposure in securities fraud litigation is limited to rare near perfect storm cases.

In his 2013 blog post "Outside Director Accountability" on The D&O Diary Blog, Kevin LaCroix observes that independent corporate directors named as defendants in D&O litigation rarely pay settlements or judgments out of their

DOI 10.1515/9781547400270-029

own assets. In a June 2013, paper by Harvard Business School professors Francois Brochet and Suraj Srinivasan entitled "Accountability of Independent Directors— Evidence from Firms Subject to Securities Litigation" looks at both liability and accountability.

The authors studied the incidence of independent directors being named as securities suit defendants and the record of shareholder votes against those directors by examining a database of 921 securities class action lawsuits filed between 1996 and 2010. They found that when companies were named as defendants in these suits, 11% of their directors were also named as defendants. It appears that the likelihood of an independent director being named as a defendant is much higher for directors serving on the audit committee (54% of named independent director defendants); for directors that sold shares (16% of named independent director defendants); or that have been on the board for the entire class period. The incidence is also higher when the lead plaintiff is an institutional investor.

Examination of subsequent shareholder votes showed that a greater percentage of votes (5.47%) regarding these independent director defendants were withheld than for a controlled sample of independent directors whose companies had not been sued.

The authors also examined lawsuit outcomes when independent directors are named defendants and found that when independent directors are named as defendants, the less likely the lawsuit is to be dismissed, which may also relate to settlements both faster and larger. Notably, the authors found that "some of our evidence points to the strategic naming of independent directors by plaintiffs to gain bigger settlements." Unfortunately, we live in a society in which litigation is seen as a commonplace element of strategy. Nevertheless, monetary payments by directors remain limited to the most egregious situations.

Efforts to Insulate Directors

Let's look at efforts to insulate directors from liability. The development of corporate indemnification statutes at the state level grew rapidly in the 1950s, and soon covered all negligent behavior. Liability insurance for directors and officers (D&O) also developed in the 1950s and 1960s, designed to cover liability, which indemnification could not address. In the mid-1980s, Delaware adopted director exculpation statutes for breach of the duty of care, and was quickly followed by other states.

Following the Enron et al. scandals, it seemed that the Delaware courts, notably unwilling to assign monetary damages to directors, might look more favorably on liability theories that increased a director's monetary exposure for wrongful behavior based on failure to undertake adequate inquiry. Many of these theories asked the courts for a finding of bad faith. Such possibilities seemed to end when, following eight years of litigation over the $100 million severance payment by the Walt Disney Co. to former president Michael Ovitz, the courts found for the directors, the Delaware Supreme Court made it clear that gross negligence (including a failure to inform oneself of available material facts), does not constitute bad faith, seeming to require some further indication of a conscious disregard for one's responsibilities to find bad faith.

Interestingly, the Delaware Supreme Court further held that bad faith was not by itself a basis for director liability but rather one precipitating condition for finding liability under the duty of loyalty. The protracted and highly visible litigation combined with the court's setting forth in embarrassing detail the deficiencies of the directors' decision-making had, however, quite a bit of impact. The tone of the Court and the implied threat of liability the next time may have increased director vigilance.

Similarly, the potential stick of director liability under the federal securities law largely failed to materialize following the 2008 collapses. The applicable liability standard that emerged for director liability was based on an assessment of whether the directors had knowledge of the wrongful disclosure or were reckless in not knowing. Regarding disclosure in a public offering of securities, however, courts have found that directors have an affirmative due diligence obligation to assure themselves of the accuracy of the disclosed statements. A decision in the WorldCom matter determined that directors can not necessarily rely on an auditor's certification when there are red flags in the financials involved. Rather than face a trial on what they knew or should have known, the WorldCom independent directors settled the litigation. They were facing a public pension fund plaintiff that insisted on personal liability for the directors instead of simply receiving insurance proceeds. Each director's contribution was designed to be approximately 20 percent of their net worth, approximately $25 million in total.

Nevertheless, while Delaware courts and others have issued opinions that publicly excoriated in harsh terms the behavior of directors and other corporate actors, it remains rare for directors themselves to face monetary penalties. Thus, the main problem regarding director behavior is not so much actual liability, or even the embarrassment of a pen lashing by a judge, but the timid behavior that may result from exaggerated fears.

Directors and Candidates Should Understand the Protections They Have

Director candidates as well as sitting directors may want to undertake, or ask counsel to provide, a review of their actual liability coverage and how it works. I have been surprised at how little many directors understand about this area, and that ignorance can provide a fertile environment in which fear can grow and decisiveness decline. Issues to look at include the source and scope of indemnification in the relevant state statutes as well as in the corporate charter and its bylaws, and the estimated ability of the enterprise in various circumstances to perform on that indemnification commitment. Some directors and companies enter into specific indemnification agreements between the company and each individual director.

Next consider the workings of the D&O policies, which for large companies are often organized into what is called a "stack" in which multiple carriers split the levels of risk. Issues to consider there are many, and it may be worthwhile to have your own counsel review the policies. Look for the level of exposure at which the policies kick in (comparable to the deductible in personal automobile or health insurance), and exactly what costs the policies cover and what they exclude.

Between the indemnification and the insurance, what you want to be sure of at a minimum is that you have no exposure for the costs of administering the litigation. You want to be double dog sure that attorney and related costs are paid directly and not based on reimbursement. You will also want to look at who chooses counsel. This is important because whether successful or not, litigation is common, may be used as an intimidation tactic, and attorneys are expensive.

One final, slightly jarring note. It is important for independent directors to focus on the fact that the insurance policies are called "Directors and Officers Liability Insurance" for a reason. The pool of money covers both the board and company officers, and their positions in litigation are more likely to be different than similar. Litigation when it succeeds often results in the plaintiffs securing their recovery by receiving funds from that pool. Keep an eye on who may have claims on the insurance money, and how much remains available for directors only. Large policies often have an adverse effect in that they can attract litigation.

Beware the Responsible Corporate Officer Doctrine

The responsible corporate officer doctrine (RCOD) arose out of two U.S. Supreme Court decisions rendered thirty-two years apart that established a treacherous concept. In each case, the Supreme Court upheld the conviction of corporate officers for crimes against the public welfare without evidence that they participated in or had knowledge of the core criminal activity. The resulting strict liability theory has been interpreted as permitting (in certain circumstances) the prosecution of corporate officers and directors for misdemeanor criminal offenses without the need to establish their intent or personal involvement in wrongful conduct. They held that corporate officers and directors could be held criminally liable for corporate legal violations when they are in a position of responsibility and authority, have the power to prevent the violation, and fail to do so.

In 2017, Supreme Court's decision not to consider the case of U.S. v DeCoster has been interpreted to remove hope that application of the doctrine will be clarified soon. Exposure to action under RCOD will likely remain a disconcerting compliance risk that directors in several key industries must monitor. To date it has been used mainly in the pharmaceutical and medical device industries, pursuant to the Food, Drug, and Cosmetic Act (FDCA).

That statute allows the government to obtain a conviction when three standards are met: (1) that "the prohibited act took place somewhere within the company," (2) "the defendant's position within the company was one that gave him or her responsibility and authority either to prevent the violation or correct it," and (3) that he or she did not do so. Prosecutors have also successfully applied RCOD theories to several other state and federal statutes including violations of the Sherman Act, the federal securities laws, and state/federal environmental laws. Their successful application has been in circumstances where protecting public health and welfare may arguably justify the finding of liability without culpability.

The possibility of applying this doctrine more broadly seems to represent a frightening slippery slope. Current pressure to find a way to assign responsibility for bad acting is high. Regulators may possibly be seeking opportunities to use RCOD to accomplish regulatory goals and ensure that somebody pays the price for wrongdoing. The Department of Justice has been very clear that it will continue to hold directors and officers responsible for corporate wrongdoing.

Whereas I have long believed that if a director stays awake, pays close attention, and believes he or she has discerned and supported the best available decision in the circumstances, the liability risk of serving as director was quite low. Because of this belief I have been willing to walk into several board roles that were seriously frightening to others. The possibility of the broad application of the RCOD may change that belief. Serving as a director has in fact become a more dangerous proposition requiring the exercise of greater care.

These principles, we hope, will be used to impose liability on individuals only in the rarest and most extreme circumstances, notwithstanding legitimate concerns regulators may have regarding wrongdoing.

Read More

"Outside Director Liability," LaCroix, Kevin M., *The D&O Diary, February, 2013*

"Accountability of Independent Directors-Evidence from Firms Subject to Securities Litigation," Brochet, Francois and Srinivasan, Suraj; *Working Knowledge,* Harvard Business School, July 2013

"Director and Officer Indemnification and Insurance–Issues for Public Companies to Consider," Gibson, Dunn, & Crutcher, July 15, 2013

"Why Corporate Executives Should Have a Separate Written Indemnification Agreement," LaCroix, Kevin M., *The D&O Diary,* August 7, 2016

Chapter 30
Navigate Corporate Hazards and Distressed Situations

There are many hazards that can hurt the company and drive it toward failure. The proximate cause of collapse, though, is always, at least in my experience, a lack of liquidity, or, in other words, running out of cash. Given how universal this is, it always surprises me that so few companies have a real process for tracking availability of cash. Though I had nothing to do with creating it, I have served on the board of a company that used a great quarterly exhibit: number of days cash on hand, given certain assumptions. They have tracked it for many years, and thus have a way better than average understanding of their cash dynamics.

That company is, however, the exception. Nobody wants their company to run out of cash and thus be driven unwillingly but inexorably into the arms of a greedy acquirer or into bankruptcy court. This is where the board can play a critical role. Though some changes that drive the loss of liquidity happen overnight, in most cases the issues have been building for a while. It is incumbent upon the board to ask the right questions, and to bring management to the table to develop a realistic recovery plan.

The difficulty confronting reality does not necessarily mean they are not good managers, but often the information they have or their interpretation of it is based on assumptions that no longer apply. Remaining inert can seem easier than tackling the changes that may be required. And for the Chief Executive Officer (CEO), the issues can be more complex. The CEO likely believes that it is his or her job to know the answer and chart the course. Feeling a sense of failure or shame may result in a closed door and lessened communication just when increased communication is essential for progress. The board, with the perspective that can come from both broad experience and a little distance, needs to focus on *any* signs of distress while cash is still plentiful, and help management to work through it.

Sometimes managers have underestimated how critical their situation was—or they were looking at the wrong data, which happens remarkably often. Others have, in the long running low interest rate environment, taken advantage of low cost liquidity in hopes of outrunning poor performance. Some have gotten caught up in the relentless pressure for short-term returns discussed above and neglected long-term health—or even willfully sacrificed it—until it is too late.

DOI 10.1515/9781547400270-030

Liquidity: What to Do When Cash Runs Low

The first and most difficult step in the active management of cash has little to do with cash. The critical first step is to acknowledge that there is a problem before cash runs low, and help bring management out of denial. Done early enough, digging into daily cash numbers may never be required. Regardless, the board needs to know how it is to be done, and why building such a tool is an imperative. And while assessing the causes of distress and possible solutions, several other steps can be taken if there is time. Get everyone, board and management, to focus on cash, and a handful of key indicators that will vary by industry but will typically include loss/gain of key customers, vendors, and personnel; communications with lenders and regulators; dates associated with major hurdles such as refinancing. These can become the basis of an easily prepared one-to two page flash report for directors and top management.

Form a Board Committee to Focus Closely on the Emergency

The next is to identify a group of board members who can form a committee of three or so members to work closely with management to address emergency needs and serve as a bridge to the full board. This group will review management's plans and assumptions in detail and consider contingencies such as whether management needs replacing or needs additional help, and needs to have both time and inclination to be available on short notice. Discussions as to where are we most vulnerable, how can we adjust our cost without losing critical customers, and so on must be had unflinchingly. It is rare for companies to be dealing with just one indicator of distress, and more typical to have to fight a multifront war.

The perspective the board can bring to this can not be overstated. Many directors are uncomfortable serving in a distressed situation due to liability concerns and/or uncertainty with respect to the scope of their duties. As a result, they often resign just when the business needs them the most. To be blunt, if they have been on the board while the company's results deteriorated, they already have whatever liability they may fear, and their best way to reduce it is to accept responsibility for the situation and work with peers and management to right the ship. In fact, the duties of the board become not only clearer in a distressed situation, but should the decision be made to file for bankruptcy protection, the court will provide a further degree of clarity as well.

The focus on cash needs to become pervasive throughout the organization. Keeping track of cash is not just about watching your bank balance. To avoid surprises, companies also need a good forecast that provides a midterm and longer view. For example, failing to pay attention to the cash component of capital investments routinely gets companies in trouble. Project net present values can look the same whether the return begins gradually at year two or jumps up dramatically at year five. But if you're not focusing on the cash that goes out the door while you're waiting for that year-five infusion, you can suddenly find yourself with very little cash left to run the business, sending you into a spiral you may not recover from.

This will require a change in thinking for most executives, who have typically delegated cash management to lower level employees. For the foreseeable future, understanding cash flow and its sources and uses is a top management and board role, and the board needs to insist. The goal is to be sure both board and management can see how much cash is available, where it is and who has what types of claims on it. Request that the CEO get a rolling thirteen-week cash flow forecast created and shared that includes expected cash receipts, disbursements, use of working capital and debt and capital expenditure payments. Until the cash crunch has been resolved, this thirteen-week cash flow forecast will become a critically important management tool used every day to make decisions.

If the board loses confidence in management or decides outside help is needed, creation of this thirteen-week cash flow forecast is the very first step that will be taken. There is no reason management can not create it, but it will require looking at data differently, so the board needs to know what is asking for, how it is created, and why it is so necessary to be sure it gets done.

Data from the last several quarters will provide the starting place, with trips to the general ledger if need be. Starting with actual experience indicates the items that need tracking, and an ability to easily test assumptions. Once it appears that every item has been captured, management and board need to review what it shows about the company's position. How much cash do we have, how long will it last based on recent consumption rate, and what can we do to make it last while we work to climb out of this position? Be sure that those cash payments that must be made on a date certain are identified. Request that the comparison of forecasted sources and uses against actual performance be shared each week. This will give you a very clear picture of where cash comes from and goes to and when.

Push your team to evaluate how critical the use of cash is, and consider what would happen if the disbursement were delayed, made late, or not made at all. This goes against the grain for those employees in the payables department who have prided themselves on staying current. Do not take their compliance with the bee order for granted, but be sure management is watching. Be sure you have provided fully for debt service, payroll, benefits, and all taxes. Do not take inbound cash or its timing for granted—look at it with a skeptical eye.

Get them to look also for possible supplemental sources of cash, such as owned real estate, planes or vehicles, equipment or excess inventory and see how fast and at what price these can be converted to cash if need be. Be sure to take a fresh look at accounts and notes receivable and accelerate collection efforts. You now have an accurate sense of what turnaround managers call the burn rate. It will help you see how fast the company is consuming cash, how long the apparently available cash will last, and whether you will likely need more before the company moves into a cash flow neutral position.

If the company clearly needs more cash than it has available to achieve stability, this tool will help you determine how much, and lenders and other sources will expect to see it and test it. Begin immediately to explore new lender financing and consider the feasibility and time required to monetize noncore assets, including business divisions.

This is a brutal process, and an essential one, not for the faint of heart. And if management is not already doing it, the board must require that the forecast be updated constantly to reflect what is happening. Done properly, it will yield an estimate of the time available to analyze the company's options and develop the plan to move forward.

It will also give you the ability rapidly to assess the impact of and respond to unexpected developments, which will happen. What if expected orders fail to materialize? Or you lose a major customer? Or a working capital lender ups its collateral requirements? Finally, it will give you the ability to identify the pressure points and the parties whose support is mission critical. This requires a review of the company position relative to creditor and vendor claims and covenants and awareness of other possible issues that can derail the process or distract its leaders.

Is This Really a Role for the Board?

Getting this involved in the granular details may strike many board members as an unseemly invasion of management's territory. But if the company is truly on a path to run out of cash, consider the consequences of not doing it. Management at this point is often paralyzed and not easily able to adjust their thinking or the data they think about daily. Thus, as the guardian of the corporation's health, it is imperative that the board help them by pushing for this work to be done. Normal course behavior will not cut it, and profit and loss statements and sources and uses analyses do not provide the I formation needed, at least in part because the interval is too long. Yes, this is the epitome of short-term thinking, but in these circumstances, it is imperative to survive the short term to reach the longer-term possibilities.

If you have not engaged bankruptcy counsel yet, this would be a good time to do so. You may need formal forbearance agreements or covenant waivers from your lenders or major creditors, and developing the correct legal documents may later be of critical importance in your ability to succeed. This is not the time to be squeamish; the cost of counsel is likely to be high, and needs to be provided for, as having the right legal assistance is imperative whether the company ever enters bankruptcy or not.

The Corporation Is Counsel's Client; The Board Retains Counsel

I have said this elsewhere, but it is worth repeating here that the responsibility for engaging counsel at this juncture rests with the board, which can include the CEO, but the retention must clearly be made by the board as the guardian of the corporation. Uncomfortable decisions regarding management nay need to be made, and the best way to provide for that without making it a foregone conclusion is for the board to engage restructuring counsel, also known as bankruptcy counsel. For the same reasons, the board should think hard as to whether it is best served by using existing corporate counsel's firm to provide bankruptcy counsel.

One more aspect to review with management. By the time cash is running low, lenders and trade typically know about it, and likely have known for a while. Lenders may very well have been asking for plans to address the issue, or for other information. Counsel will help you clarify the company's position legally, but it is a good idea to be sure that communication channels are open and functioning. It is human nature to avoid uncomfortable discussions with lenders, and doing so can compound the problem.

While of course the board wants to behave in accordance with a unified strategy, it must ensure that such a strategy exists, and it must include communication with lenders and other creditors. If they are not hearing from the company, and even worse, if management has not been responding to their inquiries, they may assume the worst and seek ways to take action prematurely.

The Next Step: Assess Viability

Armed with the knowledge of cash flow and availability as well as a sense of the time available to address the issues, the next step is to analyze the various options available for moving forward. The goal is to determine if the company as a whole or in parts is viable. What parts of the organization can be returned to profitability and positive cash flow within the time available? After understanding the cash position, this is the most urgent question, and needs to be answered as quickly as possible.

Viability analysis consists of several parts, quantitative and qualitative, aimed at identifying the building blocks available in developing the turnaround plan. The quantitative portion can rest on the cash flow model. From there, build an integrated financial model that ties cash flow to profit and loss and to the balance sheet. In most cases, financial reports provide a snapshot of a single moment in time and do not provide understanding of the key relationships that drive the business. The goal in this phase is to understand each component of the business as it adds to or detracts from cash generation. From there, a further analysis of customer demand, margin, market environment and competition is required, which in turn feeds the organizing of the components of the business into which ones to focus on fixing, which to consider the feasibility of selling, and which to shut down. The same aspects apply to any business—analyze the performance and returns of the individual segments or business units.

Do not be surprised if the financial reports the board has generally relied on are not as helpful to this process as expected. Management information systems are often designed to address the decision- making of older versions of the company, and not the enterprise as it has evolved. While this can shake your confidence, it is another reason that working from the updated cash flow forecasts is useful. It will be uncomfortable, but the board will find that it often must move forward without all the information it would like to have, so keeping eyes firmly fixed on cash will be a good guide.

The next step, and here the board plays an active role, is to think about the more qualitative elements, such as:
- What is this company truly about, and where is the problem coming from?
- What customer need are we aiming to fill, and are we filling that need? Can we continue to do so and earn a profit? How are those needs changing? Are we gaining or losing customers? Orders? Why?
- What are the key strengths of our company as it currently stands, and how are those strengths being used and deployed? How can we enhance those strengths and reduce the effect and cost of our weaknesses?
- What businesses are we in, and how do we fit within our markets? Which markets appear more likely to grow, or to shrink, and how will we work with that change? Do we, for example, have pricing power—can we raise our prices without losing share, or what happens if we reduce them?
- In what areas or businesses do we excel? Where do we fall short of expectations?

What you are looking for are the parts of the company that can emerge as a profitable business, able to sustain itself and finance its capital and liquidity needs. Identify the viable portions and isolate those that are not. Review the results and consider how to build on the potential for success of the viable portions, and to maximize recovery or minimize losses from the parts not deemed viable. Estimate how long the needed actions will likely take. With the viable, possibly viable, and not viable portions identified, we next turn to the question of what we can do with them, and in what format.

Determine what the viable portions, typically called the core business as the turnaround plan takes shape, need to succeed. If funding is required for the core business, estimate how much, what options there might be, and the time required to demonstrate business success. Finally determine what parties involved in the situation need to be convinced.

For example, even if a company has a viable core business, it may not have the liquidity available to complete needed restructuring. Its historical lending sources may have lost faith that the management, company or industry can generate sufficient returns, or perhaps the assets used as collateral have decreased in value. The company may need to source new or bridge financing. If the favorable prospects are convincing, however, the board must be sure that a compelling and practical case for success is developed.

Before that, however, think further about the best legal and operating format in which to move the core and noncore businesses forward. For example, is the core business likely to be robust enough to stand on its own, or would it and its stakeholders do better if you can stabilize it for a period to allow you to find the right strategic, rather than financial, buyer? Or is the time available so short that your best path is to put the company into Chapter 11 to affect a sale of the core business and a court supervised liquidation of the remaining assets? Are there liabilities, such as long-term leases, that can best be reduced or eliminated in the context of a Chapter 11 proceeding that are otherwise a hindrance? Can the company secure needed funding more easily from within the Chapter 11?

The fundamental question you need to answer with respect to the core business is this: Should the company be sold to new owners, or is restructuring in the current form a possibility? Either way, the possibility of a Chapter 11 filing must be faced squarely and analyzed rigorously. Is a Chapter 11 proceeding an attractive or unattractive mechanism to use in the facts and circumstances? While it can be expensive and sometimes unpredictable, Chapter 11 can relieve pressure from creditors and provide financing options not available out of court. It also gives the company what can be precious time to develop and execute its turnaround strategy and rebuild what is the almost inevitably tattered credibility of the distressed business.

A word to the wise. During this period, be sure that management and the board all hear from counsel as to their fiduciary duties, which is basically the question of identifying for whom who you are working. Fiduciary duty continues to be owed to the corporation, but shareholders and creditors may each think that the company's primary responsibility is to them. This can be ambiguous as equity value shrinks or disappears permanently or temporarily.

Bringing in Help

The board may determine that the company does not have the capacity available to manage a turnaround, or choose to consider hiring a professional turnaround management team for other reasons. An outside manager or organization can offer useful perspective and new discipline to the process, as well as added resources and skill sets. Their detachment from company history can be helpful, and their experience with turnarounds may enable you to move much faster than you can without them, which could be the difference between success and failure.

To be blunt, existing lenders and creditors with money at risk, no matter how long the company has worked with them, will be looking at incumbent management as part of the problem. They face their own internal pressures as their judgment in managing the relationship is under scrutiny. Bringing in an experienced turnaround professional can significantly ease tensions with lenders as they take comfort from the arrival of an objective party, who may be someone they have worked with in the past. These connections are valuable to you, but examine them carefully to be sure the turnaround executive is fully committed to realizing value for all.

Thus, in addition to seeking experience, you need to find someone you and your organization can trust. Management often assumes that employees will leave if they know the company is in trouble, but in fact employees have often been aware of challenges for quite some time. They are frequently relieved to learn that someone is taking responsibility for fixing the situation, and that person, free of the baggage of history, politics, or hierarchical concerns, can often gain valuable insight from them quite rapidly. Bringing in outside help can also help reduce the inevitable distraction of line executives and others whose focus on operations has never been more important.

Assessing Leadership Resources

Leading a company through a turnaround successfully is very different from managing a successful company, and it is the rare executive suited to both. It can also be very painful for an executive who has labored long and hard to build the company to oversee cutting it into pieces or shrinking it, often part of what needs to happen.

As the board takes a breath and contemplates the actions required, consider the possible leaders available. Think, too, about the possible structure as well as the impact the leader's position and selection may have on valuable customers and vendors. Whether you draw the leader from inside or bring in an outside resource, the following qualities are often most important:

- Engaged and accessible leader who can motivate people inside and outside of the organization
- Effective communicator able to rebuild tattered credibility through consistent updates
- Committed to doing what it takes to move forward for the benefit of all "stakeholders"
- Excellent listener able to assimilate information and adjust the critical path as needed
- Possessed of unshakable integrity and discerning judgment to build trust of a variety
- of parties with different and often inconsistent objectives.
- Exhibits grace under pressure who treats all parties with respect no matter how tough it gets.

Structuring the Leadership Role

With a sense now of what the leader will need to do, it is time to think about the leader's role in the organization. The role can be played by the incumbent CEO if the board and the CEO and others believe that he or she has the skills and fortitude to persevere and succeed. That said, the pressure is enormous and the emotional difficulty of taking apart or radically changing what a long time CEO has built can be personally devastating and professionally crippling.

What we most often see when we arrive in a new assignment is the closed door of the CEO's office, and an absent, unengaged board. The CEO would not be the CEO if he or she did not assume responsibility for the company, and believe he or she is expected to have the answers, be a super hero, and solve the problem. Feeling unable to do that, the temptation to close the door and hide can be very strong. Doing so is entirely understandable and a huge mistake. Thus, if the board chooses the incumbent CEO as the leader of the turnaround effort, it is mission critical that that person have support. The support of bankruptcy counsel is important, as is support from the board. Those may not be enough, as it needs to be faced that this executive is grappling with a sense of shame and guilt, and thus he needs also to rely as well on the support of his family and trusted confidantes who can help with that.

Another way to structure the leadership role is to create a purpose-built position working with a trusted restructuring professional. Many companies have successfully crested a Chief Restructuring Officer, or CRO, who takes on responsibility for leading the turnaround effort while incumbent leaders manage the business operations and maintain relations with customers. This role sometimes includes the executive powers of the CEO, and sometimes does not. It can also be structured as an advisory role.

The role needs to be crafted carefully, and should report to the board while working closely with the incumbent management team. An important aspect of this role is that it is temporary, and will disappear once turnaround objectives have been achieved. That temporary nature adds to its appeal for many companies, as it acknowledges that turnaround skills are different from normal management skills, and one executive is unlikely to embody both. It can also be used as a graceful way to let the incumbent CEO out of the hot seat while keeping him in place to reassure customers, vendors, and employees.

Communicate the Plan, and the Progress

In either case, the role of the board is critically important. Though the board can not manage the turnaround, it needs to do all that it can to raise the odds of success. This means not only selecting, supporting, and monitoring the effectiveness of the leaders, but being closely involved with the development and realization of the turnaround plan. The turnaround strategy to be implemented should be universally understood. Every employee, manager and director should be able to describe the company's turnaround strategy.

When a company's viability is in question, rumors and misinformation grow rapidly. Constant communication of clear, accurate information is critical to getting the right message out and preventing erroneous beliefs from undermining your efforts. There is no such thing as too much communication. Communication builds credibility—with employees, with financial and other stakeholders in the business, and with the press and the public. This will reinforce your strategy and help instill confidence in your ability to lead the company into the future you envision.

If you have chosen to take the company through reorganization using a Chapter 11 proceeding, that creates further communication requirements. Bankruptcy is often a misunderstood process and is very frightening to many employees, vendors, and customers alike. Be sure all interested parties understand why you are filing for bankruptcy protection, and clearly communicate the goals to be achieved by doing so. Reassure people that a bankruptcy filing is not the end of the company's life, but that it offers a set of tools for troubled companies and their stakeholders. Importantly, Chapter 11 of the Bankruptcy Code also requires that the company, known as the "debtor in possession" once the filing is approved, follow a highly structured process that includes specified confidentiality and reporting requirements and other forms of communication.

Just Do It

An endless list of things must be accomplished, often against tough odds and within a tight timeframe. Nevertheless, maintaining the status quo is not an option. You must act decisively, even in the face of reservations or concerns. There will be many tough decisions that will need to be both made and communicated. This requires discipline in making necessary decisions, not avoiding them, as well as in communication as you want to do everything you can to preserve confidence and buy in with all stakeholders. The board needs to be sure that these decisions are being made, and communication is occurring. It is always amazing to see how much can get done, and done very well, by a motivated team that believes it is empowered to make a difference.

Once the turnaround strategy has been communicated through a detailed plan, everyone Is accountable for what happens next. Throughout the process, it is important to recognize and celebrate milestones achieved and to correct the course if they are not achieved. Staying disciplined and focused is one thing; wearing blinders is another. Remain alert to changing circumstances and how they affect the prospects for a successful turnaround. Missing a milestone, or achieving one too easily, may indicate that you need to adjust your plan. Incremental success with ongoing adjustments is preferable to no forward movement at all.

The work involved in turning around a company is grueling. It can also be very gratifying as you get to the heart of what drives the business, its people, and yourself. Difficult and unexpected things will happen and threaten to knock the company off course, and you have prepared for that by following the steps outlined here. Many wonderful events will also occur, for which it is harder to prepare, but which will help to keep you moving forward toward success.

Appreciation of the Effort Put in Goes a Long Way

It takes considerable time, effort, and courage to recognize and act on the need to fix the company under your care, and to lay the groundwork for turning it around by facing facts, analyzing cash, and developing the turnaround plan. It can also require inhuman amounts of effort, stamina and sacrifice to execute the plan successfully. One of my favorite sayings is this: If you see a turtle sitting on top of a fence post, you know he did not get there alone. The board and management are in it together.

Finally, there is nothing like the tremendous feeling of accomplishment as you watch results begin to turn and management, employees, colleagues, your creditors and vendors and yes, your customers begin to breathe again. And once you have been through this once, you will find that nothing and no one can threaten your sense of confidence and personal value again.

Yes, Virginia, You Did Sign Up for This

Some directors will read this and exclaim that this is not what they signed up for, and either resign or fail to appear for critical meetings. I beg to differ. If you are a sitting director of any company, you have affirmatively accepted, with your fellow board members, the responsibility for the welfare of the company. Quailing in the face of fear and difficulty is no way to behave, and risks not only letting down your colleagues and the company you have promised to protect, but increasing your own exposure, in other words, if you as a director are not part of the solution, you will highly likely be seen as part of the problem.

Becoming the Debtor in Possession

Should the company file for protection under Chapter 11 of the Bankruptcy Code, its legal status will typically change to that of "debtor in possession" under the supervision of the court. This new legal status will remain in effect, unless for some reason the court is moved to remove the incumbent board, until the company is "discharged" from the Chapter 11 as the plan of reorganization is confirmed by court. This concept of the debtor in possession is unique to the US bankruptcy process. It is based on a wonderfully idealistic construct that incumbent directors and managers can perform as statutory fiduciaries to reorganize a business that failed under their leadership.

This is a uniquely American expression of trust and confidence, reflected in Congress's intent in adopting the Bankruptcy Code: that business reorganization cases would be used "to restructure a business's finances so that it may continue to operate, provide its employees with jobs, pay its creditors, and produce a return for its stockholders." While the process has inevitably become much more cynical as time has passed, remembering its roots can be helpful.

There are many who do not believe that the Chapter 11 process should begin with an assumption that the debtor remains in possession. This appears to be due in large part to the observation that boards of directors of many failed companies cease to function or are conspicuously absent as distress intensifies. As a result, outside professional advisors become de facto boards as well as management. With no genuine governing body, there is no principal. The advisors or agents of the debtor are their own clients. Which means there is no true accountability and that role is thrown on the court and the parties in interest. As the courts have found in many situations, it is not possible to be your own client.

These governance failures are generally not intentional. Sometimes boards are simply unaware of their continuing responsibilities. Sometimes boards are dazed in the face of crisis, and simply freeze. Some boards essentially disband. To protect debtor estates from abuse, the Bankruptcy Code contemplates various checks on the debtor in possession's freedom of action, ranging from ordinary course operating parameters to required reporting and disclosure. The Bankruptcy Code also places the debtor under the formal oversight of court appointed creditors' committees and the U.S. Trustee, not to mention that of the bankruptcy court itself. And if cause Is shown, bankruptcy courts are authorized to appoint a Chapter 11 trustee or independent examiner. Without a genuine, independent governing body, the debtor in possession becomes unable to serve as a fiduciary as required by the Bankruptcy Code and corporate law. Directors be warned, then: if the company you serve has filed for protection under Chapter 11 of the Bankruptcy Code, you continue to have serious responsibility for its welfare.

Read More

"Governance Issues of Distressed Companies," ABA Business Law Section, American Bar Association, March 29, 2018

"Fiduciary Duties of Directors and Officers of Distressed Companies," Logan, Ben H, *AIRA Journal*, Association of Insolvency and Restructuring Advisors, 2013

Executive Guide to Corporate Bankruptcy, Salerno, Thomas J., Beard Books, 2010

"Turnaround Manager's Playbook," Midanek, Deborah Hicks; Solon Group, 2017

Chapter 31
Recognize and Rectify Hazards of Board Process

As the Chinese proverb suggests, in every crisis, there is opportunity, and I take it a step further by desiring never to waste a single drop of the lessons learned and opportunities uncovered by that crisis. So now that we have reviewed the issues involved in facing difficult decisions, analyzing cash, assessing viability of various units, and dealt with the vagaries of moving through the recovery or sale process, let's look at what we have learned. We know a great deal more about our company, our industry, and our liquidity and capital resources. Imagine, too, what we have learned about our colleagues on the board and in management.

Take a further step and imagine how communication among those who have made it through the process has evolved. Everyone has likely shed their dignified carapace and engaged in direct communication. Scales have fallen from eyes, defense mechanisms have long been shed, and tight bonds formed. You have seen what your fellow travelers on this journey are made of. And you may possibly be thinking that if only you knew then what you know now.

Let us then explore what we might be able to do to gain the benefits of that knowledge without the hardship, realizing that if we can build those bonds, that trust, and that open communication we have substantially lowered the risk that we will ever go through the harrowing process of shepherding our company through a period of serious distress. Some of the obstacles to overcome are explored below, and I hope this stimulates thinking about additional hurdles you may have experienced.

Continuing Confusion as to Responsibility and Authority

To my eyes, the most significant threat to success lies in the difficulty of establishing a reasonably clear agreement among directors themselves as well as between directors and management and directors and investors as to what their job is and how to do it.

I am puzzled by articles that posit a new model of fealty to the corporation rather than to shareholders, when in fact the model that exists now IS the model that requires directors to serve as fiduciaries for the corporation, and as its agents, not directly those of shareholders. If there is confusion on this, boards will be vulnerable to being weakened by outspoken shareholders asserting bogus ownership rights. Perhaps we should urge the Securities and Exchange Commission (SEC) to adopt the notion the European Union (EU) has publicized, making clear

DOI 10.1515/9781547400270-031

and explicit that shareholders do *not* own the company and thus do not enjoy the rights and privileges of ownership.

We have examined these issues at some length herein, and I hope that readers who influence board rooms will as a result have better developed views on this subject. There is not much more I can add other than to repeat that the board is a fiduciary for and agent of the corporation, and through helping it to thrive it serves shareholders, the primary beneficiaries of its efforts. When the board has a clear view of its role, it can step more fully into its powers.

Group Think

The powers of the board are vested in the board, and not in the individual directors. This one sentence encapsulates the dilemma of fostering board effectiveness. While individual directors may have deep knowledge, excellent experience, and strong views as to the best route for the corporation to follow to achieve its goals, if the individual can not influence the thinking and ultimately the decisions of the group, that individual can not be an effective director. There are many ways that that director's efforts can be derailed by the group, both intentionally and inadvertently. Group behavior is powerful, and in blunting contributions of individuals, it can end up defaulting to taking the path of least resistance.

Board leaders often follow certain rituals of communication, such as deflecting individual comments by saying that the topic is off point or belongs in a committee discussion, or should be taken up outside the boardroom. While sometimes these comments are correct, they can easily be used by influential parties to reduce the individual director's ability to be heard at all, and of course to preserve their position of dominance. One silly constraint that occurs way more often than I like to believe: "we only have limited time as so and so needs to leave to catch a plane." It always surprises me when those words are taken seriously by the entire group, when a great deal of effort has been invested to prepare for the meeting itself, which has been planned long in advance. I must always stop myself from suggesting that so and so catch a later plane, when the business of the board has been concluded.

Faulty Filters

Executive recruiters checking references during board candidate searches will often ask, "Is this person a team player?" which can be code for "Is this person compliant, or a boat rocker?" In some circumstances, if a board member challenges major decisions, a company may actively work to discredit the person. Consider the case of Hewlett-Packard and Walter Hewlett, an academic and the cofounder's son, who controlled 18% of Hewlett-Packard stock. With his deep understanding of the computer business, he questioned the desirability of HP's proposed merger with Compaq in the fall of 2001. Even though technology mergers rarely work, his point of view was summarily dismissed. When he felt he had no choice but to go public with his objections, he was ridiculed publicly in a smear campaign.

Corporate Myths

Close relatives of sacred cows, corporate myths are generally based on what once was true, and have had a long history of instilling pride in executives and employees alike. They can be powerful long after they are no longer true, and it's the job of the board and its members to look beyond their constant repetition to determine if they are valid, and if so, are they relevant. Though handy as a sound bite, in what context is it useful to be, for example, "the low-cost producer"? The real question is whether the delivered cost is attractive to the customer. While this is a different, and much more relevant, question, the belief that the company is the low-cost producer creates complacency and inhibits the assessment of reality.

Conformity Pressure

Directors are generally intelligent, accomplished, and comfortable with power. But put into a group that discourages dissent, they nearly always start to conform. Humans have a strong desire to conform to the expectations of the group, as exemplified by Solomon Asch's famous 1958 study. Eight people in a room are asked to identify which lines on a card equal the length of other lines on the card. Seven of the participants, prepared in advance, identify out loud the wrong lines as being of equal length. What does the actual subject, the last to respond, do? In multiple trials, roughly 80% of subjects went along with the group's obviously incorrect answer. In discussion as to why subjects had responded this way, most subjects reported that though they knew the answer they gave was incorrect, they went along with the group for fear of being ridiculed or labeled peculiar.

Asch concluded that pressure to conform to the group was so strong that reasonably intelligent people were willing to call white black to fit in. Further conclusions suggested two driving elements: the desire to be liked and accepted, and the belief that the group is better informed than the subject. It appears to be difficult to maintain that you see something one way when everyone else sees it another. According to his further research, it is less difficult if the single dissenter has an ally. A minority of two reduces the tendency of each to conform to giving the wrong answer. So, if you fear conformity pressure may inhibit you on an important subject, develop an ally to fortify the position.

The State Dinner

Imagine that you have been invited to dine with the Queen, and the table is set with more implements than you are accustomed to using. You will discreetly watch what the other diners do, and mimic them, hoping that your lack of sophistication is not noticeable. Imagine as well, then, how difficult it is for any board member, especially a new one, effectively to espouse a view that goes against the expressed opinion of the majority, the old hands. Now add to that the board hierarchy, explicit and implicit.

Bullying

Do you really mean bullying? Yes, and it takes multiple forms. For example, a longtime leader may simply assume that no one else has anything worthwhile to say, and thus manage to foreclose the opportunity for others to speak.

One easy way to do this is by the artful use of Roberts Rules of Order. Though few rely extensively on them anymore, apparent knowledge of them in managing resolutions and discussion may be enough to intimidate others into silence. Another route is to patronize board members, suggesting they are too new or too tall or short to have had time to formulate useful thoughts. And, of course, another is simply to preclude questioning. Watch for it, and calmly refuse to fall for it.

Read More
"Opinions and Social Pressure," Asch, Solomon E., *Scientific American*, 1955
Roberts Rules of Order, Robert, Henry, S.C. Griggs & Company, 1892

Chapter 32
Know that Steady, Purposeful Work is the Antidote

So, what is the antidote to this possible stalemate? A common understanding of the role and a sense of purpose, a set of goals that all are dedicated to achieving, translated into a team plan in which all parties in the room have important roles to play in helping the corporation move forward. Establishing a common objective creates a logical flow to describe who does what, when and how. And moves the team from passive defense to active offense, and back again as required in a fluid situation.

Expressed another way, what ultimately produces corporate wealth is the ingenuity and skill of talented executives. Even in the face of all the needed focus on protecting the corporation and ensuring ethical and compliant behavior, boards work best when they facilitate the ability of executives to exploit emerging developments and opportunities. Board understanding of and support for executive ability to make good-faith business decisions with speed and efficiency is imperative. The effective board also helps streamline decision-making to allow executives to invest more of their time in improving the company's products and services to increase profits and ultimately returns to shareholders.

Let's look at a few approaches that may be helpful to directors seeking to be effective while being authentically themselves in board service. Bringing your humanity and the benefits of all your experience into the board room with comfortable confidence is the key to your being effective, and to contributing to making the entire group operate well. Building an effective and purposeful board is fundamentally about dealing with people, in all their glory and frailty.

Reading the Room

For new directors, taking their seat in the boardroom can be an intimidating. Existing hierarchies, alliances, and large personalities can make it difficult for your voice to be heard. I am not a social psychologist and not well versed in analysis of group dynamics. Undertaking such analysis is, however, an imperative for each director. It is easy if views are expressed too forcefully, for example, for the rest of the group to become defensive and take the opposing view, or even to express no view at all, which can lead to adoption of the default position. It is, therefore, mission critical for the individual director to develop the tools of influence and avoid becoming an outlier, as to be pigeon holed as an outlier is to

DOI 10.1515/9781547400270-032

be rendered ineffective. Your voice can not be heard, and once seen as an outlier, you may be relegated to the ineffective pile forever.

Preparing

Being heard is always easier said than done. On the simplest level, the groundwork ahead of a board meeting needs attention, by reading board and committee materials and preparing questions and comments. To bolster your confidence, you may want to consult evidence to support your views, drawing upon research reports, articles or surveys, so that you can deliver well founded commentary and be perceived as a serious contributor. Knowing your own values and being yourself also helps your voice be heard, as if you seem simply to be imitating others, you will command less respect. This does not require an aggressive approach, which will also reduce your impact, but it is about calmly and consistently expressing your values when you think you need to do so. This can require considerable skill if you are challenging established behaviors.

Owning Your Style

Presenting ideas or values that are perceived as challenges will often create resistance. Humans generally do not like having their views challenged, and when challenged, a knee jerk response can easily be triggered that results in a search for evidence to back up our own existing views rather than openness to new ideas or facts. This can be especially toxic in the small and cloistered world of the board in which directors are often not well acquainted otherwise and have no history of connective tissue to help them navigate.

In my experience, assertion does not work nearly as well as demonstration. If I tell you directors tend to conform to established behaviors, that has less credibility than if I trot out the state dinner analogy used above. Arguing in abstractions does not work as well as finding ways to lead your fellow directors and executives to form their own conclusions. One common way to achieve this is to trigger an "aha" moment with an analogy.

Finding Your Point of View—and Theirs

It can take some time and effort to understand the points of view of your fellow directors and the various stakeholders. Study their possible motivations as well as their styles. Work to identify their strengths and weaknesses as well as how they learn. Find a path of your own to offer unique value. One approach I have used in the past is to adopt the point of view of the customer when considering corporate decisions and possible impacts. If I ask myself how each step will be seen and felt by the customer, and how their purchasing and use may change as a result, I end up with a reasonable way of weighing questions and answers. I did this when I realized to my own horror that in serving a particular board I had fallen prey to the passive role: if there is anything I need to know, someone will tell me. Oops. Not necessarily so.

Much of the ability to understand your fellow board members as well as top management requires a commitment to building relationships beyond the board room. When I served my first board, I was much younger than any other director, the only female, and knew more about the company than any of the others. To develop my influence, I worked the corridors, innocently asking the others why they thought as they did, and carefully working in various facts and ideas to move their thinking. They were happy to help me, and in the boardroom, when I asked similar questions, I was quite gratified that often the seeds I had planted were reflected later as the views of these much older, and more influential, men. Board work calls on your whole person, all your ingenuity and skill, to develop ways of being effective in pursuing corporate goals.

Leading with Your Ears

Often board meetings lack a self-assured leader adept at drawing out the various opinions in the room. When this occurs, it can be difficult to get a word in edge-wise. It can help if you simply choose to see the uncontrolled flow as an oppor-tunity to gain insight. In such settings, people are often vying for the chance to speak, watching for their opening rather than listening to what others are saying. Being a relaxed and attentive listener with eyes and ears open and mouth closed can give you surprising power.

Addressing Biases

Management consultant and author Peter Drucker famously said that "culture eats strategy for breakfast." That is particularly evident in the closed environ-ment of board meetings, where egos and competing agendas, biases known and unknown, and various social games form a large part of the unwritten agenda. Power and money and careers are at stake. Before directors can commit to any strategy, culture must be examined, and particularly the intangible biases that may be in play.

As humans, we are all affected by cognitive biases. Our challenge is to be aware of them and try to minimize their negative effect. Even the most seasoned directors and executives have limited experience in recognizing various types of bias that may be at work. Optimistic bias makes us think good things are more likely to happen than bad, while pessimism leads to the opposite conclusion. Confirmation bias causes us to find ways to support our existing views, rather than disprove them. Overconfidence causes us to overestimate possible results. Hubris overwhelms us. Groupthink undermines our capacity for independent thought. Generally, we are less rational and more vulnerable to acting based on emotion than we want to believe.

People are prone to many well documented unconscious cognitive biases that exist to help us filter information in day-to-day decision-making. But these unintentional mental shortcuts can distort the outcomes when we are forced to make big, consequential decisions, infrequently, and under high uncertainty. This is precisely the type of decision we confront in the board room.

There are many well-documented biases, but these are among the most pernicious in the board room.

Overconfidence

Experts become more confident as they gather more data—even though the additional data might not make their conclusions any more accurate. Its mere existence, whether relevant to the decisions required or not, contributes to a familiar cycle. We have all seen people point to a pile of data and ignore contradictory information, becoming ever more confident in their position, which makes them even more likely to ignore contradictory information. Said otherwise, we convince ourselves that we have a winning strategy this year even though we continue doing pretty much what we've always done.

Confirmation Bias

People with shared experiences and goals often wind up telling themselves stories, generally favorable ones. One study found, for instance, that 80% of executives believe that their product stands out against the competition—but only 8% of customers agree. This human failing is especially perilous in the board room, where a small group of people who meet infrequently are often kept in a protected bubble, where ugly, messy reality is kept at bay.

Survival Bias

The strategy formulation process is particularly vulnerable to this, because we only see what production processes created and what existing customers, for example, bought. We do not see what was not produced, and not purchased. We can precisely measure the behavior of the customers we have, but what about the silent voices of the customers we do not have? We will never know the whole story. And yet we often forget about the ones we know nothing about.

Attribution Bias

We are all more than familiar with this. When a target is missed, the blame is often directed at a plausible but possibly not primary cause such as unseasonable weather or interrupted electrical or internet service. Cool headed analysis would be too dangerous as the people in the room might have screwed up. Thus, we focus on outside forces beyond our control. With failure dismissed as an externality, the management team closes ranks and decides to double down and re-establish the goal. "We lost a year, but we're going to get back on track." Equally difficult is attribution for wild success, which of course is never due to luck but instead to prowess, until it is time for it to be replicated. These are manifestations of what I call victim thinking. It is a way of saying "We are powerless," which is hard to believe.

Attribution is further complicated by the way performance data are presented, as well as by the person doing the presenting. Executives are eager to protect themselves and their resources. We may as a result see sandbagging, where fear of missing the target may drive selection of easy targets impossible to miss. Or we have those who pursue shortcuts, running their area for short-term performance in the belief that they will have moved on before their milking becomes visible.

There is always the manipulator, who believes be or she knows much more about what his or her division can do than anyone else. The resulting plays are many, but a favorite is requesting resources that are not likely to be granted, and when requests are not fully met, pointing to poor resources as the culprit for underperformance. Finally, if the supervisor can not directly observe the quality of effort, results can be noisy signals. Were those poor results a noble failure? Were those great results dumb luck? It all depends on who is telling the tale.

Building a Championship Team

The most involved, diligent, value-adding boards may or may not follow every recommendation in the proverbial good-governance handbook. What distinguishes exemplary boards is that they are robust, effective social systems in which each member fully inhabits the role and the room. What are the elements that lead to such strong fabric?

Successful teams usually have chemistry that can not be quantified but can often be built through active cultivation, much as the coach of a championship team would seek to do. Each good quality begets the next. The leader respects each team member; team members develop mutual respect; their respect for one another enables them to develop trust; that trust enables them to listen to and to share difficult information; because they all have the same, reasonably complete information, they can challenge each other's conclusions coherently because a spirited give-and-take becomes expected; they learn to adjust their own interpretations in response to intelligent questions. This cycle starts with a leader who intends to develop it, and makes the first extension of trust.

This fabric of respect, trust, and candor can be torn at any point. One of the most common breaks occurs when the CEO does not trust the board enough to share information, and waits, as an extreme example, until the night before the board meeting to dump on the directors a huge report that includes, buried in a thicket of subclauses and footnotes, a bucket of bad news. Yet this silly and dangerous pattern happens all the time.

If a board is healthy, the CEO provides sufficient information on time every time, warts and all, and trusts the board not to meddle in day-to-day operations. He or she also gives board members free access to people who can answer their questions, removing the need for back channels. It is impossible for a board to monitor performance and oversee a company if complete, timely information is not available. And it is the direct responsibility of the board and each of its members to insist that it receive adequate information. The degree to which this often does not happen is astonishing.

The CEO, the chairman, and other board members can take steps to create a climate of respect, trust, and candor. First and most important, CEOs can build trust by sharing difficult information openly. Or the chairman can break down subgroups by splitting up political allies when assigning members to activities such as site visits, external meetings, and research projects. It's also useful to poll individual board members occasionally: an anonymous survey can uncover whether factions are forming or if members are uncomfortable with an autocratic CEO or chairman. Other revelations may include board members' distrust of outside auditors, internal company reports, or management's competence. In today's, such polls are quick and easy to administer.

Dissent is Not Disloyalty

Every member of the board needs to believe that dissent is healthy and not evidence of disloyalty, and demonstrate through their actions that they understand the difference. The capacity to challenge one another's assumptions and beliefs is an imperative for a strong board. Respect and trust do not imply endless affability or absence of disagreement; in fact, I will go so far as to say they can not take root in a climate of dysfunctional politeness.

Trust and respect grow among board members strong enough to engage effectively with differing points of view and handle challenging questions. One reason I enjoy working with boards of troubled companies is that focus on the goal of recovery strips away falsity. Often, true character is revealed, and those who join forces to combat the difficulty form strong bonds that often enable them to leap tall buildings together.

Building a Portfolio of Roles

Effective boards require their members to play a variety of roles, in some cases dipping deep into the details of a particular business, in others playing devil's advocate, in still others serving as project overseer. Similarly, in some cases, the board and only the board has the clear need to act or decide, such as appointment of the CEO or final action regarding a transaction.

In other cases, the board serves as advisors and consultants or mentors to management. In others, the board and its members are directly able to help the company move forward based on personal knowledge or contacts, and in all cases the board is charged with protecting and building its own healthy fabric and the structure and health of the enterprise. Playing different roles gives directors a wider view of the business and of the alternatives available to it. Director's roles and tasks shift and change depending on the corporation's circumstances and stage of development.

Read More

"What Makes Good Boards Great," Jeffrey A. Sonnenfeld, *Harvard Business Review,* September 2002

"How Well-Run Boards Make Decisions," Michael Useem, *Harvard Business Review,* November 2006

"Making Decisions on Values, Not Biases," Doochin, Jonathan, *Harvard Business Review,* May 2010

"The Impact of Unconscious Bias on Leadership Decision Making," Brainard, Michael; *Forbes Magazine,* September 13, 2017

Chapter 33
Survive Success and Relentlessly Build Resilience

In my experience the company is most vulnerable when the money is rolling in. It is human nature to relax then, and way too easy for all parties to become complacent and take their eyes off the ball. We know what happens when management and boards fall asleep. All kinds of pathologies can be growing. We do not want our company to disappear, but instead to flourish.

To do that we as the board must ensure that we are constantly working to exemplify and build a corporate culture that is resilient, able to both acknowledge and learn from mistakes, and driven by enduring values that go beyond the value of the dollar. In the wonderfully apt statement of economist Hyman Minsky, "stability breeds instability," and our job as the guardians of the perpetual life of the corporation is to combat that tendency with every fiber of our ability.

Roland Kupers, an advisor on dealing with complexity and a fellow at Oxford University notes in his article *Resilience in Complex Organizations* that the term resilience has taken in a technical meaning as well. "In a deeply interconnected world, stresses and shocks propagate across systems in ways that evade forecasting. Climate change is linked to the Syrian civil war, which is connected to heightened concern over immigration, which precipitated Brexit. Lehman Brothers was an investable company, until suddenly it was not and it catalyzed a global financial crisis. None of these links are causal in a strict sense, nor could they reasonably be assigned a probability, but they nevertheless clearly form a web of cascading events."

We have all become familiar with the terms "black swans" and "fat tails" and in general realize that they occur far more often than we want to believe. Yet we do not always take the time to consider the consequences of such events. Our goal is not to get an A on the risk management exam, but to be sure our organization survives and prospers. The risk management conversation can easily become too abstract for humans to grasp as our eyes and ears glaze over. We need to focus on possibilities that can take the company out, or knock it to its knees, and organize our skill to protect against those things while preserving our future possibility.

Standard risk management tools assume that risks follow a normalized distribution. Black swans do not follow normal distributions, and nor do their followers, the fat tails. In 2013 the World Economic Forum published a comprehensive overview in Perspectives on a Hyperconnected World, describing the impact of complexity for policy and business. The conclusion is not that policy-makers and managers must become complexity experts. But a level of complexity literacy is crucial to navigate the modern age. Organizations will continue to face normal-

DOI 10.1515/9781547400270-033

ized risks, which require the traditional tools. It is systemic risks that require the new tools.

What emerged from the 2013 paper is a formal focus on tools that foster resilience: increasing the company's ability to recover from a disturbance, and quickly. There are several components to this effort, including building enterprise resilience, the capacity of a company to adapt and prosper in the face of high-impact, low-probability risks. Planned redundancy, for example, is a familiar resilience strategy.

Another key component of supporting resiliency is diversity. Nature shows us this, and the threat represented by increasing reliance on monocultures brings home what can happen without it. When building diversity with intention, however, we do encounter the issue of defining what kind of diversity is relevant. Kupers has adopted the term "requisite diversity" to suggest that identifying and encouraging the needed kind is a deliberate process.

As a parenthetical comment, it is worth considering carefully what "requisite diversity" means not only when considering company's employees, but many other aspects such as vendor and customer diversity, process diversity, and, of course given our subject matter, board diversity. Another way to define the idea is to change the word slightly and think about what the word diversification means to us as a way to reduce risk.

A further hallmark of the resilient organization includes the purposeful building of a strong sense of shared values that recognizes the value of connections among people. Remember that we stated above that 85% of enterprise value can be attributed to intangibles. While suspicious as to how on earth that number can be derived, it makes an important point. Said another way: "It's the people, stupid," including what they deliver and how they do so. Focus on culture is therefore an imperative for the board.

One compelling story about this is the way that the Taj Hotels went about recovery following the devastating terrorist attacks on its flagship the Taj Mahal Palace Hotel in 2008. The owners, the Tata Group, worked relentlessly to support its people, the families of those who died or were injured in the attack, as well those injured elsewhere in Mumbai. Not only were medical care, mental health and needed housing and travel support provided, but the company achieved something remarkable simply by asking their employees what else they needed, and providing it. Though the pain and suffering were huge, the entire company gained something through the process, those intangibles that make the world go around: respect, and trust.

That culture needs to support experimentation and innovation, which includes accommodating and learning from the inevitable mistakes. Invest in providing the people, the time, and the resources to look, listen, and learn outside the usual organizational boundaries. This may foster the ability to learn and move faster than competitors. Having a purposeful system for such enquiry builds resilience. And what company springs to mind as an example of this but Apple, in its various iterations.

In the world we live in, it is important to note that resilience is not simply about being able to return to the way we were before we encountered a shock. Shocks often highlight the company's need to adapt or face being forced to change by external circumstances. Cultivating adaptability and a forward-looking orientation is a big part of building a resilient entity.

The ability to look forward in the uncertain world we live in can not solely be based on extrapolation from past data, no matter how good we become at data massing and mining. We need to develop techniques that help us engage with uncertainty itself. Shell's well-known scenario planning process has been applied over the past fifty years to envision various alternative futures and structuring conversations about them; in some cases, actively changing them.

Goldman Sachs has used periodic war games for a similar purpose. What these techniques do is help us move from a position of reacting to events after they have happened to engage our minds and our imaginations, in considering how multiple possibilities may unfold. Whether they occur as imagined or not, these exercises improve our adaptability and responsiveness to signals from the world around us. Nowhere in the company is this more important than at the board level, where the typical agenda has been devoted to static data and near-term developments.

Read More

Synchronicity: The Inner Path of Leadership, Jaworski, Joseph, Berrett-Koehler Publishers; 2nd edition, 2011

"Three Decades of Scenario Planning in Shell," Cornelius, Peter; Van de Putte, Alexander, and Romani, Mattia, *California Management Review,* October 1, 2005

"Perspectives on a Hyperconnected World" Resilience Action Initiative (RAI), World Economic Forum, 2013

"Living in the Futures," Wilkinson, Angela and Kupers, Roland, *Harvard Business Review,* May 2013

"Resilience in Complex Organizations," Kupers, Roland, Oxford University Fellow, World Economic Forum, 2018

Conclusion
Own the Role and Build the Future

The existence of the board in some form is old as the hills, and durable. Much flexibility is built in, which is both helpful and can lead to confusion. Regardless, that is no excuse for the kind of passive behavior based on ritual and not rocking the boat that has led the idea of corporate governance to be dismissed or treated with derision by so many.

Change must come from within the boardroom, from directors who understand their role and responsibilities and actively inhabit the space. Many well-intentioned rules and regulations are aimed at trying to create the circumstances in which directors will wake up and take charge, but they are designed by people who are outside the board room. Simply further tightening procedural rules may have helped, but is not enough. At issue is not only how we structure the work of a board but also how we manage the board as a social system.

Only those who sit in boardroom can change the tenor of board, management, and shareholder dynamics. The goal of this book is to help each one to be as confident and constructive and courageous as possible, separately and together. If roles and responsibilities are mutually understood, trust is cultivated, and dysfunctional politeness rejected, the structure can work very well. Rigid inside/outside distinctions disappear.

The legacy of deferring to CEO is important to remember, as serving as CEO today is a lonely role. Trust between directors, the CEO, and the board is an essential currency required for moving forward. Respect for the CEO, however, can not be allowed to inhibit the expression of director opinion, just as the CEO can not play hide the ball with the board, but must instead see the directors as valuable assets. If these conditions do not exist, they need to change or someone needs to leave. Trust, respect, and candor, needed for success, are difficult to instill and maintain, and very easy to destroy. Cultivating them is an important activity for all and deserves time and attention.

The corporation began as a vehicle to fuel collective human ambition by growing trade around the world. Corporations are propelled by what they trade and the value of what they receive in return. Through application of wisdom, commercial acumen, and good fortune a corporation can become strong, resilient and enduring.

The corporate form not only works, it works well. Thanks to the innovation made possible by the corporate form, economies have flourished. Leo Strine, Chief Justice of the Delaware Supreme Court, has stated that the great value of the American—that is, the Delaware—approach to corporation law lies in the fact that

DOI 10.1515/9781547400270-034

it invests corporate managers, executives and directors, with the nearly unfettered authority to pursue business strategies through diverse means, subject to a few important constraints, such as the requirements that shareholders approve certain transactions such as mergers, vote for directors annually, and have access to books and records.

The American approach is grounded in the belief that what ultimately produces corporate wealth is the ingenuity and skill of talented managers, and that corporate law works best when it facilitates the ability of managers to react adroitly to emerging developments and opportunities. The law must enable managers to make good-faith business decisions with the speed and efficiency that modern commerce demands, and it should minimize distractions from value-creating tasks so that managers can spend more time improving the company's products and services to increase profits.

The corporate form coupled with limited liability for investors was authorized as an instrument for enhancing the well-being of society and not simply to make investors rich. Making boards and CEOs more accountable to shareholders may be a useful means to achieve the larger objective of increasing societal wealth, but this does not mean that the goal of a durably wealthier society is equivalent to the short-term interests of investors in higher stock prices. It may be that the United States should follow the example set by the European Community and formally declare that shareholders do not own the company. As argued forcefully above, tilting corporate policy toward short-term thinking is counterproductive for all.

Bold action is also a legacy of the corporate form. Guts, stamina, and tenacity are required. Board service is not for sissies, but for people who will back their judgment with conviction and remember their humanity and the importance of purpose beyond profit. It requires the engagement of not only the brain but of all five senses and more.

There is no time for complacency. We are not here to continue to follow approaches that have not been working. We are here to grow, both ourselves and our society. We are here for a reason: to make our lives and our leadership matter in moving our families, our corporations, and our global community into a sustainable future.

Index

DOI 10.1515/9781547400270-035

Made in the USA
Middletown, DE
05 April 2019